D0387246

ESCAPING NORTH KOREA

ESCAPING
NORTH
KOREA

DEFIANCE AND HOPE
IN THE WORLD'S MOST
REPRESSIVE COUNTRY

MIKE KIM

ROWMAN & LITTLEFIELD PUBLISHERS, INC.
Lanham • Boulder • New York • Toronto • Plymouth, UK

ROWMAN & LITTLEFIELD PUBLISHERS, INC.

Published in the United States of America
by Rowman & Littlefield Publishers, Inc.
A wholly owned subsidary of
The Rowman & Littlefield Publishing Group, Inc.
4501 Forbes Boulevard, Suite 200, Lanham, Maryland 20706
www.rowmanlittlefield.com

Estover Road, Plymouth PL6 7PY, United Kingdom

Distributed by NATIONAL BOOK NETWORK

British Library Cataloguing in Publication Information Available

Library of Congress Cataloging-in-Publication Data

Kim, Mike, 1976–
Escaping North Korea : defiance and hope in the world's most repressive
country / Mike Kim.
p. cm.
Includes bibliographical references.
1. Korea (North)—Social conditions. 2. Korea (North)—Politics and
government—1994– 3. Refugees—Korea (North) I. Title.
HN730.6.A8K5245 2008
306.095193—dc22
2007048855

ISBN-13: 978-0-7425-5620-1 (cloth : alk. paper)
ISBN-10: 0-7425-5620-4 (cloth : alk. paper)
eISBN-13: 978-0-7425-5733-8
eISBN-10: 0-7425-5733-2

Printed in the United States of America

♾™ The paper used in this publication meets the minimum
requirements of American National Standard for Information
Sciences—Permanence of Paper for Printed Library Materials,
ANSI Z39.48—1992

To all of the courageous North Koreans who have inspired me with their strength, perseverance, and love of life.

CONTENTS

FOREWORD

This is a story of heroes. Of North Koreans increasingly and courageously evading the dictates of the system at home to survive and risking their lives to flee the world's most repressive dictatorship. And of a heroic young Korean American, the author, Mike Kim, who risked his own life for four years on the China–North Korea border to help them.

Why is this book of critical importance to you? Two and a half million people died when North Korean dictator Kim Il Sung invaded South Korea in 1950. According to Freedom House, up to another two and a half million people starved to death as the result of his son Kim Jong Il's policies in the 1990s. With nuclear weapons now at his disposal, South Korea, Japan, and the United States could suffer losses that would dwarf even these horrendous earlier numbers.

The ingenuity and courage of individual North Koreans, colorfully related in the following pages, point the way to a peaceful solution. They show that conventional pessimism about the prospects for radical change in the Hermit Kingdom is wrong.

I am all too familiar with this pervasive and dangerous inability to see a people's capacity to stand up and gain their freedom—with encouragement and practical help from outside democrats. The overwhelming conventional wisdom about the Soviet Union and Eastern Europe for decades had been that it too was preordained to suffer forever more under the heavy hand of Communist dictatorship.

Foreword

Fortunately a sunny Californian, Ronald Reagan, became president in 1981 and stood this conventional wisdom on its head. I was then the senior State Department official in charge of our relations with the Soviet Union. I helped draft his speeches and organized and participated in his first meetings with Gorbachev. President Reagan spoke with confidence about "a world in which all people are at last free to determine their own destiny."

Despite the derision with which these remarks were met, just a few years later the barbed wire on the Hungarian-Austrian border was pulled down. By then, I was the American ambassador to Hungary and had a front row seat, even played a certain role, in the unfolding drama. Young East Germans had fled to Hungary and wanted to move on to Austria and West Germany. Under pressure, the Hungarian Communists finally allowed these East Germans passage to freedom. This was a critical step toward the fall of the Berlin Wall a few months later—and the reunification of Germany as a democratic and peace-loving state.

The parallels with North Korea are striking. Another nation artificially divided by the Communists witnesses tens of thousands of its citizens fleeing to a neighboring Communist country, in this case China—in hopes that they can eventually reach the other half, the prosperous and democratic South Korea. The most direct route across the Demilitarized Zone, the equivalent of the Berlin Wall, is largely impassable. China resists its international obligation to these refugees, just as Hungary initially did but eventually gave way.

The lessons are clear. A regular flow of refugees, particularly one that includes the young and elite, managing to get through to the free half of the country can remove the glue of fear that keeps the dictator in power at home. Just as in East Germany, if the pillars of support for the dictator begin to see that the emperor has no clothes, they will change sides.

The most important support for a dictator is his security services and their willingness to obey his orders and to use force against their own people. In the some 60 successful nonviolent democratic revolutions over the past four decades, the eventual unwillingness of the security services to obey orders and use force has been the most important factor.

Mike Kim records absolutely fascinating experiences with North Korean soldiers and border guards, and ordinary citizens' interactions with them. Border guards are freely taking bribes to let people cross the China–North Korea border in both directions. A soldier recounts that many soldiers hate their own officers so much that they would fire on them rather than the enemy if a war arose. Knowledge of elite privileges is widespread, with derogatory comments about only the elite having cars, even the most expensive Mercedes-Benz.

Mike Kim documents the emerging discontent, the rampant unemployment, the absolute impoverishment of the majority, and the necessary resort to theft and other forms of criminal behavior just to survive.

I met Mike in December 2003. He had just returned to the States after a year of working with North Korean refugees at the China–North Korea border. It was the first of many conversations that we would have about North Korea.

In July 2001, Mike took a two-week vacation to China and met with North Korean refugees for the first time. Through those meetings, he learned about the North Korean refugee crisis as he listened to their horrific stories of suffering. He was so deeply moved by those encounters that he returned to the States and quit his financial planning business to prepare to move to China. In January 2003, he left for China on a one-way ticket and with only a couple of contacts in his PDA.

While I have met a handful of people working with North Korean refugees, I know of no one else who packed their bags and moved to the border.

Throughout the course of that first year, Mike assisted North Korean refugees by providing food, clothes, medicine, and shelter. His efforts eventually gave birth to Crossing Borders, a nongovernmental organization that has set up multiple shelters and orphanages for North Korean refugees in China. The following year they expanded their operations by sending teams into North Korea on a monthly basis to provide humanitarian assistance. Since then, Crossing Borders has become one of the main groups operating at the China–North Korea border.

In 2005, Reuters interviewed Mike regarding his work. In 2006, his organization delivered testimony at a U.S. congressional hearing on Combating Human Trafficking in China. He has worked his way into North Korean circles and has gained unique knowledge about the country and its people.

The international community can learn much from this book. The concluding chapter has recommendations from a cross section of policy experts for specific actions that can be taken across a broad front to help North Koreans and thereby to bring true peace and freedom to the Korean peninsula. Mike's own policy views are an impressive mix of deep caring and moderation, of sophistication and nuance about what can and should be done. Let me therefore encourage you to go on this journey with Mike Kim inside North Korea.

—Ambassador Mark Palmer

PREFACE

This is a book about my experiences with North Koreans at the China–North Korea border. Some names, identifying details, locations, dates, and times have been changed in order to protect people's privacy and ensure their safety. The North Koreans in this book have dispersed to different locations since their interviews. Some are still hiding in Crossing Borders refugee shelters in northeast China. A few successfully found asylum in South Korea and the United States, while others were captured attempting to get there and repatriated. Some will be in a North Korean prison or gulag at the time of your reading. Then there are the courageous few who returned to North Korea to help their families and communities. Unfortunately, some of the people I write about in this book have died of disease. Others, I believe, have been executed by the North Korean regime.

It is necessary to say something about Korean names. In the Korean culture, the family name is used first, as in "Kim Jong Il," where "Kim" is the family name. For the most part, I have thus used the family name first throughout the book. In Korean culture it is also considered rude to address an older person by their first name. In order to maintain the spirit of my relationship with my interviewees, I refer to those who are older than I by their last name (e.g., Mr. Lee) throughout the book. In addition to not using first names, Koreans will often use titles when addressing each other (e.g., Teacher Kim or Pastor Lee).

Preface

Since I was born and raised in the States, people often ask how I learned the Korean language. Growing up I always spoke English with my parents at home, so I never had the opportunity to learn Korean very well. My limited vocabulary included basic phrases I used with my grandparents and other Korean-speaking relatives. When I moved to China, I had a very difficult time communicating with the Korean-Chinese there. (My Korean-Chinese staff still make fun of me to this day about how hard it was to understand me when I first arrived.) However, since I grew up hearing Korean spoken between my parents and among my relatives, I was able to pick it up at an accelerated pace and became fairly fluent as I began to speak the language every day.

As for Mandarin, I never formerly studied the language. During my first two months in China, I traveled the country with a group of Chinese Christian leaders and as a result was forced to learn basic Mandarin very quickly.

One final note: During my four years in China, many friends, colleagues, and even roommates did not know the real reason for my stay in China. When they asked me what I was doing at the China–North Korea border, I told them that I was a Christian executive or a martial arts student training in the North Korean style of tae kwon do (both of which were true). I believed that it would be best for both them and me if they didn't know the true nature of my work. When they learn of this book and my real work in China, I hope that they will understand why I couldn't tell them the true reason for my stay in China. I would like to apologize to them for all of the secrets over the years and trust that this book will go a long way in explaining a few things.

———————

To learn more about Crossing Borders or how you can support its work, please visit www.crossingbordersnk.org.

ACKNOWLEDGMENTS

First and foremost, I must thank God because if it were not for a strong and overwhelming sense of calling, I would never have packed my bags and made the move to the China–North Korea border. Second, I owe much to all of those who believed in me enough to financially support my work—especially in the early years. It was their financial support that allowed me to attempt the things that I write about in this book. Additionally, the Crossing Borders U.S. staff will always have a special place in my heart. They have shown tremendous commitment to our work and dared to dream big dreams with me. Together we enjoyed the powerful results of combining faith and humanitarian aid. And without a close group of organizational partners, mentors, teachers, and advisors, the organization would not be where it is today. I would like to specifically thank Voice of the Martyrs, Tim Peters, Pastor Ahn, and Pastor Kim—as well as other organizations and individuals that, for security reasons, cannot be named here—for their partnership and support throughout the years.

I would like to thank Ambassador Mark Palmer for introducing me to Rowman & Littlefield and for his valuable advice on my work throughout the years. I would also like to thank Susan McEachern, the executive editor at Rowman & Littlefield, for her enthusiasm ever since we first discussed the concept of this book back in 2004 and for her continual guidance since. She patiently answered my hundreds of questions as

Acknowledgments

I was working on the manuscript. Jehanne Schweitzer, senior production editor at Rowman & Littlefield, invested much time in the project and copyeditor Desiree Reid made significant improvements in the manuscript. Tom Wells, the developmental editor for the book, also provided guidance and spent many hours editing the manuscript. Peer reviewers D. C., Amy, Susie, Ed Sohn, and Abe Lee read the manuscript, including multiple revisions, and gave critical feedback; some even took days off from work to do so. Ambassador John Miller, Professor Donna Hughes, and Lisa Thompson gave significant advice on chapter 5. Tom White from Voice of the Martyrs, Carl Moeller from Open Doors USA, and Ann Buwalda from Jubilee Campaign USA offered valuable insights for chapter 7. For chapter 12, I interviewed some leading figures involved on the North Korean issue and asked them, "What are some steps that can be taken to resolve the North Korean crisis?" I would like to thank them and everybody else who took the time to talk to me. I would also like to thank Suzanne Scholte, president of the Defense Forum Foundation, for making many key introductions for interviews for this book. Additionally, I would like to thank the Honorable Song Young-Sun, Professor Charles Armstrong, and Kenny Kim for their contributions to this project.

This book would not have been possible without the work of many translators in the United States and Australia who spent countless hours translating documents and audio files of interviews with North Koreans. I also owe special thanks to Peter and Bethany in Gainesville, Florida, who let me stay at their home (and play free on their golf course!) for four months until I finished the manuscript. Finally, I would like to thank my mom, dad, brother, and sister for their financial and emotional support during this unique season of my life. My mom paid for a large part of my college tuition, making it financially possible for me to leave for China at a young age. I believe that I got much of my ability to persevere and overcome great challenges from watching her live her life. Thanks, Mom.

Introduction

In November 2004, I was in northern Laos standing in the back of a truck with six angry soldiers pointing their AK-47s at me. I was leading two North Korean refugee women through the 6,000-mile modern-day underground railroad that begins in North Korea and runs through China and Southeast Asia. We hoped to gain asylum for them in South Korea. We had just illegally crossed the border from southern China into Laos and had been captured by border patrol soldiers. As I stood there with my hands in the air, I thought to myself, "How in the world did I ever get myself into this?"

A few years earlier, in June 2001, I had been living in Chicago and had my own financial planning business. I had a steady flow of clientele and had been awarded for generating the most revenue in the office that month; I had just hired a personal administrative assistant to help manage my workload. Life was good, and my future was looking very bright. In late June, I had my assistant, Elaine, clear my schedule so that I could take a two-week trip to China. I had always wanted to visit China, primarily because I had heard many stories about the persecution of Christians there and wished to witness religious persecution firsthand. As a Christian, I was always interested in the issue and wanted to explore it further.

Pastor Joo, a man who regularly traveled to China to work with house churches, allowed me to travel with him on one of his many trips to the country. We traveled throughout China—from Beijing, to the northeast, to the south—finally concluding our trip in Xinjiang Province in northwest China. As we traveled from church to church, I was awed by how Christians in this part of the world lived. I heard testimony after testimony of religious persecution and was deeply moved by their displays of faith and devotion.

At one of the house churches, Pastor Joo pointed to Ji-Eun, one of the many adorable orphans living at the church, and indicated, "She's a North Korean refugee." A bit confused, I asked, "What's a North Korean refugee?" I was a Korean American, but I had never heard of a North Korean refugee. He explained that because of the famine and oppression in North Korea, hundreds of thousands of people were fleeing to China in search of food and freedom.

Ji-Eun's grandfather had piggybacked her for days through the mountains of North Korea without any food, Pastor Joo told me. When he had arrived at the border, he had taken her in his arms and swum across the Tumen River, which divides China and North Korea, at the risk of being shot by North Korean border patrol soldiers. After crossing the river, they had continued for days through the mountains of China, again without food, evading the police. Unable to speak Mandarin and not knowing a single person in the country, he had stumbled across the house church we were visiting and dropped off Ji-Eun. "Please take care of my granddaughter," he had said. He had then run away in order to protect her—if the Chinese authorities had apprehended him, they would have both been repatriated to North Korea. Ji-Eun hasn't seen her grandfather since.

Throughout my time in China, I met many other North Korean refugee children and listened to their horrible stories of suffering. My heart went out to them. They were living in a constant state of fear, hiding in small house churches. The church leaders told me stories of frequent police raids where the authorities came looking for refugees. Those who were not at the churches were able to escape while the less fortunate were captured and forcibly repatriated to North Korea.

Introduction

I returned to the States a bit shaken from what I had experienced. I distinctly remember sitting across from clients talking about mutual funds, retirement plans, and insurance while feeling disengaged from it all. The "underground" house churches in China and the North Korean refugees weighed heavily on my heart.

One day shortly thereafter, I was standing in front of the large world map on the wall in my room. I put my hand on China and prayed for the country. Then I put my hand on North Korea and prayed for it. At that moment I knew what I had to do—go to China.

I moved to southern California to prepare and train for one year before leaving. While in California, I took classes in intercultural studies and met with leading individuals involved in refugee work. I wanted to learn everything that I possibly could about the North Korean refugee situation before departing.

My time in California was a crucial step in my preparation for the field. With finances tight, I had to learn to be resourceful and live frugally. I made certain sacrifices and downgraded many aspects of my life. I slept on the floor, not only because I didn't want to spend the little money I had on a bed but also to prepare myself for the rigors of the field (an idea I got from Hudson Taylor, an influential British Christian missionary who served in China during the nineteenth century). I couldn't always eat what I wanted, as I had been accustomed to doing, and there were occasions when, for the first time in my life, I skipped meals to save money. In short, it was an important time for me to learn the discipline of simplicity that would be necessary in China.

My time in California was also a crash course on faith. For the first time in my life, I had to trust God for things that I was used to taking care of on my own. For example, I no longer had a source of income, and so my livelihood depended on the donations of others. This was probably the most difficult thing for me to get used to. In the end, my training paid off. Little did I know that the small trials I experienced in southern California would prepare me for much greater hardships in China.

On December 31, 2002, after a year of training in California, I sent the following e-mail to a core group of supporters: "I can't believe the time is finally here. I have a one-way ticket to China and I leave tomorrow at 1:00 P.M. . . . So, I'm finally going. Many of you have joked that you thought this day would never come. Well, I'm really going (unless I miss my flight tomorrow). I somehow managed to fit everything into two duffle bags."

The next afternoon, on New Year's Day, I was on a United Airlines flight to China. I had no idea what city I would live in, or who I would stay or work with. Once I settled down at the China–North Korea border, I determined that the next step was to find a way to come in contact with North Korean refugees who were in hiding. I wanted to help the refugees but had no clue as to how I would meet any.

I eventually met several Korean-Chinese who put me in contact with some refugees. A few small refugee shelters along the border eventually evolved into Crossing Borders, a Christian nongovernmental organization (NGO) dedicated to assisting North Korean refugees at the border. The Korean-Chinese became staff members. We have since helped hundreds of North Koreans over the years by setting up other refugee shelters, starting orphanages for abandoned children, and sending teams of Korean-Chinese staff into North Korea.

The majority of my time in China was spent with the North Koreans in our shelters. We spent a lot of time at the dinner table talking, laughing, and telling stories. Sometimes I slept over or hid in the shelters with them, and we found ways to pass time by playing cards or board games. When we got tired of playing games, we told stories late into the night about our lives. Whenever it was safe to be outside, we played badminton, volleyball, or soccer. We also took frequent hikes up the nearest mountain.

As our friendships grew, I earned their trust. They opened up and shared their deepest secrets with me—things they had never told anyone else. They have given me permission to share their stories with you in the following pages. "If more people know, then more people can help," one North Korean woman told me.

This book is an intimate portrait of the lives of my North Korean friends. As they told their stories, I often sat with pen and paper or digital recorder in hand and listened to them talk for hours. They spoke about their government's brainwashing tactics and offered their true thoughts about the regime. Civilians and soldiers discussed how North Koreans view Americans and their sentiments on war with the United States. Children told me about the suffering they endured during the famine in the 1990s, their methods of survival, and family members lost. Women and young girls described their experiences in sex trafficking and the horrible abuse they endured. Others spoke in detail about beatings, torture, executions, and the persecution of Christians in the gulags.

In *Windows of the Soul*, Ken Gire wrote, "Stories give us eyes other than our own with which to see the world." He offered the following prayer: "Reveal to me through stories something of what it is like to walk around in someone else's shoes. Show me something about myself in the stories I read . . . *Enlarge my heart with a story, and change me by the characters I meet there*" (emphasis added).[1] North Korea in its current state doesn't have much it can offer the world, perhaps just its inspirational stories of hope. It's my hope that your heart will be enlarged by these stories and that you will be changed by the characters you meet here.

We can learn a great deal from the North Koreans, the refugees in particular. They call me *Sunsaengnim*[2] (Teacher), but I have learned so much more from them. It's also my hope that some in the international community will be mobilized to take action by their stories, which teach us much about North Korea and the plight of its people. The North Koreans have much to teach us about life too. When I travel and speak about the plight of North Korea, at least one person will usually come up to me and say, "Thank you for your talk. Today I learned that

I really don't have much to complain about." I have often thought that if the North Koreans can scale their mountains, then I can make it over this next hill of mine.

My life was changed by these people and these stories, and it is my hope that they will somehow touch and inspire you as well.

ONE

The North Korean Mind

What we don't know about North Korea is so vast that it makes the Kremlin of the 1950s look like an open book.

—Arnold Kaner, U.S. undersecretary of state
under President George H. W. Bush

Although everyone is familiar with President George W. Bush's "axis of evil," most people are unaware of North Korean dictator Kim Jong Il's counterpart. Shortly after Bush placed North Korea in his axis of evil, Kim Jong Il countered with his own version. It also comprises three countries: the United States, Japan, and South Korea. If you bumped into any North Korean on the street and asked her to name the three worst countries in the world, without a moment's hesitation she would reply, "The United States, Japan, and South Korea." If you asked her to rank the countries starting with the most wicked, she would reply, as if programmed, "The United States is the most evil country in the world. Japan is a close second. South Korea is the least evil of the three."

After meeting hundreds of North Koreans, it has become clear to me that, when it comes to worldviews and politics, all North Koreans have mastered the propaganda line. They are very predictable. South Korea is the least evil country in Kim Jong Il's axis because it is, in the eyes of the North Korean regime, simply a victim of U.S. imperialism. The regime believes that South Korea has been manipulated by the United States and sees it as its duty to rescue its misguided brethren. Almost all

North Koreans will complain, as one agent in the North Korean National Security Police (*Bowibu*), the rough equivalent of the FBI, did to me, "It is because of America that Korea cannot be unified."

Japan is ranked second on North Korea's axis of evil because North Koreans (and some South Koreans) have not forgotten about the Japanese occupation of once-unified Korea. Horrific stories of persecution, rape, and murder abound. Many Koreans to this day blame Japan for the current division of Korea. They suffered a great deal during the Japanese occupation, and Koreans (North and South alike) have had a difficult time letting go of the past. Their bitterness is expressed through their refusal to buy Japanese products. Some Korean parents forbid their children to marry a Japanese person. It was no coincidence that in 1998 North Korea test-fired a missile that flew over Japan. North Korea is still asking Japan to pay reparations for its colonial rule of the Korean peninsula.

The United States tops North Korea's list, and hatred toward Americans is evident in the very fabric of the language. *Ak* (evil) may be the single most commonly used word to describe Americans. The derogatory term *nom*, similar to calling someone a bastard, is inevitably attached to the end of any word referring to Americans. For example, *Mee-guk* is the Korean word for America, so a North Korean will always call an American a *Mee-guk nom*. He would never say *Mee-guk saram* ("American person"). During a three-day visit I made to North Korea in February 2004, I heard this phrase used many times. At dinners with government officials, I was surprised to hear them use it repeatedly in front of me without the slightest bit of hesitation. In their minds, they weren't saying anything wrong; they were simply using proper language to refer to Americans.

While living in China from 2003 through 2006, I had the unique opportunity to study North Korean tae kwon do with North Korean instructors sent from Pyongyang for several years. In the process of earning a second-degree black belt, I got to know them well. When I asked Master Chung, my eighth-degree teacher, about this *Mee-guk nom* phenomenon, he replied, "Oh, we learn that from a young age. We don't know of any other way to refer to Americans. When I was a kid, if there were some kids fighting or doing bad things, you would hear people say, 'They're going to turn into a *Mee-guk nom.*' It was the worst possible insult. Even in school we learned that Americans and Japanese are the worst people on the face of the earth."

I wanted to get a second opinion, so I asked Mrs. Cha, a North Korean woman in her early thirties, about this. I took her and her family out for *pat-bing-su,* a Korean dessert made of ice cream, crushed ice, fruit, and red beans (it tastes much better than it sounds). It was the first time she had tasted the treat. As we were eating, I asked her if I was the first American she had ever met. Yes, I was, she responded. Laughing, I remarked, "I bet you were really scared of me when we first met." She smiled and sheepishly replied, "Yes, I was very scared of you because you were an American." I told her that I had just returned from North Korea and couldn't believe that they call all Americans *Mee-guk nom* there. In my meetings with government officials, they had said it as if I wasn't even there. She laughed and confessed, "I also used to say that a lot."

Mrs. Huh, a North Korean refugee woman also in her early thirties, commented, "In North Korea, they tell us that the reason our lives are so bad is because of *Mee-guk nom.* They tell us, 'Let's toughen up and make it through this.' People think, 'I don't mind eating gruel everyday as long as *Mee-guk nom* don't take over our country.'"

Mrs. Yoon, a North Korean refugee recently diagnosed with cancer, was hiding in one of our refugee shelters in China. "I used to say *Mee-guk nom* a lot," she told me. "Now I don't say that any more. Now I just say *Mee-guk saram.* In North Korea, we don't have our own rice, right? All the rice that we have is either from the United States or South Korea. How could I continue to hate Americans when they provide the very rice that sustains us?"

The Korean word for Japan is *Il-Bun.* North Koreans will always refer to Japanese people as *Il-Bun nom.* Yet North Koreans will never refer to South Koreans in this derogatory way.

BRAINWASHING: NORTH KOREA'S MOST POWERFUL WEAPON

In April 2003, I attended a North Korea symposium in Seoul, South Korea, where Suzanne Scholte, president of the Defense Forum Foundation and a leading North Korean human rights activist, gave a speech. In her talk, she referred to Colonel Joo Hwal Choi and diplomat Young Hwan Ko, the first North Korean defectors brought to the United States to testify at a congressional hearing:

> What was particularly disturbing about their testimony was not just how horrible things were in North Korea, but how this North Korean regime brainwashed its own citizens into hating us. Colonel Choi described a children's schoolbook in North Korea in which students were taught how to add with such equations as "If you threw a grenade and killed two American GIs, and your friend threw a grenade and killed three American GIs, how many American GIs would you and your friend have killed?"

In June 2003, I discussed the topic of brainwashing with two teenage North Korean boys living in one of our refugee shelters. Chul and Sung had been hiding in China for two years under extremely difficult circumstances. I mentioned to them that I had heard that children in North Korea were taught math in the way Colonel Choi described. They smiled, looked down at the floor in embarrassment, and said that it was true. "We're here talking and joking around like this now, but what would it have been like if I had met you when you first came to China?" I asked them. "Oh gosh!" one replied. "We would have been so scared of you that we wouldn't have been able to talk to you at all! We wouldn't have even been able to look you in the eyes."

The leaders of North Korea understand that the future of their regime depends on the effectiveness of their brainwashing (though, of course, they don't call it that). They take their brainwashing seriously and go to painstaking lengths to ensure maximum control over the minds of their people.

When I lived in China, I often visited a particular spot at the China–North Korea border that overlooks a North Korean village. During one visit, a local villager who had lived in the border area for many years commented, "They have no electricity for the common people over there. The only electricity that the village has is used for propaganda that is played over the speaker system. Propaganda is played all throughout the day." He added, "It is like their Bible. They have to hear Kim Jong Il's words every day—morning and night." The same holds true for many villages in North Korea.

Instilled into the North Korean psyche is a deep-seated fear of Americans. One of the regime's central tactics is to keep its citizens constantly aware that there is an enemy. This is accomplished by demonizing Americans. From birth, North Koreans are bombarded with messages teaching that Americans are the root of all evil. Michael Breen, author of *Kim Jong-Il: North Korea's Dear Leader,* tells of buying an English phrase book in Pyongyang, North Korea, that taught verb tenses in the following manner: "We fight against Yankees. We fought against Yankees. We will fight against Yankees." Another phrase was "Let's mutilate US imperialism!"[1]

A Pyongyang-endorsed biography of Kim Jong Il tells the story of how he, at eight years old, confronted a U.S. pilot who was shot down in North Korea during the Korean War. According to the book, Kim stepped forward in front of all his classmates and said, "Look at that fellow, how frightened he is and what a poor figure he is cutting. No matter how many packs of those brutes may attack us, we need not fear them. We should beat the wolves mercilessly with a stick." The biographer continues, "Then he appealed to the schoolchildren to carry on the work of aiding the soldiers on the battle line more actively in order to crush all the U.S. imperialists, since they had now clearly seen what the enemy looked like."[2]

Tom White is the executive director of Voice of the Martyrs, an organization committed to helping persecuted Christians around the world. He once spent 18 months in a Cuban prison for distributing Christian literature. He had the opportunity to visit Pyongyang and recalled being taken to a museum (see photo):

> We went to a "Museum of Hatred" in the southern part of North Korea. . . . This is a museum a couple of stories tall. Outside were several hundred elementary school children waiting for their tour. Inside were paintings of Americans driving spikes through the skulls of Korean women and children, saying that this is what the American people are. . . . We went through the two floors and it was very sad . . . all hate. It was about 80 percent anti-American . . . Then they herded all of the elementary kids in there to say this is America, this is the West, this is the enemy.[3]

An anti-American painting in a North Korea museum near Pyongyang. The caption reads, "Harrison's gang forcibly commits a brutal massacre of the people at Lake Lotus 'Bong Jun.'"
(Voice of the Martyrs)

During one of my tae kwon do workouts, Master Chung told me about some of the many anti-American games he played in class as a child:

> Sometimes the teacher hung up a picture representing America. Then when the teacher signaled, all of the children in class took a sharp object, charged at the picture screaming at the top of their lungs, and then ripped it up. During wintertime, I remember the teacher telling us to make two snowmen. On one snowman we wrote "America" and on the other we wrote "Japan." . . . With sticks in our hands, we would scream at the top of our lungs, charge at the snowmen and break it.

Games like this are still being played in North Korea and are encouraged by elementary school teachers. Imagine a country full of people who are taught and encouraged to hate like this from birth.

The North Korean regime has a variety of mediums through which it brainwashes its people: the daily news including the newspaper, speeches, literature, and signs posted throughout the country. The *Rodong Shinmun* (Workers' Party Newspaper), North Korea's main paper, is a common channel through which propaganda is dispersed. Through a North Korean contact, I once obtained 30 copies of the paper. Since it was such a rarity, I distributed copies as gifts to family, friends, and organizational donors. I gave a copy to two of my cousins who live in Seoul, South Korea. One cousin, Hee-Sun, commented on the strange language the paper used. Even though she was a fluent Korean speaker, the writing was foreign to her. Another cousin, In-Ho, who had just completed his mandatory military service, was thankful to get his hands on such a rare item and warned me, "Be careful carrying this around. If any police caught you reading this paper, they would harass you asking how you got this."

When visiting North Korea, at every turn you will find some sort of propaganda posted on the streets. One of our Korean-Chinese staff members saw the following signs when visiting Chongjin: "Hail Great Kim Il Sung!";[4] "If the Communist party decides it, we will do it"; "Let's live our own way"; "Let's beat America with a big iron stick." He said that people in the streets greeted him saying, "We live very happy lives and we live in the bosom of our warm leader."

There is also propaganda at the borders of the country made out of huge white blocks reminiscent of the Hollywood sign in the Hollywood Hills. Erected on stands, each character is nine meters high and six meters wide. Including the height of the stand, each character stands twelve meters high. In a thirty-minute drive along the border you will see multiple signs that make pronouncements such as "Hail to the Great Sun of the 21st century. General Kim Jong Il!"

The regime uses legends for brainwashing too. In Hoeryung, the hometown of Kim Jong Il's mother, Kim Jong Suk, there is a sign that reads, "Let's learn from our fellow heroine Kim Jong Suk and how she protested against Japan." She died at 32 years of age and ever since has been a national war hero. One of our Korean-Chinese staff members told of a tour guide in Chongjin telling a tour group the following story:

> Shortly after winning our independence from Japan, Kim Jong Suk came to this spot when she was 30 years old, two years before she died. All the people gathered and said, "We have heard that you are a good shot. Will you please demonstrate for us?" Do you see that big memorial stone over there? If you take a close look you will see a hole in the rock made from a bullet. Kim Jong Suk once came to this spot when she was 30 years old and shot five bullets at that stone. There is only one bullet mark because the first one hit the stone and the other four bullets hit the same exact spot.

At that point, our staff member shouted, "I think it's because she only hit the rock once and missed the other four shots." The group laughed, but the tour guide glared at him.

In March 2007, a group of Chinese college students traveled to Chongjin on a one-week vacation. While there, they witnessed first- and second-year North Korean college students in class. The students were in army clothes standing at attention in a straight line. The teacher shouted, "Let's learn from Kim Jong Suk and how she fought against Japan even though she was poor and had nothing. Let's fight against America in the same way."

The North Korean press, as a standard part of its operations, reports legends about Kim Jong Il. The Korean Central News Agency (KCNA), the main news agency in North Korea, once claimed, "Mysterious natural phenomena were witnessed on September 28. When . . . Secretary Kim Jong Il in a car arrived at the entrance to the [military] unit, the fog cleared off and the sun shone bright in the blue sky. Two apricot trees on either side of the road to the unit had 28 and 26 blossoms respectively. Seeing the mysterious natural phenomena, the unit servicemen said that Secretary Kim Jong Il is the famous general produced by heaven."[5]

This is the type of news and information that North Koreans are limited to receiving. The same holds true for literature. Author Michael Breen put it well when he said, "So far, no North Korean has been short-listed for the Nobel Prize for literature."[6]

Every village in North Korea has a white tower that says, "Father Kim Il Sung, the Great Leader lives with us forever." After Kim Il Sung died in 1994, they built these white towers as a reminder that he is always present with them in spirit. Many have commented that because Kim Il Sung was introduced to Christianity at an early age, much of the propaganda is taken from Christian ideas and biblical teaching. There are songs in North Korea that sound very similar to Christian hymns. One of our local staff members who pastors a house church in China commented, "If you took some North Korean songs and replaced Kim Il Sung with God or Jesus it would sound exactly like a Christian hymn. They even have a creed that is almost identical to the Apostles' Creed."

Examples of North Korean propaganda are abundant and in some cases quite comical. In one of our drives along the China–North Korea border, we were having a conversation about North Korean propaganda, and our U.S. Director of Operations said, "Hey, Mike, did you ever hear the story about how Kim Jong Il played 18 holes of golf and scored an 18?" I had not heard that story and asked one of our Korean-Chinese staff members, who is very knowledgeable about North Korea, if he had ever heard it. He said no, then added:

> But I do know that North Koreans don't use the English word *golf*. There is an aversion to using English words over there. Their way of thinking is, "Why should we use English words? We should use Korean words." So they called golf "putting a ball into 18 holes" and eventually shortened it to "18 holes" because it was too hard to say.

As ridiculous as this may sound, it shows how North Koreans are educated. But perhaps what's most amazing is not that the leadership teaches these kinds of stories but that the people actually believe them.

The regime depends heavily on what it calls *hakseup* to successfully brainwash the people. The word simply means "education." One South Korean friend described it as a "learning session." When I asked an educated North Korean man what *hakseup* means, he defined it in English as an "ideology session." Every citizen is required to regularly attend *hakseup,* usually on Tuesdays. When I asked what went on in these meetings, he explained, "We are required to regularly meet in small groups to memorize and to write a number of things." "What kinds of things?" "We have to copy things such as Kim Il Sung or Kim Jong Il's speeches or recite them until we have them memorized," he said. "We also often have to memorize North Korean literature and historical accounts of Kim Il Sung and Kim Jong Il." Then he whispered, "It's so boring. I usually fall asleep."

Like football towns that close shop when their team is playing, North Koreans close shop when *hakseup* is in session. I once called a tourism company in North Korea on a Tuesday several times throughout the day, only to receive no answer. I later learned that they weren't answering the phone because they were having their *hakseup* sessions. Every week on Tuesday, businesses and the markets shut down so people can attend these meetings.

When North Korean government employees are sent abroad, they continue to attend *hakseup* meetings, even more frequently. Despite their increased attendance, the regime has a strict policy that no North Korean can stay overseas for more than three years. They are required to return to Pyongyang for re-education after their three-year term is completed. In some cases, I have seen North Korean employees sent back to Pyongyang early if their colleagues suspect that they are weakening ideologically.

In addition to *hakseup,* women are required to attend a meeting called "Ten-day Life Evaluation" to confess to their wrongdoings. One participant told me, "We have to confess things such as the house being messy, not taking care of our kids well, not packing lunch for our husband." Younger people are required to attend a similar meeting called "Weekend Life Evaluation." One young woman commented, "What kind of wrong can we do? We just stay at home to cook and clean."

The following *New York Times* article about the way some North Koreans responded when their houses were on fire illustrates just how effective government indoctrination has been:

> To hear North Korea's state media tell it, in the midst of an inferno of exploding railcars and dying children, several heroic women made the ultimate sacrifice, running into blazing buildings in frantic attempts to save treasured portraits of Kim Jong Il and his dead father, Kim Il Sung. "Many people of the county evacuated portraits before searching after their family members or saving their household goods," the Korean Central News Agency wrote approvingly from Ryongchon, the railroad town where a huge explosion killed at least 161 people and injured 1,300 last week. "They were buried under the collapsing buildings to die a heroic death when they were trying to come out with portraits of President Kim Il Sung and Dear Leader Kim Jong Il." In North Korea, where the state personality cult is stronger than in Mao's China or Stalin's Russia, citizens need no reminder that their leaders are more important than their own children.[7]

Mrs. Park, a 32-year-old North Korean, worked for the army near the Demilitarized Zone (DMZ), the heavily guarded border between the two Koreas. She recalls the day she was ordered to pick up prodemocracy literature being flown in from South Korea by balloons. Mrs. Park and four other soldiers were assigned the task of collecting the literature before anyone could read it. During her shift, she found four of those balloons and disposed of them:

> I remember the balloons floating in with a colored plastic bag tied to the bottom of them. At the time, I didn't know what was in the

bags, but later I learned that they contained prodemocracy literature and pictures illustrating what life was like in South Korea. We
were ordered to collect the balloons before civilians could see it . . .
We didn't pick up the literature with our hands but picked it up
using a stick.

"Why?" I inquired. "We were taught that our hands would rot if we
touched anything from South Korea," she replied. Asked if she believed
that at the time, she said yes.

THE NORTH KOREAN WORLDVIEW

One time, I played the name game with a group of North Korean
refugees. "When you were in North Korea, did you know who Michael
Jordan was?" "No." "Did you know Bruce Lee or Jackie Chan?" "No."
(I have been to remote villages in the mountains of Ethiopia where
people knew of Bruce Lee or Jackie Chan.) "Did you know who Elvis
was?" "No." "Did you ever hear of Michael Jackson?" One teenage
boy's face lit up: "I know Michael Jackson!" He stood up, smiled, and
flashed a dance move. We all laughed. Surprised, I asked, "While you
were in North Korea, you knew who Michael Jackson was?" "No, I
only heard of Michael Jackson after coming to China."

After asking more questions, I learned that the only famous people
they knew outside their country were high-level government officials
from the United States because they were demonized so often. There is
a word in Korean, *gangpae,* which means "gangster." The North Korean
media refer to George Bush, Colin Powell, and Donald Rumsfeld as
gangpaes. The refugees were also familiar with some South Korean soccer players because Kim Jong Il allowed the 2002 World Cup games to
be televised whenever South Korea was playing. Other than that, they
didn't know the name of a single famous person outside their country
owing to their government's control of information.

On the other hand, there are the elite in Pyongyang who have traveled quite a bit and studied or worked abroad. They are much better educated and better read. I could have an intelligent exchange with them about topics ranging from sports to politics. In one conversation, one of these elites wanted to talk about movies: "You know *Titanic?* The movie with the boat sinking? Now that was a well-made movie! Did you see it?" "Yes, I did. I really liked the movie." "*Gone With the Wind,* that's another excellent movie! Have you seen it?" I had not and didn't plan to. "No, I'm too young," I replied. "That movie was before my time." I then thought to myself, "Now here's an interesting moment. A North Korean asking me about an American movie that I've never seen."

The man then said, "I don't know how you can live in a place like America. There are so many evil people in your country. How can you live with bullets flying around you all the time?" I laughed and said, "What makes you think there are bullets flying around all the time?" "Well, you see it all the time in the movies. How do you live in a place like that?"

I tried to explain to him that things, for the most part, are exaggerated in the movies and that in my lifetime I had never witnessed a gunfight. But the regime had painted a picture in his mind of what America was like, and I wasn't going to change it.

Breen tells a humorous story about a meeting in Seoul between North Korean and South Korean diplomats. Lee Bum-Suk, the head of the South Korean delegation, was driving into Seoul with his North Korean counterpart. The North Korean diplomat, noticing the city bustling with construction and traffic, said, "We're not stupid, you know. It's obvious you've ordered all the cars in the country to be brought into Seoul to fool us." Lee, known for his sense of humor, replied, "Well . . . that was the easy part. The hard bit was moving in all the buildings."[8]

The North Korean media reports, "North Korea, despite her ongoing struggle, is paradise on earth. Other nations, such as 'the south,' that do not have the benefit of *Juche* [North Korea's ideology of self-reliance] are poor, miserable places to live."[9] However, as North Koreans defect to China, they learn the truth about the world.

I once asked Young-Soon, a 16-year-old North Korean refugee, what she had learned about the world while in North Korea. "In school, we were taught that people in South Korea and Japan are so poor that they went around selling body parts to survive," she answered. "We were taught that people walked the streets of South Korea and Japan saying, 'Help me. I'm so poor. Please buy my eyes.'" She giggled, realizing now how silly it sounded.

Mrs. Kim, a North Korean refugee woman, said, "When I was little, I was taught that South Koreans live under bridges because they don't have homes to live in. Also, I was told that they wear old and ragged clothes. But then when I saw South Koreans [in China], I noticed that they were dressed so nicely. I thought, 'How could they dress so nicely when they don't even have a place to live? Nothing they wear looks worn out.' How weird. Now I know."

WAR WITH AMERICA

One morning, I went to the gym for my morning tae kwon do workout to find Master Chung sitting in his chair reading the North Korean paper as usual. He called me over and pointed to the paper: "Do you know what it says in the paper these days? It says that America wants to attack North Korea. It says, 'If America wants to come, let them come! We'll show them a real war! Iraq? That wasn't a war! Let America come to our country and we'll show them what a real war is!'" Then he leaned toward me and lowered his voice as if he was telling me a secret. "You know why America can't come to North Korea?" "Because of China and South Korea," I replied. "China won't approve and too many South Koreans will die if a war started." "No. That's not why. America can't attack because the North

The Juche Tower, a monument in Pyongyang, is a symbol of North Korea's ideology of self-reliance. (Voice of the Martyrs)

Korean army is too strong. People don't know how strong it is. Even North Korean civilians don't know just how strong the military is. The strength of the military is a secret."

I could see in his eyes that he was serious and believed every word he was saying. But in my conversations with North Korean soldiers, I was finding quite the opposite about the military's strength. In October 2006, I interviewed Chang, a 28-year-old North Korean soldier who had defected from the army. I wasn't surprised that he was a soldier, as he was taller than most North Korean men I had met. He described the conditions of the military at the time he defected:

> North Korean soldiers are physically weak right now. . . . I would say that 80 percent of the military is in a severely weakened physical state. We can't even complete our 30-minute morning exercise because we're so tired from lack of food. Drill leaders don't even push that hard any more because people can't keep up with the exercises. However, I would say that 80 percent of the soldiers are also fully ready to die for their country. Even civilians have that kind of mentality. I would say that most civilians have the mindset, "Let's go to war and die for country!" There is only a small fraction of people that don't want war. Usually it's the people who are well-off or in higher positions that don't want war. They don't want war because they're content with their situations. I think that the people's desire for war is born out of both love for their country and discontent regarding their current lifestyle.

When I ask North Koreans who they think would win a war between America and North Korea, I get mixed responses. North Korean elite who have ties to the regime always respond as Master Chung did, saying that North Korea would destroy the United States. Refugees who have spent a significant amount of time in China and have seen footage of the Iraq War always say that the United States would win. I have heard that some North Koreans are indifferent about war. Others are so annoyed at hearing about war with America every day that they just want to fight and get it over with. When I asked a 23-year-old refugee what North Koreans think of war with America, he replied, "Is there anybody that likes war? Who likes war? In war, life is hard and people die. But in North Korea, the media tells us that Americans love war."

The regime works hard to ensure that thoughts of war with America are at the forefront of people's minds. They use scare tactics to distract people from the country's economic crisis. In October 2006, I interviewed a 27-year-old North Korean man named Sang who related:

> Ever since August 15, 2006, the day we declared independence from Japan, there has been a lot of talk about war with America. You see soldiers running drills, and even civilians are being trained for war. There are drills where sirens go off and everyone flees to the mountains. Shortly after August 15, government officials gathered all the people in the village and made the announcement that we're preparing for war with America. On September 6, it came out in the papers, "We're going to war with America!"

"What's the significance of September 6th?" I asked. Laughing, Sang replied, "I don't know. I think when government officials are bored, they just pick any day and declare war with America. In North Korea, we talk about war day and night."

Chang, the 28-year-old soldier who described the weakened state of the military, told me:

> We're working on attaining nuclear weapons, but I still don't think we would win in a war with America. Most North Koreans would die and the ones that do survive would eventually flee to China. When I was in the army, we analyzed footage of Desert Storm. I remember watching that thinking, "I don't think many of us would survive a war with America." But I think most North Koreans still think that they would win a war with America. When I was in the

army, my mindset was, "Whether we win or lose, let's just do it. Those that die will die and those that live will live."

I asked Chang to describe his daily schedule in the military:

5:30–6:00 A.M.	Morning exercises
6:00–6:30 A.M.	Clean
6:30–7:30 A.M.	Eat breakfast
7:30–8:45 A.M.	Military class
8:45–9:00 A.M.	Break
9:00–9:45 A.M.	Military class
9:45–10:00 A.M.	Break
10:00–10:45 A.M.	Military class
10:45–11:00 A.M.	Break
11:00–11:45 A.M.	Military class
11:45 A.M.–12:00 P.M.	Break
12:00–1:00 P.M.	Lunch
1:00–1:45 P.M.	Military class
1:45–2:00 P.M.	Break
2:00–2:45 P.M.	Military class
2:45–3:00 P.M.	Break
3:00–5:00 P.M.	Drills (on whatever they learned in class that day)
5:00–6:00 P.M.	Break
6:00–7:00 P.M.	Dinner
7:00–8:30 P.M.	Watch the news/propaganda, sing songs, and dance
8:30–9:30 P.M.	Clean their uniforms and shoes, and do laundry
9:30 P.M.	Sleep (and take turns on night watch)

"We trained like this for one month in the summer and two months in the winter," Chang told me. "When we weren't in training, we worked on the farm so that we had enough food to eat. During those times we didn't train at all." Chang said the schedule was exhausting:

> In military class, because I was so weak and my health was so bad, I couldn't concentrate. I just tried to make it through class without falling asleep. . . . I couldn't think of anything else but food. During those classes I would think to myself, "If I could eat anything I wanted right now, what would I eat?" Most of the people in class are only thinking about two things—food and sleep.

As I was interested in martial arts, I asked Chang about hand-to-hand combat training:

> The classrooms were boring, but hand-to-hand combat was fun. During break times, we would go out and fight one-on-one. Sometimes one person would take on two or three people. Oftentimes, we were so bored that we would go out and fight each other just to help pass time. It wasn't skilled fighting. You did whatever you could to win. People would pick up a rock or anything near them and use it to fight. During those times you really saw the evil side of other soldiers. Even though North Koreans are weak physically, we have this evil in us that will allow us to win fights. We've been trained to think from a young age that we will win in any given situation. We North Koreans are evil, aren't we?

Chang sat quietly for a moment and stared at the floor deep in thought. "When I was a soldier, if we went to war, rather than shooting the enemy I probably would have fired on my officers first," he said. "There were officers that I hated, and I would have fired on them in a second. There are many others like that in the army. If they were given the chance, I think a lot of people would fire on their own officers."

North Korea is preparing for war with America. Whether or not they have any real concrete plans for action, I do not know. But I do know that they are instilling in their people an intense hatred and fear of Americans from birth and that they are training their military solely with the idea of a war against America. However, their intention is not to fight the United States but to conquer South Korea. One of the main goals of the regime is to unite North and South Korea under its leadership.

One of our Korean-Chinese staff members was imprisoned for five months in North Korea and eventually released for a ransom of $3,600. While in prison, he was accused of spying for the United States. During interrogation, while they were torturing him, one of the officers slipped and said, "You idiot! Don't you know that North Korea is preparing to destroy America? Even as we speak, we have 50 elite soldiers training in Cuba preparing to enter the U.S. and wreak havoc." The officer added (truthfully or not) that North Korea had a biochemical weapons factory in Cuba. "Our country has this kind of military power, destructive power, and these biochemical weapons can even be more destructive than nuclear weapons that the United States has," he said. "This is how easily we can destroy people or destroy the world."[10]

In one of my final training sessions with Master Chung before he was sent back to Pyongyang to be re-educated, he taught me some techniques on how to defend against an attacker using a knife. I asked him, "Where did you learn these techniques?" "I learned them in the military," he replied. "You were in the North Korean military?" I asked. "I didn't know that." "I was in the army for many years," he said. "How about you? Were you ever in the army? I've always been suspicious that you had some military training." "No. I really wish I could have had that experience, though," I responded. "Sometimes I still consider joining the Marines."

"When you return to the States, you should join," he told me. "If the U.S. and North Korea ever go to war, we might see each other. Let's make a deal. If that happens and we see each other across enemy lines, you don't shoot me and I won't shoot you."

We both had a good laugh and shook on it.

TWO

Inside the Hermit Kingdom

We have no idea what is going on. We are completely in the dark. We don't even know how many people live in the country.

—Douglas Coutts, World Food Program

As a child, I never asked my parents much about North Korea, and they never really had much to say about it. The first time I learned anything about the country was in my seventh-grade social studies class when the teacher, in a world geography lesson, explained that North Korea was an isolationist country. The second time I encountered the country was when my mom told me a story about my great uncle. During the Korean War, North Korean soldiers invaded Seoul and kidnapped eight engineers from a large electrical company. My great uncle was one of them. The soldiers took the engineers to an auditorium at a university in Seoul. In front of a South Korean audience, they executed each of them one by one, until my great uncle was the only one left. The soldiers took him back to North Korea to help develop the country's electrical system. My great uncle was one of the 84,000 South Koreans who were kidnapped during the North Korean occupation of the South.[1]

We have not heard from my great uncle since. Many years after the war, my grandmother regularly visited fortune-tellers in Korea to try to find out whether or not he, her older brother, was alive. (She regularly consulted with fortune-tellers in the past but has now converted to

Christianity.) When I recently asked my grandmother to tell me more about my great uncle, she gave me a brief, one-minute synopsis, then sighed deeply and said, "I really don't want to think about it anymore. I don't like to talk about it, and on top of that I don't really know that much. I don't know what happened to him after he was kidnapped. . . . I don't even have a picture of him."

Ever since my mom told me about my great uncle, I've often thought about him living in North Korea: What was life like for him inside the "Hermit Kingdom"?[2] For many years, it was a complete mystery to me. However, after living at the China–North Korea border for four years and visiting North Korea, much of my curiosity has been satiated and the mystery has slowly unraveled.

THE RICH AND THE POOR

According to Hwang Jang-yop, the architect of *Juche* (North Korea's ideological system) and the highest-ranking defector to date, "North Korea's economy exists first and foremost to serve the Dear Leader."[3] With the national budget, Kim Jong Il and the 600 loyalist families satisfy their every whimsical desire. Kim paid $15 million for top wrestlers from the American Wrestling Federation to travel to North Korea and entertain him.[4] He spends about $700,000 a year on Hennessy's Paradis cognac and is the company's biggest customer.[5] In 1998, when the famine was at its worst, the regime imported watches from Switzerland worth $2.6 million.[6] That number tripled to $10 million in 2001.[7] That same year, while the UN was appealing for $600 million in emergency aid for the country, Kim spent "$20 million importing 200 of the latest and costliest . . . Mercedes, which he distributed as rewards to his followers after the test-firing of a new long-range missile over Japan."[8]

As Edward Kim, editor of the *Chosun Journal*, wrote, "The regime partied while the people starved."[9] This might be one of North Korea's best-kept secrets. While the regime uses the national budget to build nuclear warheads and party, they have asked the North Korean people to make sacrifices by cutting down to two meals per day.

One Crossing Borders local staff worker commented upon returning from North Korea in January 2007, "There is a huge discrepancy between the wealthy and the poor." There may be no country in the world where inequality is greater. And people are beginning to notice the growing economic differences.

Crossing Borders sends Korean-Chinese teams into North Korea on a monthly basis. In 2006, Voice of the Martyrs fully funded our project and made it possible for us to send in about 10 teams a month. The purpose of these trips is to provide humanitarian assistance to North Koreans and give support to persecuted Christians in the country. When the Korean-Chinese teams return, they write detailed reports about their travel to North Korea and our staff meets with them to debrief them on their trip.

Returning teams always comment on the poverty-stricken state of the nation. Pastor Cho, a Korean-Chinese local staffer, wrote in his report, "We went to Aunt Young-Ran's house. She was so incredibly poor. There was no immediate food to eat, no groceries, no soy sauce, not even any *kimchi*.[10] The children were naked because they had no clothes to wear." Another returning team member commented, "They lived in dirt houses that did not have any appliances or furniture. The walls were covered with origamilike paper shaped into flowers. There was a beat-up drawer in the room. They did not have electricity, so they could not see at night. When you looked at their clothes, you could tell that they could not afford new clothes but borrowed used clothes from their neighbors."

Clothes are a precious commodity in North Korea. One North Korean woman, Ok Hui, said that one day while she was at work in the fields she spotted an old woman who could deliver a message to her mother who was in a different location. Ok Hui took off her underwear and offered it to the woman if she would send the message. Since underwear is a rare item in North Korea, the old woman agreed.[11]

The markets are filled mostly with Chinese products (although at times the government even bans Chinese products in an effort to curb illegal trade). American items are permanently banned in North Korea. One teenage refugee said to me, "Did you know that you can't wear blue jeans in North Korea?" When I asked why, she replied, "Because Americans wear blue jeans." Refugees who return to North Korea don't take any American products with them because of the high risk of being caught with them.

According to our reports, the number of beggars on the streets has been steadily increasing over the years. With the exception of a show city like Pyongyang, beggars and the homeless are rampant on the streets of North Korea. Orphaned children have become a problem of epidemic proportions. North Koreans even have a word to describe beggar children, *Khot-Jebi*, which literally means "flower-swallow."

During a period when North Korea banned U.S. citizens from traveling there, I was able to visit the country for four days through some government contacts I had developed over the years. My contacts met me at the China–North Korea border and took me into the country without any visa and without stamping my passport. On my visit, I observed these *Khot-Jebi* kids swarming the streets. One time, I tried to take a picture of them as they ran up to me asking for money, but the National Security Police agent who was assigned to me, Agent Koh, grabbed my wrist and said, "There are two things you cannot take pictures of. First, don't take any pictures of any military sites. Second, don't take pictures of anything that would make us look bad. Only take pictures of things that make us look good so that when you return home you can tell everyone how beautiful our country is." Sounds funny, I know, but that's really what he said.

LIFESTYLE

It's a bit ironic that my great uncle was abducted and taken to North Korea over 50 years ago to help develop the electrical system, yet electricity is still virtually nonexistent for the common person. Korean-Chinese staff who travel to the country often comment on the lack of electricity. A husband and wife team reported, "We brought a rice cooker to give them, but they didn't even have any electricity, so we had to bring it back." Pastor Myung observed upon his return that the food shortage "would be bearable if there was electricity, but every day there is an electrical shortage that makes it feel as if you are living in a pitch-black world . . . If I could sum it up in one sentence, I would say that the people [of North Korea] are in a living hell."

For the most part, motorized transportation is unavailable to the average North Korean. A government worker once asked me what kind of work my parents did. When I told her that my dad used to work with cars, she replied, "Maybe he could send a car for us to use. Nobody has a car here, only the privileged do."

In 2005, I visited a small Chinese village at the China–North Korea border with one of our local staff who used to live in the area. As we sat on the bank of the river overlooking a North Korean village, he said, "I used to sit here for hours trying to see if I could see a single person or a car. My dad once worked here for a week and didn't see a single person over there." Startled, he pointed to a truck in the town and said, "That's the first time I ever saw a vehicle there." A staff member who traveled to North Korea in the latter half of 2005 remarked, "The electrical shortage has even cut off any type of public transportation. The only transportation you see on the streets is army cars and an occasional train a few times a week."

In those rare instances when transportation is available, it is primitive at best. When visiting the country, I saw a blue truck with a cloud of smoke behind it struggling to move along. I asked Agent Koh about it. "Someone sits at the back of the car and throws in wood or coal," he explained. "You know how in a fire there is the orange flame and the blue flame? The blue flame has gas in it. The car takes the gas from the blue flame and uses that." But I asked my brother, an engineer who studied automotive engineering, about the orange-and-blue-flame concept, and Koh's explanation was incorrect. Nonetheless, because oil is so expensive in North Korea, cars use steam engines powered by wood or coal.

Those people who do have the rare opportunity to ride in a vehicle often talk of frequent mechanical failures. One Korean-Chinese staff who rode in a North Korean bus observed, "Because the bus was so old, it would continuously break down throughout the trip, stalling for half an hour before starting up again."

Proper heating during the unforgiving winters is another major concern for families. Siberian winds blowing from the northwest result in brutally cold winters. Wood, though the cheapest form of heating, is neither affordable nor readily accessible for most families. In October 2006, I asked a family that had recently defected how they managed to heat their homes in North Korea. One of the sons replied:

> We used wood for heat. Since people don't have money to buy wood, they go to the mountains to get it. The distance to the mountains is about eight miles, which takes us around five to six hours to walk. We'll leave at about 5:00 to 6:00 in the morning and arrive in the mountains around 10:00 A.M. We get back home around midnight.

When I asked why they arrived home so late, he explained, "In North Korea, you need a permit to go into the mountains to get wood or you have to pay. We returned home late at night to avoid the police." Because there is such a shortage of wood in North Korea, it is illegal to cut it without a permit from the government. Another of the sons said:

We're probably twice as fast as people here [in China]. We walk fast so we were able to do the hike in five to six hours. We see people walking on the streets here in China and wonder why they walk around so slowly. We each took a log about two meters long and dragged it back home. We made this trip every two or three days and we took turns going two at a time. So, thankfully our family was able to have heat every day. It was easier for us because we lived near the mountains. . . . In big cities like Chongjin, you have apartments where there is no heat. Since the buildings have no heat, it's even colder than in small houses where you can burn wood or coal. I think people in apartments are worse off for this reason.

I asked, "So basically your full-time job in North Korea was going to the mountains to get wood?" The son replied, "There's no work to do in North Korea. Even if you do work, they don't pay you. So why work?"

The average American walks 1.4 miles a week, which adds up to 350 yards a day.[12] On the days they went to get wood, these North Korean men were walking 75 times farther. And they lived near the mountains!

FEAR AND INFORMANTS

North Koreans live in a constant state of fear. Mr. Ahn, a refugee, said, "Even when I think of returning home, I have fear. It's my home, yet when I think of returning, there is fear in my heart." Our Crossing Borders workers, upon returning from the country, comment on the obvious state of fear there. People are reluctant to speak with foreigners out of fear they might say something wrong. Children will not accept gum or candy from strangers. North Koreans have all seen or heard about the black vehicle that pulls up to people's homes and takes them away, never to be seen again. There is an entire department devoted to visiting people's homes and checking radios to make sure they are not listening to any illegal frequencies.[13] Because there have been an increasing number of investigations of families living near the China border, some families are moving further inland to avoid scrutiny.

Informants are the key sources of this perpetual state of fear. Kang Chol-Hwan, a prison camp survivor and author of *Aquariums of Pyongyang: Ten Years in the North Korean Gulag*, wrote, "The informants were at every turn. There was no one to confide in, no way to tell who was who."[14] It's difficult to know just how many informants there are in North Korea. One North Korean insists that "20 percent of the population are informants." Pastor Oh, one of our staff who frequently travels to North Korea for business, believes that one out of every two people are informants.

Refugee informants pose an immense challenge to our work and threaten to sabotage it. The regime sends spies to China posing as refugees in an attempt to infiltrate humanitarian aid and church networks. We have had several encounters with refugee informants, but one in particular did the most damage.

Mrs. Joo, a refugee, was under the direct care of Missionary Lee, one of our local staff members. She attended his house church every week and expressed a growing interest in learning more about Christianity and the Bible. When I met her, she sang along to all of the hymns, prayed, and even told me how she converted to Christianity.

After the service was over, Missionary Lee and I were discussing his upcoming trip to a particular village in North Korea when Mrs. Joo interrupted, "That's my hometown." She said that she was planning on returning home for a few days and offered to meet with Missionary Lee and help him with his work. But when they met in North Korea, Mrs. Joo turned him in to the National Security Police, saying that he was a spy working for the U.S. government.

Missionary Lee was imprisoned for six months and suffered a great deal (more on his story later). He endured beatings and torture, and nearly died. The North Korean government eventually released him after we paid a ransom of $3,600. Upon his release, he wrote a report saying, "I found out that Mrs. Joo was a North Korean spy. . . . When I was being tortured, I remember seeing a report she had written, describing everything she saw and heard from that worship service— even things regarding Teacher Mike. The report was as thick as a book."

EMPLOYMENT AND UNEMPLOYMENT

The regime has its hands full dealing with emerging discontent over lack of employment opportunities. Mr. Shin, a refugee in one of our shelters, offered, "I would say around 95 percent of people in North Korea don't have jobs." While this may be an overstatement, the vast majority of the population is unemployed, as interviews with North Koreans and our local staff confirm. Pastor Sohn, a Korean-Chinese staff member, observed during his visit, "There are many unemployed men sleeping under the shade of a tree in the middle of the day . . . Many of the factories that these men worked for have closed down. . . . The morale of the town has hit a low point."

People once coveted government jobs because they paid well compared to other work. Now the tables have turned, and it is seen as somewhat of a curse to have a government job. Men are forced to work long hours for the government, often without pay, and those that don't show up for work risk imprisonment. In the Soviet Union, people who worked for the government used to say, "We pretend to work and they pretend to pay us." One finds the same situation in North Korea today.

Mrs. Suh, a Korean-Chinese staff member, says, "People were better off selling products on the streets because working for the factories doesn't pay very well. However, many men are forced to work in these government-run institutions. They are not free to work where they want, and these men rarely receive income for their work. Women, on the other hand, are able to freely conduct their own business and find income by selling in the markets."

A role reversal has occurred: In patriarchal North Korea, it is now the women who are usually the breadwinners. When I visited the country, I found that only women were working in the stores and markets. Mr. Bae, another Korean-Chinese staffer, reported upon his return from the country:

> Early in the morning you will see women carrying goods to sell on their shoulders. In North Korea, women are better at supporting themselves and their families financially than men. Women will wake up early to work in the marketplace. They will spend the whole day in hard labor. Then they come home late at night to prepare dinner and take care of their families. The men in North Korea are still stuck in the old ways of thinking that men are more important than women.

The lack of job opportunities has forced women, children, and the elderly to become entrepreneurs. People scramble for any type of available work that will provide a meager income. Selling or trading coal, seafood, produce, and Chinese products are just a few ways that people make their living. A person can make about 12 cents a day selling coal. Hyun-Soo, a resourceful 14-year-old boy, is able to earn about 25 cents a day by picking up coal that falls off the sides of trucks and then selling it. Those with more money will open businesses such as bars, pool halls, and karaoke clubs. Some venture into illegal businesses such as drug or human trafficking because of the potential for lucrative profits.

Traditionally, a government employee made around 3,000 to 5,000 North Korean Won (KPW) per month, which is equivalent to about U.S. $2 to $3.[15] In the summer of 2005, I said to a group of refugees, "I heard that the average salary in North Korea is around $2 to $3 a month." They all laughed, and one replied, "That was long time ago. Now, you're lucky if you can even get $1.25 per month." Government salaries have decreased to the point where they are nonexistent in most cases. Many employees will work for a whole month only to find that the government cannot pay them for their labor. Yet they are still required to work every day.

I have heard of cases in which factory workers are paid salaries, but such instances are rare. In May 2007, one of our staff members visited a factory in a large city in North Korea. "The employees looked like they were in terrible physical condition," she said. "They wouldn't let us take pictures inside the factory because they didn't want us showing other people what the employees looked like and the environment in which they worked." She added that the factory had electricity and that there were workers' quarters where employees could sleep. They received a salary of about $1.50 per month.

In addition to the problem of unemployment, the incredible depreciation of the North Korean Won has been disastrous for the economy. The regime claims that its official exchange rate is 141 KPW to the U.S. dollar (as of December 2006)[16] and tries to use this figure for international trade. But, in reality, the market rate (or black-market rate) of the KPW is much weaker—currently around 3,200 KPW to the U.S. dollar. Throughout my time at the China–North Korea border, I documented the fluctuating exchange rate of the KPW (see table). In a period of just four years, from May 2003 to April 2007, the Won weakened nearly fourfold. The effect of this on the North Korean economy and individual families has been devastating.

Changes in Exchange Rate, North Korean Won (KPW) to U.S. Dollar (USD) (number of KPW per 1 USD)

May 2003	April 2004	October 2005	March 2006	April 2007
875	1083	2500	3042	3167

Due to the depreciation of the North Korean Won, imports from other countries, China in particular, have become increasingly expensive. Imported food from China has become unaffordable for the North Korean people and raised the cost of their own food. The price of food in markets in North Korea has now skyrocketed to the point where it is virtually impossible for the average family to afford three square meals a day. Additionally, a decline in humanitarian aid from the international community has created a fear that there will be a rice shortage, also driving up the cost of food.

The best rice in North Korea, which is poor by Chinese standards, now costs about 25 cents (800 KPW) per kilogram. (In the United States rice costs roughly $1 per kilogram.) It has held somewhat steady at this price for about two years now (since April 2005). Assuming that a government employee does get paid his monthly salary of 62 cents (2,000 KPW), with his full salary he can only purchase 2.5 kilograms of white rice per month, which would be about 10 to 12 small bowls of rice. In other words, one month's salary cannot even buy one bowl of white rice a day for one person—let alone feed a whole family. Even if a husband and wife both received such monthly government wages, that money would not be enough to buy one bowl of rice a day for one person.

When I showed these numbers to Professor Mark Rush, an economics professor at the University of Florida, he commented, "They have to be going into a lot of black market activity. I would imagine bartering plays a big role there. I just don't know how those people live . . . How would you live there?"[17]

Families in North Korea are constantly in crisis mode as they scramble to survive and make ends meet. Most families cannot afford to eat white rice and substitute corn gruel instead, which is about half the cost of rice. White rice is reserved for the upper class in North Korea. The average family can only afford to eat rice on special occasions such as birthdays and national holidays. A North Korean refugee boy named Ja-Hoon recalled, "Every year on my birthday I received a bowl of white rice."

BRIBERY, CORRUPTION, AND STEALING

Bribery has been institutionalized to the point where it is difficult to get anything accomplished in North Korea without paying a bribe. Pastor Lee said, "In North Korea, if you have money you can do anything." Mr. Bae, who visited North Korea in mid-2005, observed, "When you go out on the streets, you see soldiers smoking cigarettes and corrupt government officials that will not help you without a bribe."

Customs officials constantly harass our workers when trying to enter North Korea. Even though they have their visas and all of the necessary paperwork, customs officials will hold them for hours until they finally offer a bribe. Two local staffers who traveled to North Korea in early 2007 reported, "I gave him [a customs official] two packs of cigarettes along with $25 stuffed inside, asking him to be lenient with us. As a result, we were placed first in line during the afternoon inspections. . . . Other people were forced to throw away as much as six bundles, but we were able to pass through without losing a single set of clothes."

In addition to bribery, stealing is now becoming a necessary means of survival in North Korea. Because of the economic crisis, people are left with no option but to steal if they want to live. Pastor Moon stated, "Good people can't survive in North Korea. They can't survive because they don't know how to steal. You have to steal in order to survive." Pastor Kim, upon his return from the country, reported, "While many years ago it was considered a crime to steal in North Korea, stealing is no longer considered a crime. People do not look upon it negatively anymore. It is understood that people need to survive and in order to do that they must steal."

Many of our refugees have confessed that they stole regularly as a means of survival. Mrs. Roh, an elderly refugee, confessed, "At night, we would sneak into factories and steal salt. We also stole oil because they had to have oil to run the machines."

When I asked Kyung-Hwa, a 16-year-old refugee girl, what aspect of life in North Korea was the most difficult, she said that stealing was the hardest. When I asked why, she replied, "My father had to go out for work that he didn't get paid for. If he missed work, then he would go to prison, so he couldn't earn money for the family. He had to go do his government work. And my sister didn't know how to do anything . . . Everyone steals from each other over there. . . . If you can't do something bad, then you are naive and you won't survive."

Even stealing among family members has become a problem. Min-Hee, a teenaged refugee girl, said her brothers "took whatever appliances that were in the house . . . and sold them. Then they would go out and spend all the money. It was because of them that our house was ruined."

Because of the mounting financial desperation and the increasing number of thieves, it has become unsafe to travel at night. Pastor Kwon, who visited North Korea in mid-2005, recounted, "In 2005, the central government ordered that no one should be walking the streets at night. Robbery in the middle of the night has been so prevalent, that no one is allowed to be out after dark."

Sang-Min, an ex–North Korean soldier, told me about the problem of stealing in the military: "One hundred percent of those in the military steal. There is not a single person in the military that hasn't stolen—even those with stars on their shoulders. Officers will give soldiers an order like, 'Go out and get me some cigarettes.' You're thinking to yourself, 'Where in the world am I going to get some cigarettes?' So you have to go to someone, slap them around a bit, and take cigarettes from them. So, from early on you learn to steal. I've got a lot of sin I've piled up."

VIOLENCE, ALCOHOL, GAMBLING, AND DRUGS

North Korean men are some of the most violent people I have ever met. Violence is somehow encouraged by their culture. It seems that every

North Korean man has some experience with either martial arts or boxing. As a result, it is not uncommon to see fights break out on the streets of North Korea. "There's a lot of fighting," Master Chung told me. "I've been in many bar fights." Smiling, he showed me a scar on his knuckle. "I punched some guy in the mouth, and his tooth stuck to my knuckle."

In our shelters it is a great challenge to get North Korean men to live together in peace. In fact, some organizations have a policy of not allowing men to live together without any supervision. Our staff who manage the refugee shelters gladly accept women but are always reluctant to receive men. Mrs. Kang, a shelter manager, once left two refugee men in their early thirties alone for one day. After running her errands, she came back at the end of the day to find both of them bloodied and bruised. They had gotten into a fistfight and left bloodstains all over the apartment.

In major cities in China, you'll find North Korean restaurants with employees from Pyongyang. The word on the street is that some of the waitresses at these restaurants are spies trained in the martial arts. I once ate at one of these restaurants with two friends who were also tae kwon do black belts. My South Korean friend, Byung, who was an instructor and fourth-degree black belt, whispered, "If you look at their knuckles you'll see that they're bruised and scabbed from training." Young-Min, a Korean-Chinese, was a third-degree black belt and a bit of a womanizer. He had a crush on one of the waitresses and asked her, "What degree black belt are you?" She was a petite woman in her late twenties, a little over five feet tall, and about 115 pounds. She gave a flirtatious smile and ignored his question. He continued, "I'm serious. We would like to know. We're all tae kwon do black belts here." Pointing to Byung and me, he said, "He's a fourth degree and he's a first degree." She finally asked, "What degree are you?" "I'm a third degree," Young-Min told her. She then playfully replied, "Let's put it this way. If we fought, I would beat you."

Byung and I had a good laugh as Young-Min's face turned red. He smiled, lit up a cigarette, and didn't say anything else.

As in many Asian countries, drinking is a significant part of the culture in North Korea. Mrs. Kyung, a refugee woman who owned a bar there, said, "Even if men have a hard time buying food, they'll manage to find some way to buy alcohol." One of our Korean-Chinese staff added, "Even though they don't eat properly, they will drink some alcohol everyday. It's a way to relieve stress. By drinking, they find relief for a moment."

I always had a difficult time understanding how North Koreans could afford alcohol under such dire circumstances. Dr. Norbert Vollertsen, a German doctor who worked in North Korea from 1999 to 2000, suggests that there is state-sponsored alcoholism in North Korea. By making alcohol affordable and readily available, the regime is able to successfully pacify and control the people. Vollertsen remarked:

> When I was a medical doctor there, I always wondered about so many young, especially male patients, in the hospitals . . . Their eyes were quite yellow. So I diagnosed that they were suffering from hepatitis. Then after one or two weeks I learned what is going on in North Korea. It's a state of alcoholism—state-sponsored alcoholism. When you can get nothing in any shop in North Korea, you always can get *soju*[18]—that is the very cheaply produced alcohol in North Korea. It's so toxic that when I once tried it, I had a headache for two or three days . . . It's always available. In every shop you go, there's nearly nothing. There are empty shelves, no rice, no corn, no bread, nothing for the children. But alcohol, you can always get it. Even in the most removed area of North Korea. And that's why I call it "state-sponsored." . . . It is to keep the people happy.[19]

Gambling and drugs are also prevalent. One husband-wife team that visited in November 2005 wrote, "Nearly all the North Korean men who were 17 years or older used 'ice' [the street name for crystal methamphetamine]. . . . The women used drugs, too. . . . The North Koreans were also heavily involved in gambling. They say that once you start a game, you can end up playing for three days straight. For this reason, they used drugs to stay awake and to endure the lack of sleep. A few people, knowing that we came from China, asked the owner of the house whether we were interested in buying some drugs."

When I told a friend who used to have a crystal methamphetamine addiction that some North Koreans were using the drug, she commented, "It seems to fit the North Korean culture . . . When taking 'meth,' you're not hungry and you don't feel the pain of hunger. I would eat a pizza-pocket or a slice of pizza a day and I was okay. . . . At the same time you can work really hard and your level of focus is very high. You also don't need any sleep. During that time I was sleeping about one hour a day."

There are many North Korean drug dealers in China. In June 2007, three North Korean drug dealers (a 28-year-old male, a 52-year-old female, and a 59-year-old female) were captured in northeast China and deported. I have never heard of a North Korean drug dealer being executed in North Korea. We suspect that the three were not punished upon returning to their country since drug trafficking is encouraged and even sponsored by the regime. High-ranking North Korean defectors have testified before Congress saying that the government is overseeing the production and export of heroin and methamphetamine. The *New York Times* reported that in April 2003, "Australian authorities arrested the crew of a North Korean freighter on charges of smuggling $80 million in heroin. Secretary of State Colin L. Powell accused the North Korean government of being 'a regime that thrives on criminality.'"[20]

A PRODUCT OF THE REGIME

From reading this chapter, one can easily gather that North Korea is a very bizarre place—unlike any other country in the world. When I visited it, I felt as if I had just stepped into an Orwellian "twilight zone." It was a surreal experience. Nothing seemed normal. To borrow a line from George Orwell's *1984*, "though the sun was shining and the sky a harsh blue, there seemed to be no color in anything, except the posters that were plastered everywhere."[21] The mood was dark, and the people appeared lifeless.

While it is not unusual to find things such as poverty, unemployment, violence, alcoholism, theft, or corruption in any country, the degree to which they plague North Korea is astounding. It is one of the poorest countries in the world today. It also has one of the highest, if not *the* highest, rates of unemployment. Violence and alcoholism are rampant. The high levels of theft, violence, bribery, corruption, and oppression have caused North Koreans to become distrustful and manipulative people, more so than anyone I have ever met. But I am not morally condemning them—they are a product of the North Korean regime. A country does not end up this way by chance. The North Korean leadership has created this "living hell."

THREE

Famine

[North] Korean children should never starve while a massive army is fed.

—President George W. Bush,
in a February 2002 speech in Seoul, South Korea

In *Beyond Borders*, a movie dedicated to "relief workers and the millions of people who are victims of war and persecution," a relief worker named Sarah Jordan (Angelina Jolie) asked Nick Ward (Clive Owen), a medical student, "What's the first thing you do when you get a cold?" "Chicken soup, aspirin, scotch," Ward replied. "Do you ever just have the cold?" Jordan asked him. "No," Ward said. "No. And that's us, right?" Jordan replied. "We drown it, we kill it, numb it, anything not to feel . . . Here they feel everything. Straight from God. There's no drugs. There's no painkillers. *It's the weirdest, purest thing—suffering.* And when you've seen that kind of courage, you know that . . . we have no idea what courage is."

The North Koreans have suffered greatly and courageously endured what the United Nations has referred to as the greatest famine since Ethiopia in 1984. The country has lost more than 10 percent of its population to starvation alone. During the height of the famine in the late 1990s, Jasper Becker writes, people "would wake up each day and immediately check with their neighbors to see who was still alive."[1] Mrs. Sohn, an elderly North Korean woman now in her eighties, actually thinks back to the time of the Japanese occupation with nostalgia: "At least people didn't starve to death back then."

The situation improved drastically after 2000, but poor economic policies and a series of floods and bad harvests have caused another major food shortage in recent years. We still receive reports of people dying as a direct result of starvation. When he returned from the country in mid-2005, Mr. Koo reported, "In Nampo, 20 people starved to death this year." Refugees say that in Musan, a mining town near the Chinese border, half of the 130,000 people have either died or fled.[2]

Estimates of the total death toll generally range from two to three million. Hwang Jang-yop, the highest-ranking North Korean defector, asked a senior official in the agricultural office before leaving North Korea how many people had starved to death. The official replied, "In 1995 about 500,000 people starved to death . . . In 1996, about one million people are estimated to have starved to death . . . In 1997 about two million people will starve to death if no international aid is provided."[3]

WHAT NORTH KOREANS EAT

The number one concern for North Koreans is food. Everything else is peripheral. Mrs. Choi, a refugee, recalled meeting a man in North Korea "whose sister was a Christian. She told me to believe in Jesus. I asked her if God would give me food. She said that He would hear my prayers. I told her not to lie to me."

North Koreans are primarily concerned with how they are going to feed their families. They wonder if they will be able to harvest enough food in the upcoming farming season to survive another brutal winter. Anything in the home that can be bartered for food is sold.

The average family in North Korea now eats only two meals a day. Their main staple is corn gruel. Mrs. Chung visited North Korea in early 2006. She found that the situation "has improved much from the past. They can eat at least two meals of corn gruel each day." When I asked Dong-Sun, a recent defector, what he had eaten in North Korea, he replied, "We ate corn gruel. Is there anything else to eat besides that in North Korea?" Mrs. Lee, a North Korean mother of two, said, "If you can eat corn gruel for 365 days a year, your family is well off."

The following reports from Korean-Chinese staff who visited the country from January 2005 through May 2007 give an idea of what North Koreans are eating today:

> If a family could eat corn gruel twice a day, they were considered to be fortunate. . . . Even when they eat tofu, they have no soy sauce to eat it with, so they eat it mixed in saltwater. . . . They say they never get to see any oil or meat.
>
> The rice is so dry and tough. They say that it's just not tasty to eat. The vegetables are eaten raw because they do not have spices and oils that they can cook with. Salt, oil, soy sauce, and pepper are very expensive, so they cannot afford them. Oil is also very rarely available to the people as well.
>
> Dinner consisted of *kimchi* and potato plant stems. The married couple said that they could eat rice beginning in June if they worked hard at their business. Because they had visitors from China, they bought tofu . . . They told us they haven't eaten any kind of meat for three years.
>
> In areas 15 kilometers away from Musan, people have not eaten rice for over 10 years.
>
> When I visited a family . . . they were only able to give a small corn on a cob and a bowl of porridge made of powder. The amount that they gave was not able to fill our stomachs.

Only the wealthy can eat white rice or any kind of meat in North Korea. "Before coming to China, I think I've only eaten beef once before," Jin-Sook, an 18-year-old refugee girl, said. "It's so expensive and we don't have many cows in North Korea." Sang-Kyu, a refugee whose family had above-average living standards, added, "Meat is so expensive that we buy a small amount of meat and use it to make soup because there's not enough meat to go around." Ki-Hoon, a former refugee who returned to his hometown in North Korea, remarked, "In North Korea, beef is so valuable that we say one cow is equal to the value of one person. Beef is so precious that we call it *bo-yak* (oriental medicine)."

Under such dire circumstances, North Koreans have had to become creative to survive. "In North Korea, fall is the time when we harvest," Suk-Chul said. "During that time, rats take food from the fields and store it away underground for the winter. We looked for those underground holes and took the food from the rats." A young refugee girl interjected, "Some families even eat rats. I heard that it's good." Surprised, I asked Suk-Chul about it. "Of course—rat is meat, isn't it?" he replied.

Pets hardly exist in North Korea because most have been eaten. Na-Young, a 13-year-old refugee girl who was repatriated to North Korea in November 2005, recalled, "On my birthday my mom bought me a rabbit. But later we were so hungry that we had to eat it."

The North Korean government has asked families to help their country by cutting down to two meals a day and has suggested that they try alternative foods, such as "roots, bark, seaweed, husks, and cobs to make noodles or 'cakes.'"[4] Many North Koreans have had to resort to eating grass and tree bark in order to survive, especially during the height of the famine. Yun-Hee, a refugee woman in her mid-thirties, said, "Sometimes when there was a shortage of corn meal, we mixed it with grass to sustain it for longer periods of time. Sometimes we didn't even have corn meal or grass, so we went without food." Young-Kuk, a refugee boy, told me, "We ate the grass that the pigs eat, with some salt. And some of the grass we ate was poisonous, causing our faces to get bloated, so much that we couldn't see."

In the summer of 2004, I met Mrs. Song, who at 80 was the oldest North Korean I had ever met. When I asked her how she survived during the height of the famine, her voice trembled with emotion as she spoke:

We were lucky if we ate once a day. We ate if we were lucky enough to find grass from the mountains. . . . But there was barely any grass. We ate anything we could get our hands on. We peeled tree bark . . . During those three to four years many people died. . . . There were so many graves that the government tried to hide them to make it seem like all those people never died. Back then, people didn't even look like people. . . . Because when people were starving, they got sick. Starvation brings illness, you know? . . . People [would] rinse their empty salt jar with water and drink it as their last meal. . . . People even ate children.

I have heard several accounts of cannibalism in North Korea. Ms. Park, a refugee woman, recalled one event in the summer of 1997: "I

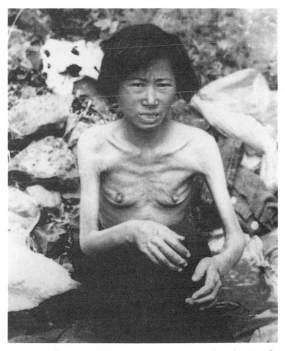

"A North Korean refugee managed to escape from the city of Hyesan in the northernmost province of North Korea to Changbai, a Chinese city close to the North Korean border, but she died of starvation two days after this picture was taken in 2000."[5] *(Life Funds for North Korea Refugees)*

didn't see it for myself but there was a 28-year-old male who was caught for eating a 4-year-old child. I didn't see him eat the child, but I did see him publicly executed for the crime." Though I have not been able to verify them, I have heard several similar accounts.

As we concluded my interview with Mrs. Song, her overseeing pastor stated, "I hope she can live more comfortably now. She has had a hard life and has gone through too much already." Mrs. Song whispered, "I want to live well."

CHILDREN AND FAMINE

In North Korea, it is often the children and the elderly who are the first to die from starvation. Pastor Yi, a Korean-Chinese staff member, told me that during one of her visits to North Korea, a son pointed to a bowl of rice on the table after eating a bowl of corn gruel and said, "Mom. I'm going to eat this." His mom replied, "No. You can't eat that. It's for your dad to eat when he gets home from work." The boy shouted in defiance, "No! I'm going to eat this!" "Son, you can't eat the rice," his mom firmly reprimanded him. "It's for your dad." The child then threw a tantrum and shouted, "I want to eat this rice right now!" Pastor Yi commented, "I felt so bad for that child. This kind of thing is going on all over North Korea. There is a lot of fighting over food."

Indeed, there is probably no country in the world today where there is more fighting over food. Kang Chol-Hwan, a prison camp survivor and author of *Aquariums of Pyongyang*, wrote, "Hunger quashes man's will to help his fellow man. I've seen fathers steal food from their own children's lunchboxes. As they scarf down the corn, they have only one overpowering desire: to placate, if even for just one moment, that feeling of insufferable need."[6]

Min-Jung, a 17-year-old refugee, cried as she told this story: "I was out of the house and my dad gave my brother a piece of bread to eat for lunch and he also gave him a piece to bring to me. My brother really wanted my piece too, so after eating his bread, he finished half of my bread on his way to meet me. I came back home. I guess we missed each other. I asked my dad for lunch and he told me that my brother had it. So I waited and waited because I was so hungry. He finally came back and he was soaked. He was totally drenched [from the rain] . . . I asked my brother for my bread. He hesitated and didn't give it to me. I was so hungry so I swore at him a lot. Then he gave me the half-eaten bread as he was crying. Now that I look back, I feel so bad for him. My brother was so weak because he wasn't eating well. His arm is only half of my arm size. Whenever I think of my brother, I keep remembering that day."

In the summer of 2005, one of our Korean–Chinese teams traveling to North Korea observed, "There were incidents where a woman would be eating a bowl of noodles at an outdoor noodle stand and a child would take the bowl from her and run. When the child was caught, he got a harsh beating . . . Others who were hungry came and ate the noodles that were covered in dirt."

Children in North Korea are clearly malnourished. "Due to malnutrition, these children have big heads, feeble arms and legs, and protruding stomachs," one local staff member observed. "Seeing how life was so hard, my heart hurt just thinking that these children will have to grow up in this situation." Malnutrition has significantly stunted the growth of North Korean children. In 2002, a UN European Union survey reported, "An average seven-year-old boy in North Korea is now 20 centimeters shorter and 10 kilos lighter than his brother in South Korea."[7]

Their stunted growth will be a permanent reminder of the suffering they have endured. When a North Korean child defects to China, his undersize is an issue. Because they do not look their ages, most refugees subtract three to five years from their ages in order not to raise any suspicions. Sang-Mi, a refugee girl staying at a house church, said, "At church, everyone is so tall. The pastor told me to say I'm younger, because I'm so small. I'm really 17 years old, but because of my size, I tell people at church that I'm 15."

Mrs. Yoon, a North Korean woman in her late thirties, says she still cries when she thinks of a six-year-old boy named Chung-Ho who she met on the streets in North Korea:

> I was going to the market to buy some food when I saw a boy sitting on the ground, pounding the floor with his fists. He was wailing at the top of his lungs. He cried, "Why was I born into this world? Why did my mom give birth to me?" He was cursing the day he was born. I was so saddened by the sight and noticed that he wasn't wearing any shoes . . . He had his feet wrapped in cloth. I approached him, and he told me his story. The boy had no home and no parents. He was one of the many orphans I saw in North Korea. He was all alone, living by himself, and slept in a stairwell at night. That day he was caught trying to steal some food and was beaten by the store owner. I felt terrible for the boy, so I bought him some corn gruel.

Mrs. Yoon paused for a moment to regain her composure, then added, "When I saw the boy in that state, I cried a lot with him. He was so hungry that he ate the bowl of corn gruel in one gulp. After he finished his meal he got on his knees and bowed to me, touching his head to the floor over and over again, saying, 'Thank you, Auntie. Thank you.'"

In a PBS documentary titled *Korean War Stories*, Irving R. Levine, a former NBC news correspondent, tells of a moment etched in his memory from the Korean War:

> I can remember walking in single file with a company of American soldiers. And sitting on all sides was wreckage and human misery. And the one sight that will remain with me forever and is burned in my mind as if I was looking at it now is of a little Korean child sitting on a curb weeping bitterly. And one of the soldiers in this file turned to his fellow soldier and said, "What's the kid crying about?" And the other soldier responded, "*He's just learned that he's a Korean.*"

As I sat in my living room in China and watched this documentary, I was deeply moved by Levine's story. He was speaking of the Korean War, but my thoughts turned to North Korea and how things are not so different now. The reality is that there are millions of children sitting on a curb or in a stairwell at night, weeping bitterly because they are North Korean.

As in many countries plagued by extreme poverty, parents in North Korea do not see the value of education when they are struggling to put enough food on the table. Pastor Cha, a Korean-Chinese staff member, reported, "Parents tell their children not to go to school because it only makes them hungry and they would be wasting valuable time that they can use to work and get more food." Pastor Huh related, "The children are unable to study in school because of the hunger. The children not only have a hard time studying because of the hunger, but parents actively discourage children from going to school. Parents see education as a luxury they cannot afford and instead tell their children to find ways to make money for the family." Contrast this with the emphasis on education in South Korea, where high school students are under unbelievable pressure to do well academically and regularly study until 2:00 to 3:00 A.M.

The famine has also impaired the intellects of North Korean children. Generations of children are growing up not only with stunted physical growth but also stunted brain development. In a *Foreign Policy* article addressing the problem of malnutrition in the world today, Bjorn Lomborg wrote, "Children lacking iodine do not develop properly, either physically or intellectually. . . . An iron deficit stunts growth and impedes mental abilities—stealing up to 15 IQ points."[8]

DISEASE AND FAMINE

As Mrs. Song, the 80-year-old refugee, pointed out, where there is starvation, there is disease. Some people collapse on the streets of North Korea because of anemia. One study revealed that "women begin to menstruate anytime from 18 years to 21 years. What this suggests is very low nutrition. Also there is tremendous bleeding associated with childbirth, showing that the women do not have enough iron."[9]

Many people die because their bodies are too weak to fight off minor illnesses due to malnutrition. In the early months of 2006, Pastor Yoon reported, "Apparently many children died after eating food imported from China. The reason was that the food was past its expiration date and was eaten while it was moldy. The children already suffered from malnutrition, so once they got food poisoning they could not be treated."

Many refugees enter our shelters with illnesses. Some are life threatening. One of the most rewarding aspects of my job has been seeing sick people fully healed. Mi-Young defected to China in August 2005 and entered one of our refugee shelters with a severe case of tuberculosis (a common disease in North Korea). She and her mom sold everything they had in order to make the journey to China in hopes of finding medical treatment. A doctor in China risked losing his job to examine her, and we learned that treatment would be costly—more than $10,000. After searching for a donor, Tim Peters, a longtime partner in our work and founder of Helping Hands Korea, stepped forward and said that he would cover the medical costs.

When I first met Mi-Young, she did not smile much. In retrospect, it's clear that her sickness affected her self-esteem. Her mood was always solemn and her countenance dismal. Today, she is a completely different person. On the day she was to be released from the hospital, I went to visit her and it was the first time that I saw her smile. She is now one of the most playful of all of the North Korean teenagers I know. Mi-Young is studying Mandarin and hopes to go to culinary school and be a chef one day.

There was a time when I did not understand the severity of the medical needs of our refugees. When I first began my work at the border, I was receiving an overwhelming number of calls from local staff about refugees who needed medical help. Crossing Borders simply didn't have the financial or human resources to obtain treatment for all of the refugees. Medical treatment was costly, and helping only a handful of refugees could completely wipe out our annual budget. One day Pastor Kim, an elderly woman who managed several refugee shelters, called and said, with deep sadness in her voice, "Teacher Mike, the sick refugee woman I told you about several months ago died yesterday." I felt a tremendous sense of guilt; the loss shook me up. I then did a lot of soul-searching and asked myself, "Is there anything I could have done?" From that point on, I vowed to give each medical case my utmost attention. But medical expenses continue to be one of our most costly line items and as a result we still lose people to disease in our shelters.

THE PUBLIC DISTRIBUTION SYSTEM AND HUMANITARIAN AID

Baegup is a Korean word that I never knew existed until I began meeting North Koreans. It simply means "food distribution." North Koreans have traditionally been dependent upon the public distribution system in order to have enough food to survive. However, since the early 1990s the government has been gradually decreasing food distribution to the point where it is pretty much nonexistent today.

Some North Koreans, based on their location and type of employment, still receive government rations, but they are very rare. One family said they received six kilograms of rice from the government one particular month. Another family said that they received occasional *baegup,* but only 50 percent of what they were supposed to receive each time. However, a vast majority of North Koreans say that they have not received food from the government since the early 1990s. When I asked one refugee woman about government food distribution, she laughed and replied, "Food distribution? What food distribution? How long has it been since the government gave us food? Ever since 1992?"

The regime continues to tell North Koreans that food distribution is on the way, but its promises seem empty. Several of our Korean-Chinese teams visiting the country in the fall of 2005 reported:

> They [the government] said that they would distribute rations, but nothing has developed so far.
>
> There is still no distribution of goods to the people from the government. . . . There are rumors of distribution from the government to come within the month, but it's never for sure.
>
> The Ministry of Food Administration has not distributed the food rations that were promised in the beginning of October [2005]. Only members of the Korean Workers' Party have received a little.

On March 26, 2007, Reuters reported that North Korea had admitted to food shortages of a million tons.[10] A couple of days later, a UN official said that North Korea was facing one of its biggest food shortages in the past decade.[11] The shortage has created the need for humanitarian assistance. However, the question is often asked whether humanitarian aid actually gets to the North Korean people.

In 2004, I met two soldiers who had just defected from Pyongyang. One of the men wrote lyrics to propaganda songs in North Korea, while the other wrote the melodies to those songs. They told me about a time when Germany gave thousands of tons of beef to North Korea. When the beef arrived in Pyongyang, German government officials were there to oversee the distribution process and to ensure that the people received the food. One of the soldiers recounted, "We were given specific instructions. We were told to give money and pay for the beef in front of the German officials. Then upon exiting the building, National Security Police agents were waiting to collect the beef and give us our money back." The other soldier commented, "I think it would have been better if Germany never gave us humanitarian aid. If they never gave it to us then we would never have had to smell and touch the beef. It was torture to be that close to beef and not be able to eat it." It is now widely known that foreign aid is rarely given to the people. Instead, it is often distributed among party leadership and the military.

The Honorable Song Young-Sun, a member of the South Korean National Assembly, emphasized the importance of verifying the proper delivery of humanitarian aid when given through official channels:

> North Korea takes our [South Korean] fertilizer, but they don't use it. They sell it to Southeast Asia where they can charge a good price. North Korea has its own fertilizer factory, but that fertilizer has too much acidity. That is why all of the land in North Korea is full of acidity and the harvest is so bad. They need much better quality fertilizer. But the quality of the fertilizer that we give them is so good, and therefore so expensive, they sell it to a Southeast Asian country and use their own fertilizer instead.[12]

By now, the evidence is clear that humanitarian assistance through government channels is ineffective and in most cases simply feeds the party leadership or the military. In order to successfully get food to the people, it must be given through unofficial channels. There are three such channels: businesses, which serve as an excellent platform for establishing a presence in the country and feed the people; the Korean-Chinese, who have unparalleled access to North Korea and can effectively distribute humanitarian assistance; and refugees who return to North Korea. I like the last method since it empowers North Koreans to help other North Koreans.

However, the big obstacle to employing North Koreans is finding people who you can trust. It is no easy task to find a North Korean who you can entrust with a significant amount of money. Only after we have observed and gotten to know a refugee for several years will we do so. Dong-Min, a 28-year-old North Korean, is a devout Christian and is one of the few we have trusted in this capacity. After completing several years of leadership training at a house church in China, he returned to North Korea and now distributes humanitarian aid through the funds we give him. He periodically returns to China to meet with our staff and receive more funds. The last time I met with him in China, he described the challenges of his work:

> It's difficult for me to share with others sometimes. I know I should give and help other people. But even what I have is not enough to live well . . . It's really difficult sometimes. I often wonder, "Is a young 28-year-old like me supposed to live like this?" . . . Honestly, sometimes in anger I don't pray before I eat. I think to myself, "God, I have these missions funds here, but why do I have to live eating like this every day? Can't I eat good food?"

I told Dong-Min that he needed to make sure that he was taking care of his needs and should eat three square meals a day. But I guess he felt guilty eating "so well" when others around him were suffering. I further explained that if he didn't take care of his needs, he would quickly burn out (a lesson I was also learning).

INTERNATIONAL BEGGAR

In July 2004, I helped sponsor a visit by the North Korean National tae kwon do team to China, where they performed a series of exhibitions. They put on an excellent show; their athleticism, high-flying kicks, brick-breaking, and sparring demonstrations were very entertaining and impressive. After one exhibition, I was invited to a private party where the team gathered to eat, drink, dance, and sing karaoke at the local North Korean restaurant. After dinner, the athletes took turns singing North Korean propaganda songs on the karaoke machine. They forced me to take the microphone and sing along to songs that I did not know. After the singing was over, they cleared out the tables and had a dance party as one of the waitresses played music on the keyboard. I wheeled out my old dance moves from the late 1980s and fit right in.

The group was a lot of fun and I was enjoying myself when one of the masters traveling with the team pulled me aside and said, "Mike, we need a battery for one of our cameras. Things have been a bit tight financially for the association. Will you buy it for us?" When I asked how much it was, he said it would cost about $50. I was a bit annoyed, since I had already sponsored the team. "You're telling me that the North Korean Tae Kwon Do Association can't afford a $50 battery?" I asked. "I've already helped sponsor the team and you're asking me for $50?" Upset, I walked away.

Some might say that I overreacted, but I was fed up with North Koreans asking me for things and trying to manipulate me for an extra buck. When I visited North Korea, local government officials, seeing that I was an American, persistently attempted to con money and bribes from me. In addition, many North Korean refugees in our shelters have repeatedly deceived us; they have even stolen money from us in some cases. And now this tae kwon do master was trying to milk me for another $50.

I have often wondered: Why are North Koreans always asking for things? Why do they always play up their poverty? Why are they so manipulative? While such behavior may be common in any third-world country, North Korean refugees who I have befriended in our shelters have repeatedly warned me, "Don't ever trust a North Korean."

I think the reasons for their behavior lie in Kim Jong Il and the North Korean regime. The regime encourages North Koreans to play up their poverty. For example, the government provides temporary visas for those who have relatives in China so that they can visit them and ask for money and food. Also, whenever a foreigner visits North Korea, local government officials bombard him with requests for investments and donations. Kim Jong Il sets the example for his citizens by playing the role of the "international beggar."[13] He asks other countries to provide things such as food and oil while he uses the national budget to build up the military and add more nuclear warheads to his arsenal. What is particularly unique about North Korea is that Kim Jong Il, through his international policy, has created a national culture that is dependent on charity. Begging, asking for things, and manipulating are simply a way of life in North Korea.

FOUR

Road to Refuge

Give me your tired, your poor,
Your huddled masses yearning to breathe free

—Inscription on the Statue of Liberty

In the fall of 2005, I took a group of visitors from the United States to the Tumen River, which borders China and North Korea. As we stood there, my American friends were in awe as they saw for the first time North Korea just 30-some yards across the river. "Should we go for a swim?" I joked. Everyone laughed, but before we knew it, Pastor Choe, a Korean-Chinese staff member, stripped down to his boxers and jumped in. Since it seemed to be culturally acceptable, the rest of us followed his lead. The water was brown, and I could taste the mud as I swam. We played "chicken," seeing who would dare swim closer to the North Korean side.

We were laughing and having a great time, but most people who visit the China–North Korea border comment on their sense of eeriness there. Helie Lee, author of the national bestseller *Still Life with Rice*, describes her visit to another river that divides China and North Korea in her book *In the Absence of Sun*:

> An eerie fear crawled through my flesh as I stood on the Chinese side
> of the Yalu River, gazing across the murky water into one of the most
> closed-off and isolated countries in the world. I couldn't believe it.

Even as my boots sank into the doughy mud, I had trouble coming to terms with the fact that I was actually standing there. Through the heavy layer of fog, I saw North Korea's sharp, mountainous landscape just across the watery border, which was about sixty yards wide and barely waist deep. The riverbank was strewn with rocks and stretched for about forty feet to the base of a tall stone wall. The wall didn't have floodlights or coiled razor wire along the top. It wasn't built to keep people from trying to get out; it was there to prevent the outside world from seeing all the decay, dirt, and disrepair just behind it. But the armed soldiers, posted every ten to fifteen yards along the rocky riverbank, would shoot down anyone who did try to escape over it and to the other side of the river.[1]

As I swam in the Tumen River, a million thoughts raced through my head. The first was rather personal: "I hope I don't get sick from swimming in this dirty water." Then my thoughts turned towards the refugees. Hundreds of thousands of North Korean refugees have swum across this river (or walked across when the water level was low or the river was frozen during the winter). But for them it wasn't a leisurely activity, it was a matter of life and death. I tried to put myself in their shoes and imagine myself escaping a cruel and ruthless regime. What would it be like to swim across this river knowing that I could be shot by a North Korean sniper at any moment? What would it be like to defect and venture into a strange and unfamiliar land where I did not know the language or a single person? Then I thought of the many refugees in our shelters who had defected with a spouse, child, or a family, and the reality of it all began to sink in.

Why do refugees risk so much to make this journey?

WHY REFUGEES DEFECT

Food is probably the most common reason why North Koreans defect. The poorest families are driven into a corner and left with no other

Tumen River, which divides China and North Korea (author photo)

choice but to defect to China to find food if they do not want to starve to death. Other families are simply sick of eating corn gruel every day.

Hannah, an amazing woman in her early thirties from southern California who quit her job as a sixth-grade teacher to join the Crossing Borders field staff for one year, and I once hiked for eight hours in the mountains near the border to meet an elderly refugee couple. They had refused to come down from the mountains out of fear of being captured. It was supposed to be a five-hour hike, but Pastor Chung, the local staff member leading the hike, headed up the wrong mountain at one point. Many times, Hannah and I didn't think we were going to be able to make it. But a mixture of good conversation, music on my iPod, and the beautiful scenery helped me persevere. By the seventh hour it had grown dark, and Pastor Chung said, "We would be in trouble if there was no moonlight." After a grueling eight hours, he finally announced, "Only 200 meters left up this slope!" We made the final push, and at the top of the slope we saw a small shack at the crest of the hill. The guide knocked on the door and shouted, "Hello! It's me! We've come to eat some good food!"

Mr. and Mrs. Hwang opened the door and welcomed us in. I looked inside the one-room home and was amazed at how simply they lived. We exchanged greetings, and Hannah commented, "You have a nice home!" The woman flashed a big smile and said, "Yes it is. Thank you. It's very comfortable living here." Though it's rude to lay down in front of your elders in Korean culture, our bodies were so utterly exhausted that we had no other choice. All of us, except for Pastor Chung, who managed several refugee shelters in the mountains, plopped down on the floor. The wife pulled pillows out for us; at that point, it didn't matter to me that those pillows were filthy or that they were used by people who didn't bathe for weeks or months at a time. (Several weeks later, Hannah checked my hair for lice.) Lying there on the floor, I asked Pastor Chung how far we had hiked. He did a quick calculation in his head and said at least 15 miles.

Mrs. Hwang prepared a simple meal of radish soup we ate with rice that was still left over from the morning. As we devoured the food, I asked the couple why they had come to China. Mr. Hwang replied, "We came to China in search for food. We wanted to live well for once in our lives." I was amazed that this was their idea of "living well." Mr. Hwang added, "We especially wanted to be able to eat meat." When I asked how often they ate meat, he replied, "Whenever we can catch a badger or a raccoon." They were content living in a shack in the mountains eating vegetables that they grew themselves and badgers and raccoons whenever they were fortunate enough to catch one.

Family is another common reason why refugees defect. Families will often send one or two family members to China in order to make some money and then return to North Korea with it. We have many refugees in our shelters that are diligently saving up money to one day return to North Korea and help out their families. When I asked one young girl why she defected, she answered, "I wanted to earn a lot of money and go back to North Korea. We were considered really poor there, and people even called us beggars. Whenever I heard that, I really wanted to earn a lot of money here [in China]. So I came here with that determination."

Once in a while, a life-threatening disease will bring North Koreans to China. Yulee, a refugee woman in her thirties, recalled, "During the time that I was in prison, I had not gotten my period due to poor nutrition. But once my period started, it didn't stop. I was released from prison in October. In January, after three months of bleeding, I went to see a doctor. The doctor said that I needed surgery. I needed money, but I had nothing. The doctor came to our house and . . . said I had cancer and that surgery may not cure it. . . . I knew that I needed to go to China if I wanted to live. . . . The river was up to my neck. It was flood season. I had to climb a rocky cliff. I knew if I were to get proper medical help, I had to climb this mountain."

Another reason why people leave for China is a growing interest in all things Chinese. An infatuation with China is spreading throughout North Korea. Pastor Lee, a local staff member, commented, "They want to learn more about China because there is no hope in North Korea." Another local staff member remarked, "Before you couldn't even talk about China. Now everyone wants to go to China." Mrs. Kim, a refugee, said that when she was in prison in North Korea, "I prayed that God would take me to heaven. In North Korea, I believed that China was heaven because God was in China but not in North Korea."

Refugees also defect because of religious persecution. There is a growing population of refugees who stay in China so that they can worship freely without persecution and learn more about the Bible (more on that later). And refugees defect out of the simple desire for freedom. Young-Ja, a young refugee in her early twenties, said, "Even if I die, I'll never go back." When I asked her why, she replied, "Because you're constantly harassed by the government. You can't think and speak ready." Mrs. Huh, an elderly North Korean woman, commented, "I've suffered in this place for 50 years. With this government, I haven't been able to say a single word. That's alright if I had to live my life like that, but I don't want my kids to have to live like I did. Can you help them escape to China?"

ROAD TO REFUGE

In March 2004, Crossing Borders staff attempted to simulate the refugee experience by hiking one of the trails that is often used to defect from North Korea to China. We used footage of our hike to make a documentary called *Road to Refuge,* which we showed at events in the United States. Starting at the Tumen River, we documented the path of a refugee from the North Korean border to the nearest Chinese city. I learned many things from the experience, the first being the strength of the North Korean border patrol. Right along the river on the North Korean side, there is a small military base that houses 40 soldiers. There are also underground camouflaged posts where soldiers hide and try to catch defectors. Chinese villagers say that sometimes you will find the bodies of refugees floating in the river after they are shot by North Korean soldiers. One local villager estimated that in certain areas there is a post about every 200 meters along the border. A North Korean who lived near the border estimated that guards were stationed every 500 meters.[2] If a refugee is fortunate enough to have a contact in the military, they may be able to cross the river by paying the guard $25.[3]

The second thing I learned was the reality of human traffickers hunting down refugee women. Several hours into the hike we came across a disturbing site. There was a single house along the path that looked a bit out of place. Dogs barked viciously as we passed by, and some people ran out of the house to see who we were. Mr. Cha, a Korean-Chinese man who married a North Korean refugee woman who had defected using the same path, explained the purpose of the house: "Those dogs bark whenever anyone passes by this trail. They are used to alert the owners when North Korean refugees pass by." The owners of the house were beneficiaries of a lucrative human trafficking business. Any North Korean woman caught on the path became a victim of sex trafficking and was sold to the highest-paying Chinese man.

The final lesson I learned was just how physically challenging the journey was. Refugees who use this particular path enter China with the following simple instructions: "Hike over that mountain. Find the main road and follow it for 15 hours to the nearest city." We only hiked for four and a half hours until we reached the main road. We had the liberty of ending our journey there and taking public transportation, but the refugee would have to continue for another 15 hours to the nearest city.

THE JOURNEY

If you took the most direct path from North Korea to China, it would only take a few hours to make the hike. However, in order to evade border guards and the police, refugees have no choice but to hike for days through the mountains. When I asked Sang-Mi, a 16-year-old refugee, how long it took her, she said, "Around two to three days, including the hikes across the mountains and stuff . . . I laugh about it now, but it was really hard back then because we couldn't afford to get caught. We would hide in the mountains." Mrs. Jang, a refugee woman, said it took her about 20 hours. When I asked if it was difficult, she replied, "Not too hard—in North Korea we don't have cars, so we're used to walking."

Some refugees choose to hike at nighttime when visibility is low and to sleep during the day. When I asked a family of defectors how they slept in the mountains, one of the sons replied, "We would just lay on the ground and sleep. It was so cold, we were freezing." Young-Il, a

21-year-old, recounted, "I would put my head down to sleep, but I could never sleep well. I was afraid to go into a deep sleep because I knew I might not wake up again."

Every refugee must cross the river in order to defect. Mi-Young crossed with her parents when the water level was high. She began to float because of her distended belly. At one point she slipped and pulled both her father and mother under water. "We almost died," she recalled.

"My father yelled at me, 'Hold on!'" She told her mom to go ahead without her. "We came all the way here for you," her mother replied. "How can we just go ahead without you?" In the end, her father grabbed both of them firmly by the hands and pulled them through to the other side.

Yulee described her river crossing: "We had to hike in the mountains. The snow was piled high. There were four of us traveling together. The descent down the mountain was very dangerous. The other woman was screaming as she fell. I figured I could die whether I went down the mountain or not. I knew that there was food in China. I went headfirst, tumbling down the mountain. I was covered in snow. We crossed the river into China, and I had not even realized it as the river was frozen." Sung, a refugee teenager, also crossed the river when it was frozen, but he fell in. After pulling himself out, he hiked for 24 hours to the nearest city. "I really thought I was going to die," he said later.

Refugees often choose to defect during the winter because the river is frozen and they generally don't have to worry about swimming. If you visit the Tumen River during the winter months, you can often see the footprints of refugees in the snow. "Even North Korean cows defect and will go back and forth," Pastor Kim chuckled.

RECENT TRENDS

There are a number of factors that have made it increasingly difficult for North Koreans to defect. For one, the North Korean regime is try-

Several narrow bridges span the Tumen River, which divides North Korea and China. The bridges are used primarily to transport goods such as oil, coal, grain, and textiles from China into North Korea. Both sides are heavily guarded to keep North Koreans from using them as an escape route into China. (author photo)

ing to clamp down on defections. In August 2006, it executed three North Korean soldiers for taking bribes and allowing North Koreans to defect to China.

In addition, the regime is handing out harsher punishments for border-crossers. Traditionally, a repatriated refugee could hope to be released after spending three to six months in labor re-education facilities. Human Rights Watch reported a policy change in the summer of 2004, however. Refugees are now being punished with longer and harsher sentences.[4]

A final challenge for would-be defectors is that Chinese villagers are becoming increasingly hesitant to help North Korean refugees. In the past many people would gladly open up their homes for a night and feed refugees, but this is no longer the case. One reason is that the Chinese government issued an edict stating that it would fine and potentially arrest anyone guilty of feeding or housing a refugee. A sign in the border region posted in Chinese reads, "It is forbidden to financially help, harbor, or aid in the settlement of people from the neighboring country who have crossed the border illegally."[5]

A second reason is the increasing number of cases where refugees assault and steal from Chinese people (especially the elderly). If you visit some Chinese border villages, you will see signs warning people against helping North Korean refugees. One reads: "On January 23, 2003, at 11:30 P.M., a horrible incident took place in Banseokjin Byunkyungtun of Hunchun City. A North Korean soldier openly fired his rifle on Chinese soil and wounded a resident with his knife, a clear violation of the China–North Korea agreement. The photo shows the injured resident and the leftover shells." Another sign reads, "On January 29, 2003 . . . a North Korean agent robbed and viciously murdered two civilians living near the border. . . . Pictured are the two civilians who were murdered by the North Korean agent."

FEAR AND HIDING

China has an agreement with North Korea to repatriate all North Korean refugees. While the Chinese government once looked the other way and allowed refugees to live in China, it has now adopted a "zero tolerance" policy. As a result, refugees in China are easily exploited and live in constant fear of being captured and repatriated.

On a trip to the border, I learned that one small village had been hiding a refugee woman for a year. When I asked how they managed to hide her, one of the villagers replied, "When the police come, they go from house to house checking for any refugees. We also just send her [the refugee] from house to house. While they're checking one house, we send her to another house." The man chuckled and seemed pleased with the cleverness of his plan. An elderly woman added, "Sometimes we send her into the mountains to hide over there"—pointing to the mountains about 100 yards away.

Missionary Lee, a Korean-Chinese staff member, described how he hid his North Korean refugee wife, Mrs. Lee: "We ripped away [the wall behind the closet] and made it into a sliding door. This way she could hide behind the closet. When the police come, they open the closet and see nothing inside since the back panel is down."[6]

Mrs. Ahn, a refugee in her early thirties, has had many close calls. But she has managed to evade the Chinese police:

In China, we had a dog, and it would bark whenever someone came by. One morning, my kid was playing outside and my husband went out to get something. So I was home by myself preparing breakfast for my family, and my dog started barking . . . So I looked outside, and policemen were there. When the police drive in, refugees can hear them and have enough time to run away quickly. This time the policemen were walking. . . . We made a compartment in which one person could hide. I quickly went into it. Some of them came in saying, "Is anybody here?" When they walked in, the breakfast table was ready and set, but no one was around. They came in . . . and searched different rooms in the house. They opened all the doors to check if anybody was there, but after looking for a bit they left.

Mrs. Ahn told me of a similar instance:

> My family usually slept in the upper room just in case something happened. One night, we heard a car coming near us. My husband said, "Escape, now!" But I said, "How can we? The policemen are already here." I just stayed there. . . . He told me to at least hide in the closet downstairs. But I just stayed there. They finally walked in and opened the closet to see if anybody was hiding in there. For the whole time, we were in the upper room keeping very quiet. . . . They must have looked through the closet checking everything. After they left, my husband said, "It's a good thing that you didn't go into the closet."

These refugees were the fortunate ones who were able to avoid capture. However, the reality is that many refugees are captured in China and repatriated. China has several detention facilities along the border where they temporarily house refugees before sending them back to North Korea. I visited the Tumen detention center (one of the larger ones) in 2004 with a Korean-Chinese staff member, and he said that 40 refugees were repatriated every week there. At least 6,000 North Koreans were repatriated in 2000, according to the U.S. Committee for Refugees and Immigrants.[7] In October 2003, the Chinese government had half a dozen detention facilities along the border repatriating 200 to 300 North Koreans every week.[8]

Young-Kuk, an 18-year-old refugee, told of how he was captured by Chinese authorities. He was attending a house church service on a Sunday morning when two policemen came knocking on the door:

> The policemen called me over, saying, "Hey, come over here," but right then I knew I was caught. I came over to the back where they were, as if I suspected nothing, and asked them what they wanted. The police officers were wearing plainclothes, but I just got this feeling about them. I walked outside with them while discreetly putting my Bible away. Just as I was about to make a run for it, one of them grabbed my wrist. One was Korean-Chinese and

the other was Chinese. They began questioning me, and I told them that they could ask me whatever they wanted to know. But the Korean-Chinese policeman started cursing at me. He asked me how long I had been here [in China]. He said that he knew I was from North Korea and asked me how many times I had been in China. He also told me to go get help from my relatives and to tell them to come. Of course I didn't, since I knew they wanted to fine them. So I lied and said I didn't have any relatives.

Young-Kuk was sentenced to six months in a North Korean prison. He pulled up his pant leg and showed me the bloody scabs from the beatings. Pastor Sohn, his overseeing pastor, pointed to the white film on his leg and explained, "He caught some sort of skin disease from the prison floor. It's so dirty that a lot of people catch a disease that rots their skin. It spread all over his body, but it's getting better now."

HOW MANY REFUGEES IN CHINA?

In 2003, the United Nations High Commissioner for Refugees (UN-HCR)[9] estimated that there were 100,000 North Korean refugees in China.[10] The South Korean government has put forward the same figure.[11] The U.S. Department of State has concluded that the number is closer to 30,000 to 50,000.[12] On the other hand, NGOs and the media have reported that there are anywhere from 200,000 to 400,000 North Korean refugees in China. In 2006, High Commissioner António Guterres put the figure at 300,000.[13]

In September 2006, I met with Sean Woo, chief of staff for Senator Sam Brownback. When I told him that I believed there were 100,000 North Korean refugees in China, he referred to two documents obtained from the Chinese Public Security Bureau that were dated January 10, 2005. Melanie Kirkpatrick released excerpts of the documents in a *Wall Street Journal* article. One of the documents reads, "The number of illegal immigrants from North Korea that have stayed in China has increased every year . . . To date, almost 400,000 North Korean illegal immigrants have entered China and large numbers continue to cross the border illegally . . . As of the end of December 2004, 133,009 North Korean illegal immigrants have been deported."[14] Another document from the Yanbian Finance Bureau dated October 19, 2004, said that there were more than 93,000 refugees living in the Yanbian Prefecture alone.[15]

The fact is that no one really knows the true size of the North Korean refugee population. That refugees are in hiding makes it very difficult to come up with an accurate number. One thing that is certain, though, is that every year the number of North Korean refugees in China grows. While many refugees return to North Korea or find asylum in another country, the vast majority stay in China. While the current number of defections may be lower than in previous years, Crossing Borders local staff has observed a gradual increase in the refugee population in China over the years.

KOREAN EMIGRATION

Flight from northern Korea has an unusual history. People have emigrated from the region for the last 150 years. In the 1860s, "a series of droughts and bad harvests" forced Koreans in the northern provinces across the Tumen and Yalu rivers in search of better living conditions.[16] In the late nineteenth century, Korean emigration increased, with people fleeing to China and Russia because of "worsening economic conditions and political instability."[17] In the early twentieth century during the Japanese occupation, emigration accelerated again. In 1946, during the land reform, about 300,000 Koreans went from the north to the south. In the late 1940s, millions migrated to the south when the Communist regime was consolidated. Then about three million fled south because of the Korean War.

Professor Charles Armstrong, director of the Center for Korean Research at Columbia University and author of *The North Korean Revolution, 1945–1950*, told me, "Transport of movement comes to an end with the Korean War because both regimes make it more difficult for people to go from one country to another. There is virtually no migration from North Korea to China until the collapse of the North Korean economy in the 1990s . . . The northern part of the Korean peninsula has traditionally been the poorest part of the country. So when the opportunity comes for people to leave, whether to the South or across the border into China, they do so."[18]

We are now in the twenty-first century, and people are still fleeing North Korea. Hundreds of thousands of North Koreans have fled to China over the last two decades. Refugees say that the number of defectors would be much higher if the border was even more porous. Mr. Jung, a refugee, stated, "I would say around half of the people [in North Korea] want to go to China. . . . The problem is they are afraid of being captured or they don't know a safe route into China." Jang-Ho, another refugee, estimated that 60 percent of the North Korean population would leave if they were guaranteed safe passage.

CHINA'S POLICY ON NORTH KOREAN REFUGEES

Many have concluded that if China were to allow North Korean refugees safe passage through the country, there would be a mass exodus of refugees and the North Korean regime would implode. James Brooke wrote in the *New York Times* that if China were to open up its border to the North Koreans, "It would take only six months for there to be a flood. The cities would be empty."[19]

China claims that North Koreans in China are not refugees but "economic migrants," temporarily in China in search of food and money. When high-ranking government officials from the United States visit China and press Chinese officials on the North Korean refugee situation, the Chinese officials will often reply, "What refugees? We only have economic migrants here." Using such logic, China forcibly repatriates North Korean refugees and by doing so continues to violate agreements reached at the 1951 Convention on Refugees and its 1967 Protocol, to which China is a signatory. Article 33 of the 1951 Convention on Refugees reads:

> No Contracting State shall expel or return a refugee in any manner whatsoever to the frontiers of territories where his life or freedom would be threatened on account of his race, religion, nationality, membership of a particular social group or political opinion.

The moment a North Korean refugee defects, they have committed an act of treason punishable by death in North Korea. Their lives and freedom are at significant risk when forcibly repatriated. Refugees who have been in contact with American or South Korean foreigners and specifically those who have had any contact with a church are at even greater risk of imprisonment, torture, and death. Suzanne Scholte, a North Korean human rights activist, says:

> To me it is the most avoidable human rights tragedy that's occurring in the world because China's policies have created the refugee crisis. . . . China defends their policy towards the refugees by claiming these people are economic migrants because they are coming to China, not for political reasons, but because they are starving. But the moment they cross the North Korea–China border, they have committed a crime against Kim Jong Il's regime, because North Koreans are not allowed the freedom to travel. It is well documented that they will suffer persecution when they are sent back. Most certainly they will be jailed. Most certainly they will be tortured. And in some cases they will be executed for the crime of leaving the country.
>
> Because of this brutal treatment to those who are repatriated, the U.N. Special Rapporteur Vitit Mutharbhorn determined that North

Koreans were in fact "refugees sur place"[20] and deserved refugee protection. So, here you have the United Nations, of which China is a member, establishing that these people are indeed refugees and are deserving of protection under international law. How does China respond? . . . It blocks the UNHCR from access to the refugees and makes it difficult for the refugees to reach the UN-HCR's office in Beijing.[21]

Michael Horowitz, another North Korean human rights activist and a senior fellow at the Hudson Institute, suggests that greater pressure needs to be put on the UN to confront China on the issue:

Some of the other [steps] would be to place greater pressure on the U.N. to take a more robust position against China for China's naked, open violation of its treaty obligations with the UNHCR. . . . Now, I understand [Ban Ki-moon] was foreign minister in a government whose prime policy was keeping Kim Jong Il in power, but he is now the secretary general of the U.N., presumably committed to human rights. He speaks out about human rights all over, except in North Korea. I think we can put much heavier pressure on the U.N. to take a more determined position on the human rights abuses, the gulags, the mass starvation, and the terror that goes on in North Korea. I would like to see the U.N. moving much more directly vis-à-vis North Korea. The good news is, with Ban Ki-moon in there, vulnerable as he would be to determined calls for the U.N. to speak out about the situation in North Korea, we can do it.[22]

Michel Gabaudan, a regional representative for the U.S. and Caribbean Office of the UNHCR, told me:

The [UN] High Commissioner when he came to China in March 2006 told [the Chinese] very clearly and made a public declaration saying that deportations [of North Koreans] are a violation of international law because while some of these people may not have come out of North Korea for reasons that qualify under the Convention [on Refugees], the risk they're exposed to by being deported qualifies them as refugees under what we call the "sur place" claim. Which is, they may not be a refugee for the reason they left, but the punishment they would be given for having left illegally is so out of proportion with the supposed crime that was committed, that would qualify them as a refugee. . . . We told the Chinese very clearly [that] . . . deportation, the return of these people against their will, is a violation of the Convention and therefore the international agreement that China has willingly subscribed to.[23]

In May 2007, I contacted a former diplomat I will call Jim, who has many years of experience helping North Korean refugees find asylum through the underground railroad in Asia. I called him on his cell phone while he was operating on the Mekong River near the Golden Triangle (where Thailand, Myanmar, and Laos meet) to ask him for his thoughts on China. He told me:

I think that China is the key. China plays North Korea and just uses North Korea as a puppet. If the Chinese want North Korea to jump, North Korea will jump. . . . In my opinion . . . they could solve this overnight. . . . Some people would say that's very extreme and that China doesn't have that much control. But just from the different levels that I've dealt with and heard of, in other countries, in Thailand, and in some of the negotiations in Laos, in Cambodia, with the embassies, and the back-door involvement of China, I just see that they do have a great influence over the North Koreans. They could cut them off from everything overnight: from money, from oil, from food.[24]

Many agree with Jim that China is the key. China has the unparalleled ability to potentially bring about a resolution to the North Korean crisis, specifically the refugee crisis. Yet China continues to drag its feet on the issue. The solution, then, lies in applying pressure to China through raising international awareness and influencing individual governments and the UNHCR. Some activists are looking to the 2008

Olympics in Beijing as an opportune time to apply pressure to China and bring the North Korean refugee issue into the international spotlight.

In addition to raising international awareness, building a coalition of governments that could apply combined pressure is also an excellent strategy. The International Parliamentarians' Coalition for North Korean Refugees' Human Rights (IPCNKR)[25] is an important step forward in this regard. As the name suggests, the IPCNKR is a coalition of parliamentarians from 19 countries (including South Korea, the United States, the United Kingdom, and Japan) with the specific goal of promoting human rights for North Korean refugees.

As Suzanne Scholte said, the North Korean refugee crisis is the most avoidable human rights tragedy in the world today. The North Koreans are, to borrow a phrase from Dr. Martin Luther King Jr.'s "I Have a Dream" speech, the "veterans of creative suffering." The sobering reality is that the catastrophic suffering of the refugees at the China–North Korea border is a fabricated crisis and a direct result of China's sordid policy towards the refugees. If China stopped violating agreements reached at the 1951 Convention on Refugees and discontinued the repatriation of North Korean refugees, it could instantly bring an end to the vicious cycle of exploitation and suffering at the China–North Korea border.

FIVE

Sex Trafficking

Injustice anywhere is a threat to justice everywhere.

—Dr. Martin Luther King Jr.

In *Human Trafficking*, a powerful movie depicting the horrors of sex trafficking, an Immigration and Customs Enforcement agent (played by Donald Sutherland) held a press conference in which he addressed the problem of human trafficking. "An ounce of cocaine wholesale—$1,200—but you can only sell it once," he stated. "A woman or a child—$50 to $1,000—but you can sell them each day, every day, over and over and over again. The markup is immeasurable. *Human trafficking, ladies and gentlemen, is the business of the future for crime organizations.*" Many Chinese "businessmen" have already arrived at this conclusion and are capitalizing off vulnerable and naïve North Korean women just across the border.

When it comes to human trafficking, North Korea is simply in a category of its own. Ambassador John Miller, the former director of the State Department Office to Monitor and Combat Trafficking in Persons and a professor who teaches courses on human trafficking at George Washington University, commented:

> While there are slave trafficking similarities with other countries, North Korea is almost *sui generis*. I can't think of another country

in the world where you have, even by conservative estimates, around 50,000 to 60,000 sex trafficking victims in an adjoining country, who are both victims and unacknowledged by the destination country—in this case China. There are a lot of unusual circumstances here. Coupled with the export of forced labor slaves to other countries, you have one of the worst situations in the world.[1]

In the State Department's 2007 "Trafficking in Persons Report," North Korea was once again given the least favorable rating, a Tier 3, which reflects the government's failure to meet "the minimum standards for the elimination of trafficking."[2] North Korea has been given a Tier 3 rating every year since it was first ranked in 2003. Only three other countries have received Tier 3 ratings every year they have been ranked: Burma, Cuba, and Sudan.

There are a variety of forms of human trafficking, such as forced labor, bonded labor, child-soldier slavery, domestic servitude, factory slavery, and farm slavery. Of all the forms, sex trafficking occurs most frequently. Human trafficking in North Korea is primarily sex trafficking (although forced labor is also a problem).[3]

The vast majority of the people who defect from North Korea are women. For a long time I believed the percentage of female defectors to be near 60 to 70 percent, as did many other activists. And of the 6,700 North Koreans who had found asylum in South Korea as of July 2005, 4,000 were women—almost exactly 60 percent.[4] However, I have noticed an upward trend, especially in recent years. While in the past 60 to 70 percent of the refugees in our shelters were women, now 85 percent are.

The reason for the increase in the percentage of female refugees is the growing sex trafficking industry at the China–North Korea border. Traffickers are getting better at what they do and expanding their operations. Further, although tighter security on both sides of the border makes it more difficult for North Koreans to defect, traffickers have contacts among the North Korean border guards so that women can cross with relative ease. As security at the border continues to tighten, we'll probably see a further increase in the proportion of defectors who are women.

How many of these North Korean women are victims of sex trafficking? Estimates have usually ranged from 70 to nearly 90 percent.[5] In September 2006, we took a formal survey of the North Korean refugee women in our shelters. Shockingly, 97 percent of them were sex trafficking victims.

THE BUSINESS OF SEX TRAFFICKING

As North Korean women enter unfamiliar terrain in China, not knowing a single person there and unable to speak the language, they are, in the eyes of traffickers, prime candidates for exploitation. Traffickers patrol the borders looking for young, vulnerable North Korean women who have just crossed into China in search of food, freedom, and money. Once captured, in a foreign land without any rights, they are at the mercy of the traffickers.

We strive to find these women as they cross the border before the traffickers do. Our well-organized house church network extends throughout northeast China into the border regions, where we have a number of families living along the Tumen River. Whenever a North Korean refugee comes knocking on their door, they will call us so that we can take the refugee into our shelters.

However, traffickers also have a strong presence at the China–North Korea border. They camp there and try to capture women immediately as they cross the river. It is a lucrative business for them, and they invest a great deal in it in order to maximize their profits. They have purchased multiple homes along the river and have dogs that will alert them whenever anyone is hiking along the trail. Any unfortunate North Korean woman who attempts to hike that path will certainly be kidnapped. Lisa Thompson, an expert on sex trafficking who works for a faith-based NGO, told me that she didn't know of another case where traffickers wait along a border to capture women as they cross.

Through the testimonies of trafficked women, we have learned a great deal about the business of sex trafficking at the border. Traffickers use two main methods to abduct the women: They kidnap them as they cross the river into China, or they pitch them lies when they are still in North Korea, often about some bogus high-paying job in China.

Mrs. Myung, a 32-year-old refugee, was kidnapped as she crossed the border and then sold to a Chinese farmer. She had left her sick and starving mother in North Korea with the intention of quickly making some money and returning to help her. When I interviewed her, she was deeply pained by the thought of her mother living all alone; she didn't even know if her mother was still alive. Seven years had passed since she had been sold, and she now had a six-year-old son, Jong-Su, with the Chinese farmer who paid the highest price for her. She had a hard life, working all day on the farm. I noticed that her hands were still dirty from that day's work in the fields. Her family was so poor that they couldn't afford to send Jong-Su to school. We agreed to provide monthly support to her family so that Jong-Su could attend school.

Ok Ja, a trafficking victim living in one of our refugee shelters, was approached in North Korea by a Chinese executive who met with her and her mother. "We have a very good job for your daughter in China," he told her mother. "She'll be working in a factory making a lot of money and will be able to regularly send money back home to help the family." A fearful Ok Ja told her mom she didn't want to go. But her mother replied, "Ok Ja, trust these people. It will be best for our family." Ok Ja followed the men to China and was sold for $1,200 to a Chinese man who physically abused and raped her.

Oftentimes, North Korean accomplices aid the Chinese traffickers. They are very effective because they can easily recruit and gain the trust of North Korean women. An International Crisis Group report titled "Perilous Journeys: The Plight of North Koreans in China and Beyond" says that these accomplices receive $63 for each woman they lead across the border.[6] Yulee, a woman in her early thirties, recalls being lied to by a North Korean man who claimed that he had work for her in a nearby village:

> He said that there was work in the next village and that I didn't need a heavy coat since it was very close by. On the way to the village with the man, we crossed a river and the water only came up to my ankles because it was fall. I took off my shoes and rolled up my pants. We went into a home that was about 50 meters from the river. As soon as I walked into the house, I knew that I was in the wrong place. I knew I was no longer in North Korea. The furniture, the windows, the flooring were all different from what you would see in North Korea, even in the wealthier homes. I saw three big blocks of tofu in the kitchen. . . . In the house there were three other women who had been sold. . . They were crouched on their hands and knees.

After abducting North Korean women near the border, traffickers face the challenge of getting the women further inland past Chinese security checkpoints. This is not an easy task as the Chinese police are actively searching for refugees, especially in areas closer to the border. But with a great deal of research and planning, traffickers are able to smuggle the women further inland. Usually, multiple cars are used: A lead car goes first and alerts the trailing cars of any security checkpoints on the way. Yulee recounted:

> When they closed the trunk, they [three other refugee women] were screaming in pain [from being cramped]. Because I was taller with long hair, they took away my North Korean clothes, did my hair and put on make-up, and sat me in the front seat thinking that I could pass for a Chinese. Two men came with us. Another car met us with two other people. I was so scared. On the way we saw two police cars. I was so nervous and sweaty. . . . The three

ladies had spent two hours in the trunk and were crying when they got out. Two other men came, so now there were four men accompanying us four women. They spoke in Chinese. It seemed to me that they were saying to each other, "You pick the one you like and we will travel on the train pretending to be couples." We were all in different cars of the train. When we got off the train, two taxis were waiting. I told myself that as long as I am here, I am dead. I told myself that as soon as I have some money, I am going to run away.

After refugee women are brought further inland, the sale is arranged. Chinese men, usually poor farmers, sometimes with disabilities, come and take a look at the women. Traffickers have the refugees lie about their ages in order to maximize profits: Older women will decrease their age by several years, and teenagers will increase it by a few. If a refugee is too young (and too short), the traffickers will continue to feed her three square meals a day and wait until she grows to a proper height. Yulee described how she and the three other women were sold:

> The ages of us four women were 17, 27, 35, and 38. I was 27, but the man told me to say that I was 22. I would bring in more money by saying that I was younger. The 17-year-old was told to say she was 19 because she was too young . . . A 23-year-old man asked how old I was and said I was too old. He took the 17-year-old. Another man with long hair who looked like a grandfather took the 35-year-old woman. A third man took me. He signaled "8" with his hands as my price for 8,000 RMB (USD $1,000). He bargained down from 10,000 RMB (USD $1,200). The man seemed happy with the price. He had long hair and was 33 years old. . . . One of the villagers said in English, "What you name?" I learned some English in school, so I nodded. He wrote "name" and I wrote my name in Chinese. They asked my age. . . . I couldn't count up to 27, so I just shook my head as though I didn't know.

Sex Trafficking

REPERCUSSIONS OF CHINA'S ONE-CHILD POLICY

China's one-child policy has created the need for a foreign supply of women. The policy has had an alarming impact on Chinese society, where boys are more valued than girls (as in many Asian cultures). Thus, parents get ultrasound tests to determine the sex of the baby and abort female babies until they successfully have a boy. If a female baby is born, parents will sometimes kill her or leave her to die. This has created a shortage of women in the country, especially among the younger generation. As a result, one of the major concerns of parents is that their sons will one day be able to marry. The Working Group on the Girl Child published a report titled "A Girl's Right to Live" for the UN Commission on the Status of Women. The report stated that between 2015 and 2030 "there will be 25 million men in China who have no hope of finding a wife."[7] The Chinese even have a term for these young men—"bare branches" (*guang gun-er*)—"because they are branches of the family tree that will never bear fruit."[8] Lisa Thompson says that India and China:

> have huge problems with gender disparity—an imbalance in their population between men and women. There are so many more men because of this cultural preference for boys. It's like a giant vacuum. What do you do with the tens of thousands, if not hundreds of thousands, of men who can't find a wife? The predictions are going very high about the number of men who are never going to find a spouse, at least not a Chinese or Indian spouse. . . . China and India are becoming dependent on a foreign supply of women.

The growing gender imbalance in China is even more evident in the countryside. Economic development in China has spurred a rush for the city, as women and men leave rural areas in search of higher-paying jobs. It is the poor and the physically disabled who are left in the countryside to continue making a living by farming. The poor farmers in northeast China see no other option but to purchase a North Korean bride if they want to get married.

Human trafficking in northeast China has also affected the North Korean gender balance, especially in border villages. The trafficking has resulted in a shortage of women in North Korea as well. Men complain that it is becoming more difficult for them to find wives. Pastor Suh, a local staff member, reported after returning from a border village in North Korea, "In Wiwon, they say that around 45 percent of the women have come to China."

In the last two years, we have been receiving reports that the North Korean authorities have been arresting human traffickers. In mid-2005, Pastor Nam, a Korean-Chinese staffer, commented upon his return from North Korea, "The use of cell phones was outlawed. The reason was said to be to curtail human trafficking. Those caught were exiled and were only allowed to return from the countryside after three years of hard labor." Mrs. Kwon said that two members of a family she had visited in North Korea were executed on charges of human trafficking in China. Another Korean-Chinese staff member reported in mid-2006, "In particular, North Korean defectors, human traffickers, and people who have reportedly received help from Christians are banished by the North Korean government to a location 50 kilometers from Musan."

When I mentioned to Ambassador Miller that we were receiving reports of arrests and executions of traffickers in North Korea, he pointed out:

> These reports require evaluation, which is hard to do with North Korea. The three standards for efforts to combat slavery are prosecution, protection, prevention. The U.S. certainly encourages punishment of traffickers. But you have to make a judgment. Does this reflect a sincere effort to stop trafficking? Can you be sure that the traffickers are being punished, or is it somebody they just picked up off the street? That's the problem with North Korea. They could

be show trials. There are some countries I suspect that go out and pick up people off the street and say they are traffickers and then they execute them. More information from the North Korean government is needed here as well as more openness to outsiders before any credit can be given.[9]

Yet I believe that the reports of arrests and executions of human traffickers are, in fact, genuine. I do not mean to suggest that the North Korean government cares about its own people; rather, it is trying to stop the sex trafficking simply because the trafficking is creating a gender imbalance that threatens the regime's future.

A struggle is taking place between higher- and lower-level government officials over the trafficking. Border patrol soldiers and corrupt local officials in border towns allow defections and cooperate with human sex-trafficking rings because they personally profit from these activities. However, it is the policy of the North Korean government to stop defections and trafficking because both jeopardize the future of the regime. The struggle is illustrated by the execution of two border patrol soldiers, an officer and a sergeant, in early 2007. Amnesty International reported, "They were arrested following an investigation by government investigators into the flow of North Korean nationals crossing the border into China."[10]

POVERTY, ABUSE, AND RAPE

Most trafficking victims end up in extreme poverty since poor farmers usually purchase them. Eun-Hee, a trafficked woman, told me of her reaction when she first saw her new home in China: "I thought, 'Is this a house or a shed?' It looked like if I pushed on it, it would fall down. It was worse than North Korea where I had a concrete house. There were a lot of spider webs. I thought, 'Is this a house that a person can live in?' It was a lot cleaner in North Korea . . . I took some paper in the house and wallpapered the walls. My mother was a seamstress, so I made some curtains and hung them."

In a large majority of cases, the North Korean women are victims of domestic violence. The men are often alcoholics and abusive, viewing their North Korean brides as nothing more than pieces of property. On March 6, 2006, a Crossing Borders staffer testified at a U.S. congressional hearing:

> North Koreans are in the ultimate position of vulnerability with the only alternative to following a trafficker into China being starvation, suffering and possibly death. Knowing this, traffickers take advantage of the dire situations of young North Korean women and coerce them. . . . Many of the promises of a "better life" are never fulfilled and many of the . . . marriages are to physically disabled or alcoholic husbands with the end result often being abandonment or physical abuse.[11]

In July 2005, I received a call from Pastor Kim, one of our shelter managers in another province, about Soo-Jin, a young refugee woman who was being abused by her Chinese "husband." "There is a North Korean refugee woman in our village whose husband is hitting her," Pastor Kim said. "The man is an alcoholic and is beating her up pretty bad." I asked the pastor if he wanted me to come out to help, but he said it was too far and asked what I thought they should do. We then devised a plan to help the woman escape. As a result, she now lives in one of our refugee shelters.

Yulee described the physical abuse she endured at the hands of her "husband" after she was sold: "He had a mental impairment. When I refused to sleep with him, he hit me. His mother and sister also hit me. I would rather die than sleep with him and fought with the family for seven months. I received severe beatings . . . I had a bloody nose, ears, and a swollen head. I cried every night."

Trafficked women are often tied down to chairs or beds until they willingly comply with the families' wishes. Sometimes the whole family is involved in enslaving the victim, and she is expected to work for all of them. If the woman does not obey the family's orders, they will beat her until she gives in. If she shows signs of compliance, the family might give her a small degree of freedom by untying her for short periods of time to clean, cook meals, and fulfill sexual obligations to her "husband." Whenever the family leaves the house, they will tie her down, until total control is established.

Sadly, rape and sex trafficking go hand in hand. Refugee women are often raped by their traffickers and then raped again by their buyers. So-Young, who stands less than five feet tall as a result of malnourishment in North Korea, is a 21-year-old victim. On February 4, 2000, after So-Young crossed into China with some of her friends, a group of traffickers lured them with lies of salaries of $36 a month. She was then raped by her traffickers and sold to a 50-year-old Chinese man who raped her again. So-Young recounted:

> They transported us in the dark, so we didn't know where we were going. We didn't know they were going to sell us. We really didn't suspect anything at first. But even when we began suspecting something, we dismissed it, thinking we were too young and small to be sold [So-Young was 16 years old at the time]. It became weird when they started mumbling things to each other, and we didn't know what they were saying. It was then that we started suspecting, "Is this person trying to sell us? No, we're too young. They wouldn't try to sell us." We just dismissed it again. But the next morning, they took my friend. She's much taller than I am. They told us that they found a place for her to work, so she happily went with them. But later on, I found out that she had been sold. With me, because I was so small, they were going to wait for me to grow taller before selling me.

Having grown up in North Korea, So-Young had never heard of God before, but in a moment of desperation she found herself uttering a prayer. "At that time, I only had a slight conception of a heavenly place. I was so disgusted, and I just called on God[12] with tears, crying out, 'God in heaven. Help me!' It was just that one time that I cried out to him."

So-Young was sold to a home near a house church. There she met a deacon who helped her escape. She believes that being sold to a house near a church was an answer to her prayer.

In the end, Chinese authorities capture and forcibly repatriate many trafficked women. Yulee remembered:

> After I had been there for a month and a half, someone came knocking on the door in the middle of the night. It was the police, five men and one woman. . . . They said they were taking me to register me as a Chinese citizen. I didn't know what they meant, so I followed. I was taken to a room filled with women handcuffed in two's. I started to cry. They were mean and treated us harshly. I counted 150 women. They loaded us into three big buses and took us to the train station. Some of the women did not have shoes or socks. Some of the policewomen felt sorry for us and were kind enough to give their own clothes to the women. They told us to come back to China. Some even gave their names to the women to contact them the next time they come to China. Some of the police were crying for us.
>
> Back in North Korea, I was in a holding area for 20 days until my brother came for me to be transported to prison in my hometown. There, they punish you if you move or talk the wrong way by making you sit very still for hours. I started to menstruate, and it didn't stop. It was December and very cold. My pants became soaked in blood and were frozen solid. The prison guards didn't care. A family friend who was like an uncle to me was in a high position at the prison. When he found out that I was sick, he placed me as a guard at the door of the prison and I didn't have to do any labor. There was a hospital right in front of the prison. I lied to my "uncle" and told him I was going to the hospital and ran away.

Yulee defected to China a second time, making her way into one of our refugee shelters. In February 2007, shortly after she arrived, she died of cancer.

Sex Trafficking

In the movie *Human Trafficking,* one of the trafficked women asked an agent after being rescued, "Do you think it's possible when you have lost your humanity to ever find it again?" Certainly this is one of the greatest challenges we face in our work—to help women recover from their horrendous abuse and find their humanity again. When people ask me what we need in the field, I often say, among other things, that we need trained people to counsel these women.

I interviewed Jean Young Lee, a friend who is a clinical psychologist, to get her thoughts on what these North Korean women might be going through. She said that they most likely are experiencing post-traumatic stress disorder (PTSD) or post-traumatic stress symptoms. She emphasized the significant impact that trauma has on a person and their general ability to function. "Some researchers would say that traumatic events get stored physically in the brain, similar to how memories get stored in the brain," she pointed out, adding that trauma victims often suffer from fear, flashbacks, and nightmares—all of which are common among refugee women in our shelters.

Trauma and Recovery, a book by Judith Herman about trauma and the process of healing, has helped me better understand what the trafficked women in our shelters might be going through. Herman writes, "Remembering and telling the truth about terrible events are prerequisites both for the restoration of the social order and for the healing of individual victims . . . When the truth is finally recognized, survivors can begin their recovery."[13]

North Korean women do not typically discuss their trafficking experiences, however, and they rarely "tell the truth" about all they have been through. In fact, after the event, they often choose to ignore it and never speak about it again. When I asked one young refugee woman if her traffickers had abused her, she put her head down and whispered, "It's embarrassing." Some experiences are too humiliating and painful for the victim to talk about, and their silence inhibits their healing.

It is also necessary for society to recognize and understand the testimonies of trauma victims. However, this is not easy. Herman states, "It is difficult for an observer . . . to see more than a few fragments of the picture at one time, to retain all the pieces, and to fit them together."[14] Our Korean-Chinese staff, while making great efforts, have a difficult time processing and understanding the experiences of the North Korean refugee women. Counseling is a foreign concept to them (and to Korean culture in general). As a result, they are not equipped to handle the psychological and emotional needs of these women. Trained counselors who can speak the language are a major unfulfilled need in the China–North Korea border area.

ORGANIZED RESCUES

An important aspect of our work is helping trafficked women escape from their buyers—something we refer to as "organized rescues." This is a common part of the operations of other NGOs operating at the China–North Korea border as well. When I asked Professor Donna Hughes, a professor of women's studies at the University of Rhode Island, if she was familiar with similar organized rescues anywhere else in the world, she responded, "International Justice Mission organizes raids on brothels, but they always act with law enforcement. They don't act outside of law enforcement. There's lots of corruption, but they try to find some officials that aren't corrupt and try to organize raids to get girls out of brothels." Of course, our work is independent of law enforcement.

To date, we have helped several women escape their homes. So-Young tells how she escaped through the help of the Christian deacon in her village:

He asked, "You go to work at 6:00 A.M., right?" . . . They told me to get out of the house around 6:00 A.M., but I said that would be too late . . . because the family would be eating breakfast at that time. . . . I told them that 5:00 A.M. would be better. The problem was that no matter how early I tried to get up in the past, I could never get up before 5:30 A.M. I normally woke up around 5:30 A.M. or 6:00 A.M., even 6:30 A.M., so I was afraid I wouldn't be able to wake up. But when I opened my eyes the next morning, it was exactly 5:00 A.M. So I got up. But then I was questioned, "You normally wake up around 5:30 A.M. or 6:00 A.M. Why are you up so early today?" . . . Another person thought I woke up early to prepare some food, but I was planning on escaping! So I acted like I was combing my hair and made a run for it. As I ran, my heart felt hot. I knew how to pray, and all I could do was pray for help. I didn't want to be caught, so I ran out into a big road and hid behind a tree. The deacon's son came and picked me up in his car and took me into the city.

We also helped Mrs. Rhee, a trafficked woman in her early thirties, escape. Her family had given her more autonomy than most trafficked women are granted, so it was easy for her to leave the home. When her Chinese husband found out that our organization had helped her escape, he was furious and hunted down Pastor Kwon, the local staff member who was her overseeing pastor. He and a group of friends found Pastor Kwon and kidnapped him, taking him to a room on the third floor of an apartment. They tied him to a chair and interrogated him about Mrs. Rhee's location. When he refused to give it up, they threatened to kill him. After they exited the room to discuss what they were going to do with him, he overheard his kidnappers say, "Let's just kill him and throw his body in a *doenjang* jar [a large, 3.5-foot ceramic jar used to store soybean paste] and hide it." When Pastor Kwon realized he was going to die, he managed to untie himself and jumped out of the window from the third floor. He sprained both of his ankles upon landing but still sprinted towards the street to find a taxi. He ran for his life as the men, who had heard him jump, chased him. But he jumped in a taxi and safely got away.

As he was being driven away, he called me and said that he needed to meet with me immediately. Since the Chinese husband knew where he lived, Pastor Kwon had his wife and children quickly evacuate the home and meet him at one of the house churches in a secret location in the city. When I arrived at the house church, I saw Pastor Kwon lying in bed with two bags of ice around his ankles. His wife was crying at his side. "I told him that he shouldn't do this type of work," she said as I walked in. "It's too dangerous."

CHILDREN AND TRAFFICKING

Unfortunately, children are sometimes the unintended victims of trafficking.[15] In October 2006, Ji-Yun, a 13-year-old refugee girl, told me the tragic story of how she and her mom defected:

> I came to China on September 6, 2004, with my mom and this one man. . . . The man piggybacked me because I was so tired. We walked for two hours. It was 5:00 A.M., and I was too tired, so I slept. When I woke up, my mom was gone. . . . I don't know what happened to her. I was so scared that I just started running.

Thankfully, Ji-Yun met a family in our house church network and was brought into one of our orphanages. We're still not exactly sure what happened to her mother. Our guess is that her mother either abandoned her or was captured by human traffickers. We think her mother was captured, because if she intended to abandon Ji-Yun, she probably wouldn't have gone through the trouble of bringing Ji-Yun out of North Korea.

As an increasing number of North Korean women are trafficked and sold to Chinese farmers, many Chinese–North Korean children are born. Since these children are born into environments of extreme poverty, they are oftentimes neglected and abused. In many cases, they are abandoned when the North Korean refugee mother either runs away or is captured and deported. The father is left unable to care for the child, and due to financial constraints, sickness, or disability, he will give up the child. In other cases, the father simply does not want the child anymore.

We have set up children's shelters, which we refer to as Second Wave shelters, along the border to address this growing problem. Abraham Lee of Crossing Borders testified before Congress:

> The children in our Second Wave shelters have a Chinese father and North Korean mother. Their mothers were subsequently repatriated, re-trafficked or have simply disappeared with the father unable or unwilling to take care of the children. Mina is an 8-year-old girl who studies hard in school and who loves to smile and laugh. Four years ago her North Korean mother disappeared, apparently having abandoned her young daughter and her dying Chinese father. With his deteriorating health, her father was unable to care for her and Mina suffered in poverty and inattention. Thankfully, she was able to enter our shelter and with Chinese citizenship has a hope for a brighter future through constant love, care, and an opportunity to attend school. Unfortunately, many of these young children never get this opportunity and are often left to fend for themselves.[16]

One of the greatest joys for me has been seeing the transformation in the lives of these little ones after they enter our shelters. We are currently working on expanding the number of Second Wave shelters and planning on taking in a greater number of children in the future. Funding, resources, and the challenge of operating underground currently limit the growth of these children's shelters.

In September 2006, I met with Senator Sam Brownback at his office in Washington, D.C., to discuss two issues: the trafficking of North Korean women and abandoned Chinese–North Korean children. As we were discussing the Second Wave shelters, he turned to a legislative correspondent in the room and asked her to draft a letter to the Chinese government requesting that they consider legalizing Second Wave orphanages. If the Chinese government would agree, this would allow NGOs to expand their orphanages and help abandoned Chinese–North Korean children on a much larger scale.

The number of Chinese–North Korean children in northeast China is rapidly growing. Mrs. Lee, a Second Wave local staff member who lives in a village near the border, commented, "At the local elementary school, 17 out of the 30 kids in the second grade have North Korean mothers . . . The government is trying to figure out what to do about them." It is becoming a growing problem in northeast China, and one that we expect the government will not be able to ignore much longer. Crossing Borders staff anticipates that there will be some positive changes in Chinese legislation in the near future on Chinese–North Korean children.

WOMEN WHO HAVE MADE THE BEST OF A BAD SITUATION

Surprisingly, a small minority of trafficked women, given a choice, might say that they don't want to leave their Chinese husbands. Even though deceit, kidnapping, and rape may have occurred early on, the women have acclimated to their new lives. Some might even say that they are content with their new situations. In rare instances, the Chinese husband may be an honest man who takes good care of his North Korean bride.

Pastor Kang, a Korean-Chinese staff member, even criticized Hae-Young, a refugee woman, for abandoning her Chinese husband. She had already been captured once in China and repatriated. She knew that if she wanted to defect from North Korea a second time, she would have to use the human trafficking network. She agreed to be sold by traffickers again, as it was the only way she could enter China safely. Pastor Kang said, "I knew her husband. He was a good man. He used his life savings to marry her. She knew that she would be sold the second time she came to China, and still she deceived that man and ran away. I feel bad for the guy."

When I discussed the phenomenon of trafficked North Korean women accommodating to their new situations with Professor Hughes, she said:

> I think that is what happens in really oppressive systems. Those that are victims of oppressive systems accommodate themselves to it. They learn to first get along and accept the circumstances of their lives, and eventually are able to find some sort of accommodation to it. I think that really has to do with understanding a system of oppression. If you asked those women, "If you could go back . . . and had any choice you wanted, would you have made this choice?" I suspect that many of the women would have said, "No, but now that I've done this, well, I found out that this guy really isn't so bad. This life isn't so bad. I think of how terrible it would have been if I had stayed in North Korea." . . . That's really how they feel. I wouldn't want to criticize them for feeling that way, but on the other hand, they have accommodated themselves to a pretty oppressive system.

Hughes drew an interesting parallel to Sudan, where thousands of Dinka women were abducted from the south and trafficked to men in the north. After the Sudan Peace Agreement was signed in 2005, some Dinka women did not want to return to their homes in the south. Hughes explained, "They had decided that they were now married to this man, and maybe even more importantly, they had children and they cared about those children and they may have had to leave them behind to return to the south. . . . They have now married northerners. They have families . . . and do not want to be forced back to the south even though they could be repatriated under new agreements."

As I tried to understand how women can accommodate to a system of oppression, I called a good friend of mine who had confided that she had been raped by an acquaintance. I knew that she had continued in a relationship with him after being raped, so I asked her if she could help me understand the mind-set of the North Korean trafficked women who stayed with their Chinese husbands. She said:

> The mind does whatever it can to adjust to that situation. . . . I to-tally think that it's a survival instinct. If at that time I admitted to myself, "Oh my God, I was raped," I don't think I would have been able to emotionally handle it. After I was raped, I had to try and make the relationship work out. If I had to come to the reality that I was raped and it was just a one-time thing, I would have probably committed suicide. I had to adjust myself to the situation. . . . You just get used to it, and you know of nothing else. . . . I found myself being concerned with making sure he was okay and that he was happy. I thought to myself, "If he's happy, things are stable and things are going to be okay."

Judith Herman writes of a bond that forms between the victim and the perpetrator. "Captivity, which brings the victim into prolonged contact with the perpetrator, creates a special type of relationship, one of coercive control. . . . In situations of captivity, the perpetrator becomes the most powerful person in the life of the victim, and the psychology of the victim is shaped by the actions and beliefs of the perpetrator."[17]

Trafficked women make mental adjustments to try to make the best of a bad situation. "What compelled them into these set of circumstances is something very oppressive," Hughes said. "But you could even say it's much better for their mental health that they in fact decided that they're going to have to try to accommodate themselves and that the situation wasn't so bad after all. . . . I think we need to understand, psychologically, that we learn to live with all sorts of circumstances in our lives. . . . We learn to look around and say, 'What's the best choice I can make in this set of circumstances?' That doesn't mean that if you weren't confined to a very limited set of circumstances that you would make the same choice."

Lisa Thompson aptly commented on the women who find a certain level of contentment in their new Chinese homes: "The fact that it turned out well for these people, that is a miracle . . . But there is something propelling them to take these risks in the first place: The fact that they're poor; the fact that they lack education; the fact that they're trying to support someone back at home. There are some really serious negatives that are propelling people to play Russian roulette with their lives. And the fact that some people played the game and it turned out well—that's luck for them. But what about the millions of people for whom it didn't turn out well?"

Some North Korean women really do play Russian roulette with their lives. They are so desperate to get out of North Korea that they consciously take the risk of being sold to Chinese men.[18] But they have absolutely no control over their future if they are trafficked. They cannot choose their husband or home—they are simply sold to the highest bidder. They are at the mercy of the traffickers, and on a whim could end up in horrible straits.

SIX

Gulags

If there's magic in boxing, it's the magic of risking everything for a dream nobody sees but you. It's the magic of fighting battles beyond endurance, beyond cracked ribs, ruptured kidneys, and detached retinas.

—Eddie Dupris (Morgan Freeman) coaching Maggie Fitzgerald
(Hilary Swank) in *Million Dollar Baby*

Every North Korean refugee is a dreamer who risks everything in hopes for a better life. The fortunate ones cross the river and live out the "Chinese dream" with food in their stomachs and a newfound quasi freedom. The unfortunate ones are captured and enslaved in China or sent to North Korean gulags to suffer "cracked ribs, ruptured kidneys, and detached retinas." The vast majority of prisoners in North Korea have been charged with minor offenses such as listening to a foreign radio broadcast, accidentally sitting on a newspaper photo of Kim Jong Il, or making a negative comment about the regime in passing. Ahn My-ong Chul, a defector and former prison guard in North Korea, recalled that most prisoners "made one small mistake." One woman was arrested after singing a South Korean pop song titled, "Don't Cry for Me, Younger Sister."[1]

The North Korean gulags have a variety of forms: detention facilities, interrogation facilities, punishment camps, forced-labor colonies, criminal prisons, and political prisons. North Korea has the most political prisoners in the world, with estimates ranging from 150,000 to 200,000. NBC conducted investigations of the prison camps and discovered that they are gargantuan. At least three camps are larger than the District of Columbia in area, and one is three times its size.[2]

Every North Korean has heard about the political prisons (*kwanliso*), which were created when the Communists took over in the late 1940s. Even mention of the word *kwanliso* causes North Koreans to shudder in fear. Ji-Yoon, a 24-year-old refugee woman, said, "Everyone has heard of it. You know that people go there to get punished. But other than that, you don't talk about it or hear about it too much." When people are reported to the authorities, a black vehicle pulls up to their house and takes them away.

CONDITIONS IN PRISON

There are major food shortages in the North Korean prisons, which should come as no surprise. If there isn't enough food in the homes, there certainly isn't going to be enough food in the prisons. Mr. Yang, a former prisoner, says, "People there are so hungry that they would eat the maggots in the outhouses and even earthworms in the manure . . . I saw it in my very own cell. Some people would get so hungry that they ate centipedes." Prison survivors often describe how they endured starvation for extended periods of time and the intense fatigue they felt as a result. Young-Kuk, a 19-year-old refugee who spent a year in prison after being repatriated, recounted:

> We had to work extra hard, especially when they were watching us, and we put some bounce in our step hoping that we would receive food at the end of the day. But for three days, they didn't give us anything to eat, and I didn't even feel the hunger pains at that point . . . Sometimes they would give us pieces of Chinese bread, but we

didn't have appetites, so we gave away our bread and only wanted to drink the water. I lost a lot of weight. The soldiers hit me severely and starved me for three days while I was detained. They worked us really hard in the freezing cold and didn't feed us . . . We were bound together by the wrists in pairs, and it was very difficult to maneuver around. We were in a place where there was flowing water from a river, and because it was winter and we were so fatigued, we drank from the stream. But at night, I would suddenly start shaking and feel my insides going crazy from hunger and fatigue.

Out of all of the North Korean prison survivors I have interviewed, only one person has ever said that they were fed sufficiently while in prison. Mrs. Chung, a refugee who had served in the military, was sent to a North Korean prison upon being repatriated. She said that they fed her radish leaves and a bowl of rice and beans while in prison. When I expressed my surprise that she ate so well in prison, she replied, "I think it varies, depending on how things are at that current moment." She continued:

In the beginning, there wasn't enough food. There weren't enough spoons either, so they would place only a certain number of spoons per group. I sat at the very front. All the newcomers had to. The front was the coldest, because the guards left the windows open for ventilation. Those who sat near the windows felt the freezing wind blowing on them. Only small spoons were given because the guards feared the prisoners might commit suicide by eating a spoon. We had to use small spoons like that. Others had to use their fingers to eat.

Water is a precious commodity in prison. One refugee woman said, "There was no such thing as a shower in prison. I didn't shower for the whole time I was there, which was four months. There was barely any water . . . I drank any water that was available. I even drank the water I washed up with."

The prison cells are small and uncomfortable. In some cases, they are specifically designed with the intent of creating discomfort. After interviewing North Korean refugees in Seoul, Michael Breen wrote, "The cell [in one prison] was so small that there was only room to sit. Spikes prevented prisoners from leaning against the walls."[3] In-Ho, a young refugee man, said, "There isn't that much room to move in the cell, because it's so crowded, and it's even more uncomfortable if you do shift. And if you move, others quickly take your spot, or the guy next to you keeps hitting you. We were all scrunched in there. We all fell asleep in the same position, so in the morning our legs were almost paralyzed. That was the first time I experienced that kind of pain." Ms. Chi, another prison survivor, recalled that "when it was time to sleep they had us all sit in a line sitting in between each other's straddled legs; then we all laid down at the same time. That was how we slept."

Conditions are extremely unsanitary. Former prisoners describe a pungent and intolerable stench inside the cells. As a result of the uncleanliness, disease is rampant. Skin disease, hepatitis, and tuberculosis are commonly transferred among inmates in prisons. As the physical condition of a prisoner worsens due to disease or starvation, guards will release them when they are near death so that they don't have to deal with the body.

Former prisoners often comment that it takes a great deal of skill and shrewdness to survive in prison. One has to learn how to appease the guards and get along with fellow prisoners in order to make it out alive. "You can't survive that place unless you've got some evil in you," one refugee said.

Money is one of the keys to survival. Suh Sung, a South Korean gulag survivor and author of the Japanese bestseller *Unbroken Spirits*, said that he more than once saw an inscription on the prison walls reading, "With money, you're innocent; without, guilty."[4] This is true in North Korea as well. For many, money can buy a shorter prison term. Sometimes, people can buy their way out of prison altogether. Money can even determine life or death. Mrs. Hong, a repatriated refugee who served one year in a North Korean prison, said, "When I was caught in

China, my [Korean–Chinese] husband gave me $60 to take back to North Korea. He said, 'Hide it and use it to live and eat well while you're in prison.' He is a poor farmer and doesn't even have enough money to live on, so I said 'No, I can't take it.' He kept on insisting, so I finally agreed to only take $12." Curious as to how she was able to smuggle the money in, I asked her, "How did you get the money past the guards?" She explained, "I folded up the bill into a tiny ball and then covered it with Saran wrap. Then I pushed it into my rectum and hid it there. After I was admitted into prison, I took it out . . . I used the $12 to buy noodles and bread in prison."

I had previously heard of North Koreans wrapping money in Saran wrap, swallowing it, and retrieving it later. When I asked Mrs. Hong why she didn't do it this way, she replied, "It's dangerous to swallow the money because it can damage your stomach. Most people do it this way now." She added, "These days it's difficult to take money into the prisons. Now the guards know that prisoners are hiding money like this. So when you first arrive in prison they will check your stool two or three times."

FORCED LABOR

North Korean gulags play a central role in the economy. The regime depends on forced labor for every industry imaginable: logging, mining, construction, and other industrial enterprises. Prisoners are given strict daily work quotas, and if they don't meet them, they will not receive food that day. Items such as jackets, boots, and sweaters are produced in the prisons and then exported to other countries. An MSNBC report indicated that products made by North Korean prisoners might end up in U.S. stores "having been 'washed' first through Chinese companies that serve as intermediaries."[5]

Repatriated refugees are worked the hardest of all the prisoners. Young-Kuk explained, "They would work us harder because we ate so well while we were in China. They made us carry heavy loads, and when they beat us, they would use all sorts of things with which to hit us . . . I wondered if I would make it out of there alive, and looked for any opportunity to escape. But there were no such opportunities."

Mrs. Park, a refugee woman in her forties, described what her days inside a North Korean prison were like: "We started our physical labor early in the morning. We began working at 6:00 A.M. and then ate breakfast at 8:00 A.M. . . . We had to cut wood. They had us in groups sawing wood together and had to count '1, 2, 3.' Oftentimes we worked straight through the day until dinnertime." In some cases, prisoners are made to perform cruel and meaningless labor. Mrs. Park continued:

> Even if there was no work for us to do, they made up meaningless work for us. There was a big pile of large rocks. The guards would say, "Separate the rocks! Move all the big rocks to the right side and all the small rocks to the left side!" Hours later after we finished, they would then say, "Now put the rocks back into one big pile!" When we finished with this they instructed again, "This time reverse it. Move all the big rocks to the left side and all the small rocks to the right side!"

As Mrs. Park spoke, I was reminded of stories I had heard in a history class at the University of Illinois at Urbana–Champaign about Jewish prisoners in Nazi concentration camps. They were forced to senselessly move large rocks from one side of the compound to the other and then back again until their spirits were completely broken. It has been said that the prisoners died not only from exhaustion but also from the purposelessness of their work.

BEATINGS, TORTURE, DEATH

If North Korean prison walls could speak, they would tell horrific stories of beatings, torture, and death. One North Korean prison survivor wrote to me of "the cries of the North Koreans as they're beaten . . .

their tears of hunger . . . moaning in pain that doesn't end . . . their dark faces with no smiles . . . I picture these faces and I see a picture of the shadows of hell." There is a strict code of conduct in prison, and anyone who fails to follow orders is severely beaten. Dong-Il explained:

> They call you by your number. If they yell "Number 1!" then you have to respond by saying which cell you're in. Once they call you, you're supposed to respond within 10 seconds—or was it 5 seconds?—and kneel before that officer facing the wall, stating, "Number 1 from cell number 1 has come out!" Then they'll acknowledge you and then tell you to do something, like put on your shoes, and then take you to be interrogated. You have to respond a certain way and within the guidelines they tell you. . . . There are many regulations. For instance, you're not allowed to speak foreign languages. I've forgotten a lot of them, but you had to know them and memorize them every day. We had to recite them really loudly all the time. The appointed room leader was really harsh to us, because he would get beaten if we were caught not doing things correctly. Even if one person messed up, we would all get in trouble.

Women, children, and the elderly are all subject to beatings and torture. Mrs. Lee, a refugee, explained, "When it comes to beatings, they don't look at men and women differently." Ms. Lim, another refugee, added, "However, it is only the men who are electrocuted with cattle prods. Women aren't electrocuted, but we are kicked, hit with sticks, and have our hair pulled out until we bleed." Another former prisoner showed me a bald spot on the right side of her head. "I was hit on the head repeatedly with a hammer," she said.

Mr. Min witnessed the horrors of torture: "Who you are is not important to them. You can be an elderly man or woman . . . it doesn't matter. They swear at you and beat you relentlessly. I've seen it all. Sometimes, the guards would demand that prisoners put their hands on the floor. Then they would step all over [them]. I would hear horrific cries. I've seen people lose all their fingernails like this."

Kwang-Ho, a young teenager, told me, "Some people think kids don't get hit in prison or that they get hit less. This isn't true. . . . Sometimes kids get hit more." Sook-Hee, a 16-year-old, was caught attempting to find asylum in a foreign embassy in China. She and nine other teenagers were caught and repatriated to North Korea. Five of them died in prison; the other five survived and were released. Sook-Hee recounted, "My punishment was sitting in a chair every day for 15 hours. From 7:00 A.M. in the morning until 10:00 P.M. at night, I had to sit perfectly still in a chair. I wasn't allowed to move an inch or say a word. They had a surveillance camera on us and watched us from another room. If one person moved, everyone was beaten. We were served lunch and dinner in our chairs. That was the only time we were allowed to move."

Mrs. Kim, a refugee in her late thirties, described one beating she witnessed while in prison: "There was another person arrested together with me. She was beaten so much that it made me sick to watch it. I was disgusted. They repeatedly hit and poked the woman with a sharp stick. They kept on hitting her until her flesh ripped. I was sitting right next to her and it made me shudder."

Pastor Shim, a Korean-Chinese staff member, reported after he returned from a North Korean village, "It is known that the prisoners in the central prison are fed with glass debris embedded in a bowl of rice. This happens quite regularly and is not a one-time incident . . . Stories about the so-called glass rice have been spreading."

Prison guards are encouraged to beat, torture, and kill prisoners and are even awarded for it. Ahn Myong Chul, the former prison guard mentioned earlier, recalled, "They trained me not to treat the prisoners as human beings. If someone is against socialism, if someone tries to escape from prison, then kill him. If there's a record of killing any escapee, then the guard will be entitled to study in the college. Because of that some guards kill innocent people." He continued, "I heard many times that eyeballs were taken out by beating . . . And I saw that by beating the person the muscle was damaged and the bone was exposed, outside, and they put salt on the wounded part. At the beginning I was frightened when I witnessed it, but it was repeated again and again, so my feelings were paralyzed."[6]

One former prisoner described the death of Mr. Doh, a fellow inmate:

On June 17, 2005, they beat him so severely near his head that he became mentally unstable. They also decided to punish him by forbidding him to move for three hours. If he spoke, they beat him. If he farted, they would beat him. My teachers, if one stays seated for a long time, his legs start to hurt. Well, when he moved his legs to relieve the pain, they again beat him. Once in a while, he'd say something like, "Just kill me if you're going to beat me to death!" Because of this, the guards kicked him and stepped on him until he was half dead . . . For 10 days, before I was temporarily transferred out, he was beaten by the guards every single day. Then when I had returned after 15 days, he had changed so much that he became unrecognizable—a completely different person. He used to be a healthy 40-year-old man—approximately 5' 7" tall and 165 pounds. Now, he was nothing but bones. . . . They'd beat him every morning with thick bats because he wasn't able to walk properly. He started developing bloody puss all over, along with severe diarrhea. When he couldn't control his diarrhea, they beat him and confiscated his meals—a few spoonfuls of rice. He got so hungry that he started to eat dirty rags that were used to clean the toilets.

Mr. Doh, unable to endure the constant beatings and torture, died in July 2005. When I asked a group of refugees if a lot of people die in prison, a woman in the group answered, "People don't always necessarily get beaten to death, but people are so weak that they die from a light beating." A teenager in the room added, "If you're sick, you can easily die. When you're weak, the smallest blow can kill you."

In some prison camps, it has been reported, as much as 20 to 25 percent of the prison population dies every year.[7] While it is difficult to come up with an accurate number, some researchers estimate that a million North Koreans have died in prison.[8]

There are also increasing reports of public executions in the country. One of our Second Wave local staff members returned from a trip to North Korea and wrote in her project report, "There were three former refugees who were publicly executed by a firing squad. The family I stayed with encouraged me to stay and watch, but I told them I had too much work to do back in China and had to leave."

In 2005, a video of two public executions was smuggled out of North Korea by the Japanese NGO Life Funds for North Korean Refugees. While the North Korean government denied the event took place, the video circulated around the world. One man and one woman were executed for defecting to China. They were blindfolded, and stones were stuffed into their mouths in order to prevent them from shouting out criticisms of the regime. In the video, three riflemen stepped forward and fired three shots at the man. The man's body fell limp to the floor, and a government official shouted a message to the audience through a megaphone, "You have witnessed how miserable fools end up. Traitors who betray the nation and its people end up like this."

Mrs. Ryu, a refugee, cried as she shared a story about a fellow inmate who was in her eighth month of pregnancy:

> The guards shouted at the pregnant woman, "Whose baby is this? Is it from a North Korean man or a Chinese man?" The woman whispered in fear, "It is a Chinese man's baby." With their big heavy boots, several of them kicked her repeatedly in the stomach. She vomited blood, and it came out of the sides of her mouth. That night, her stomach was hurting badly and a lot of blood was coming out of her. She gave birth to a dead baby. We were horrified and cried so much that night. Shortly after she delivered the dead baby, the guards went out to eat, leaving her alone. She jumped from the second floor of the medical clinic and escaped from prison.

Ethnically motivated infanticide is common in North Korean prisons. A North Korean woman carrying the baby of a Chinese father will be severely punished, and the baby will be forcibly aborted. In "The

Hidden Gulag," David Hawk wrote, "Repatriated pregnant North Koreans thrown into the interrogation-detention system face ethnically-motivated infanticide and forced abortions." In the political prisons, he writes, "except for a very few privileged couples, the prisoners were not allowed to have sex or children . . . And there are sporadic reports of killings of pregnant women who were raped or coerced into sex by prison guards."[9]

COLLECTIVE PUNISHMENT

The regime practices something called *collective punishment*, whereby up to three generations of a dissident's family can be jailed for the "crime" of one person. In the prisons of North Korea, you will oddly find people who have never committed a crime in their lives. Their crime is simply being related to someone who committed a "crime." Hawk comments, "What is unique to North Korea's situation that I have not encountered anywhere else is the *collective punishment*, the guilt-by-association aspect where not only the perceived political wrongdoer but his family up to three generations is also imprisoned, and not in the same camp. The punishment is . . . for the entire family."[10]

Shin Dong Hyok, a 26-year-old North Korean man, was born in a political prison camp in North Korea and punished for the "crimes" of his parents. After 22 years in prison, he escaped and eventually found asylum in South Korea, where he told his story. Since he was born in a political prison camp, he had no knowledge of the outside world. He commented, "I didn't know about America, or China or the fact that the Korean Peninsula was divided and there was a place called South Korea."[11] He added that while in prison, he did not know of Kim Il Sung or Kim Jong Il.[12]

In an interview with the *International Herald Tribune*, he described the moment of his mother's execution, "Before she was executed, my mother looked at me. I don't know if she wanted to say something, because she was bound and gagged. But I avoided her eyes . . . My father was weeping, but I didn't cry. I had no love for her. Even today I hate her for what I had to go through because of her . . . However I try, I can't forgive her."[13]

There are rumors that after Hwang Jang-yop, the architect of *Juche* and the highest-ranking defector, escaped from North Korea, Kim Jong Il ordered a purge of 2,000 people with ties to him.[14] Survivors of gulags have reported that they saw members of Hwang's family being punished in prison because of his defection. Hwang's daughter reportedly killed herself by "jumping off a bridge as she was transported to the Korean Gulag."[15]

Kim Hyun Hee, a North Korean agent responsible for planting a bomb on Korean Air flight 858 in 1987, killing 115 passengers, wrote a book titled *The Tears of My Soul* in which she detailed her training in espionage and the events leading up to the terrorist act. Shortly after the explosion, she was captured by authorities and was flown to South Korea to be interrogated; she ultimately received the death sentence. Kim repented for her crime and, in a shocking turn of events, was pardoned by the South Korean president, Kim Dae Jung. In her book, which she dedicated to the families of the victims of flight 858, she wrote, "My confession to the South Korean authorities had to be regarded by my government as the worst possible treason. Because of my failure, and because of my disgrace, my family would almost certainly be taken from their homes and interred by the North Korean government in some horrible slave labor camp, probably for the rest of their lives. I had not only ruined my own life, I had also irrevocably ruined theirs."[16]

In a familial society like North Korea, collective punishment successfully paralyzes many North Koreans politically. Ms. Seo, a former kindergarten teacher, commented, "If you have one life to live, you would gladly give it to overthrow this government, but you are not the only one getting punished. Your family will go through hell."[17]

Gulags

GLIMPSES OF HUMANITY

Young-Kuk first told me about his prison experiences over a cup of tea at a café in China. As Young-Kuk described how he was beaten and tortured, he smiled and even laughed at times. I said to the others in the room, "It amazes me that after he has suffered so much he can laugh about these things." Young-Kuk interjected, "We laugh in prison too. When it gets too hard, we have to laugh a lot. This is how we survive." Young-Ja, a 16-year-old refugee girl, added, "If you don't laugh, you can't survive. You'll die right away."

Occasionally, prison camp survivors will tell stories of generosity and love inside North Korean prison walls. Young-Kuk said:

> There was another person there who was somewhat similar to me. He had been caught in China and had gone through much heartache. The more I looked at him, he and I were so similar. He lost his parents and his younger siblings. Everything was taken from him, even his clothes, so I gave him a pair of my trousers and shared with him the food I had. As I was doing that, the other people in the prison looked at me so strangely. They wondered how I could think about others before I took care of myself, sharing even the little I had with someone else.

Young-Kuk also spoke of an older man who, in turn, took care of him: "There was another older person who I called uncle. . . . After everyone got their food ration, they would come back and give him another portion since they knew him well in there. . . . He gave his extra portion to me to eat, treating me like a son."

Even in one of the darkest and cruelest places in the world, precious friendships are formed. Young-Kuk recounted:

> Even before I would get a chance to take a bite [of food], people all around me, young and old, would ask for some. I couldn't share with everyone, and even one extra spoonful would be so little, but

I would share with people I thought most needed it. But through all that, *hyong* [elder brother] never asked me for food. He would say, "Why are you being so foolish and giving all your food away? You should eat." He was the closest friend I had in there. It was so little, but I gave him a couple spoonfuls of food telling him to eat it. But he looked at it and said, "I can't eat this. This is your food. That would be taking away from your food." So we looked at each other and agreed to eat it together.

Even in an utterly inhumane place such as the North Korean gulags, there are glimpses of humanity among the victims, moments of humor and generosity. North Koreans are some of the greatest survivors that I know. They love life too much to give up, even when faced with impossible odds. They find a way to hold on to hope in the most desperate of circumstances.

SEVEN

Christianity and North Korea

If power is combined with trust, we can overcome even Heaven.

—Kim Jong Il

In April 2004, I left my home at the China–North Korea border and flew into Seoul for a week of meetings. After I finished all of my work in Seoul, I took a two-hour bus ride from Seoul to Taejon to visit my dad. On the highway, I saw a gigantic billboard that said "Jesus Loves You" in large yellow letters. I was a bit startled at first since I had spent the previous two months in China and North Korea—places where such expression would be completely forbidden. I thought to myself, "How strange that South Korea and North Korea are such polar opposites when it comes to Christianity." In that sense, the two countries could not be more different.

When you walk the streets of Seoul, signs of Christianity are everywhere. There are churches, Christian bookstores, and subway preachers. A neon cross or church stands at nearly every corner. South Korea has the largest church in the world: the Yoido Full Gospel Church. In 1992, the church boasted a membership of 700,000 (roughly 16 times larger than the biggest church in North America), made possible through multiple weekend services and satellite locations.[1] South Korea is also second only to the United States in the number of missionaries it sends abroad. Christianity is part of the very fabric of South Korean culture and society.

When you walk the streets of North Korea, on the other hand, you will be hard-pressed to find a single trace of Christianity. Besides the three government church buildings that have been erected for propaganda purposes, there are almost no visible signs of the Christian religion. In fact, the regime has altogether eliminated the word for "God" (*Hananim*). Mrs. Lee, a refugee in her late thirties, told me, "There is no such word as 'God' in North Korea . . . If someone came to North Korea and used the word 'God,' I wouldn't have been able to understand what they were talking about." In North Korea you have some of the smallest churches in the world today: Two or three individuals form a "church," as they gather late at night with a flashlight in hand and conduct services hiding under a blanket.

FEAR AND HATRED

There is deep-seated fear and hatred of Christianity in North Korea. A North Korean dictionary defines "church" as "an organization that spreads poisonous anti-government ideas to take the people's rights away, disguised as a religious activity."[2]

Dong-Min, a teenage refugee, told of seeing a television show in North Korea on the topic of churches: "The television show said that church is an American thing. They warned that Christians will give you candy and try to trick you. Then at the first chance they have, they will kidnap and sell you . . . When I first came to China I was so scared to go to a church asking for help. When I had no money and nowhere else to go, [however], I had no other choice."

Pastor Kang was once leading a group of refugees in a Bible study on the topic of love. "We all have people we don't like," he said. Then he asked Mrs. Kim, one of the refugees, "What kind of people do North Koreans not like?" Mrs. Kim humorously replied, "People like you"—pastors.

An anti-American and anti-Christian painting in a museum near Pyongyang (Voice of the Martyrs)

From North Korea's inception, Kim Il Sung has done everything in his power to stomp out Christianity. Thomas Belke, in his book *Juche: A Christian Study of North Korea's State Religion,* wrote, "In 1945, the Communist Korean Workers' Party began the massive anti-religion campaign by systematically destroying about 2,000 churches and 400 Buddhist temples. Countless atrocities and murders were committed against the 50,000 Catholics and 300,000 Protestants."[3] Kim Il Sung announced the success of his campaign to eradicate Christianity in a 1962 speech: "Through court trials, we have executed all Protestant and Catholic church cadre members and all other vicious religious elements have been sent to concentration camps."[4] Final estimates suggest that Kim Il Sung destroyed over 1,500 churches.[5]

I often ask refugees about their knowledge of Christianity while they were in North Korea. Eun-Young, a young refugee woman, told me she had never heard of Christianity there, "not even once." Kun-Sun, another young woman, said, "I never heard of Jesus, church, or Christianity until I came to China. In North Korea, you can't believe in God, but people are always searching for spiritual things. People illegally do fortune-telling in hopes to find out about the future."

Out of the hundreds of North Koreans I have interviewed, only one said she had heard of God or Jesus while in North Korea. When I asked Mrs. Song, the elderly woman who defected to China when she was 77 years old, if she had heard about Jesus Christ in North Korea, she answered, "Yes I have, since I am old. It was a long time ago when I was younger . . . right around the time of the Korean War when I was 25 or 26."

In its current attempt to keep Christianity out of the country, the North Korean regime has had to contend with the many refugees who return from China as Christians. A U.S. Commission on International Religious Freedom report stated, "There is a department of religion at Kim Il Sung University, but graduates and faculty are said to be involved in training security forces to identify repatriated refugees who may have become Christian adherents during their time in China."[6] When a refugee is repatriated to North Korea, the first question they are asked by prison guards is, "When you were in China, did you become a Christian?" The second question is, "When you were in China, did you meet any missionaries or foreigners?" Refugees know that to answer "yes" to either question would mean a life sentence in a political prison camp or even death.

Mrs. Suh, a refugee who converted to Christianity in China, was captured in April 2005 and repatriated to North Korea. After serving a lengthy prison term, she was released and defected a second time to China, where she found her way to one of our refugee shelters. When I asked her how she responded to the first question guards asked her, she replied, "If I answered yes, I wouldn't be here today."

North Korean Christian refugees are thus forced to lie about their faith when re-entering the country, if they want to live. Dr. Carl Moeller, the CEO of Open Doors USA, an international organization that provides support to Christians who face persecution because of their faith, commented, "The very fact that the North Korean government asks [about the religion] of apprehended refugees indicates that they're aware that there's a growing movement of North Koreans becoming Christians in China."[7]

If a Christian refugee is captured in a house church in China or there is other incriminating evidence against him, he will in most cases make excuses. "I only went to the church because I had nowhere else to go," he might say. Or, "The church was the only place I could find help." Or, "I didn't believe in God while I was there, I just accepted their help." If a person is unable to convincingly deny their faith, it will certainly mean life in a political prison camp or in many cases, death.

Mrs. Suh told the story of another refugee she met at the time of her capture: "There was a woman who was caught [in China] at the same time as me. She was wearing a cross necklace at the time of her capture and didn't have time to remove it. It was obvious to the authorities that she had been attending church while in China, and there was no way she could deny it . . . When I left the prison, she was still there. After I was released, I asked a friend in the same prison about the woman who was caught with the cross necklace. She said that the woman wasn't there anymore. I'm assuming she was executed."

CHRISTIAN ROOTS

Those who are unfamiliar with Korean history will be surprised to learn that the nation of North Korea has very strong Christian roots. Reverend Robert J. Thomas, a young missionary from Wales, first tried to introduce Christianity to the peninsula in 1866. He traveled to Korea on an American boat, but upon his arrival the members of the crew were met with great hostility. The governor of Pyongyang ordered his men to attack the ship and to kill every person on board. Reverend Thomas leapt from the boat and shouted, "Jesus, Jesus" in Korean and held out a Korean Bible. As he offered it to a Korean man, the man cut off his head. Kim Il Sung points to this moment as the beginning of North Korean anti-American struggles[8] and claims that it was his great-grandfather who led the attack against the ship.[9]

The Korean man who beheaded Thomas took the Bible home and used the pages as wallpaper in his guesthouse. He eventually converted to the Christian faith. In 1891, when an American visited the area and asked about the unique wallpaper, the owner told of how for many years people had come from all over to read the walls.[10] Christianity spread throughout the peninsula, and the Korean church grew. In 1907 it experienced a great revival that started in Pyongyang and swept throughout the peninsula.

Ironically, Kim Il Sung's parents were both devout Christians. His father, Kim Hyong-jik, attended a school that was run by American missionaries and later became a Presbyterian elder. Kim Il Sung attended church with his parents until he became an atheist later in life. Reverend Billy Graham, on his second visit to North Korea in January 1994, had a conversation with Kim Il Sung about Christianity. In his autobiography, *Just As I Am,* Graham recalled, "I also took the opportunity to speak very directly about my own faith in Christ—a faith that, I reminded him [Kim Il Sung], his own mother had professed. He acknowledged that she had taken him to church sometimes when he was a boy, although he admitted with a smile that he had always wanted to go fishing instead. He listened respectfully to what I said but made little comment."[11]

THE NORTH KOREAN CHURCH

Although Kim Jong Il has made it one of his highest priorities to completely wipe out any hint of Christianity, we continue to receive reports about the presence of the underground church in North Korea. There is a story of a little 11-year-old North Korean girl who made the journey from North Korea to China alone. After hours of hiking through mountains and crossing the river, she showed up at the steps of a Chinese church, where she explained her situation and asked for help. The church deacons were amazed that she made the journey alone and asked, "Little girl, how did you know to come here for help?" She replied, "My grandfather told me, 'Look for the cross and go there. Those people will help you.'" Even in a closed country such as North Korea, information about the church spreads in the North Korean underground.

We receive a large number of reports from our Korean-Chinese teams indicating that they regularly encounter Christians inside the country. In early 2006, Pastor Cho, a Korean-Chinese staff member, visited his relatives in North Korea. "My cousin, aunt, and my three nephews are Christian," he reported. "That night I prayed with them that God would protect us. They had a painting of Jesus on the cross, which was published by an old Catholic church. It was hidden and covered with paper under a box, and I took it out to have a look when there was no one around."

When I asked Mrs. Jough, who visited the same month, if she encountered any Christians, she said yes. "They were people who had gone to China, received Bible teaching and have now returned. All they do is pray. That is because they have no Bibles and cannot sing hymns."

Pastor Kim, a house church pastor in China, recalled meeting a person in North Korea "who became a Christian in China. When I suggested that we close our eyes and pray, he refused, saying that he could not do so with other people present. I told him that it was okay to pray with his eyes open. He said that he would pray for freedom of religion in his country and for his people. . . . This believer has a lifestyle of continual prayer and has had more experiences of God than people like you and me. Because he has such a strong conviction . . . it was I who was challenged. He was an amazing believer."

Mr. Ha visited North Korea in mid-April 2006. "They can't gather together, so they pray on their own," he recounted. "As far as I know there isn't anyone teaching them, but since they already have more than 100 Christian books sent to them, they read and study those texts to teach themselves spiritually. The group has grown in size through spreading the gospel and now includes seven cell groups in different areas. They all gather round to help one another in times of difficulty and encourage each other to remain and grow in faith."

Christians from North Korea will sometimes take great risks to sneak across the river into China for a few days to receive Bible training.

On May 10, 2003, I took a four-hour trip to the China–North Korea border to meet with four North Korean Christians. The meeting took place in a small, dark room about 100 yards from the border. Two of the women were leaders of an underground church and had crossed the river into China for the meeting. We were very cautious and whispered as we spoke. When I asked, "What brings you here to China?" one of the women answered, "I want to learn more about God." In the short time that we had, I asked as many questions as I could. "How many members are there in your church?" I asked the women. "Ten to fifteen," one replied. "How many Bibles do you have in your church?" "We have six. Every time we come to China, we take one more Bible back to North Korea." One of the pastors present preached a sermon, and two of the women were baptized.

Even in the heart of Pyongyang, there are Christians who secretly live out their faith. Pastor Jun, a Korean-Chinese staffer, returned from a trip to Pyongyang and spoke of an elderly North Korean woman who worked at his hotel. When the two of them had a moment alone, he said to her, "Believe in Jesus. If you don't know about him, I'll tell you about him." The elderly woman stared at him in shock, without replying, so he repeated himself. Still she was silent. Only after he repeated himself again did she respond. After recovering from her shock, she ran to the door and closed it. Putting her hand on her heart, she exclaimed, "Oh! I believe in Jesus. I believe in Jesus. Thank you. Thank you." The pastor replied, "Wonderful! Then you must know some Christian songs." She immediately sang hymn 460 for him in a low voice. The English version of the hymn is titled "God's Great Grace," but in Korean the literal translation is "What I've been through to this day." As she sang, tears fell from her eyes, and the pastor cried with her. When she finished, she said, "I can't sing that song out loud, but every day I sing it quietly in my heart. A day doesn't pass by when I don't sing that song and pray to Jesus."

Missionary Yoo, an elderly Korean-Chinese woman in her seventies, is a veteran missionary to North Korea who leads a network of 116

Christian families there. When I asked her to describe her visits to North Korea, she said, "I write down for them the Apostles' Creed, the Lord's Prayer and hymns 405, 338, and 256. We sing together all night in fellowship. . . . When I go to North Korea, I just cry and cry as I see the situation they're living in." When I asked Missionary Yoo how they were able to sing without the police noticing, she replied, "We sing late at night. We gather with one or two other people and sing very quietly. When we sing or pray we have to make sure the kids are sleeping, or if we meet during the day we send them outside." Children are trained in schools to report their parents if they notice any suspicious activity at home. "When we sing, we close all the windows," Missionary Yoo added. "The North Korean police are known to sit outside windows and spy on people to listen to what is going on in the house."

No one really knows how many Christians there are in North Korea. There is an annual summit where the largest organizations engaged in underground work gather to network, share ideas and information, and volunteer resources. At the last summit in Seoul, 100,000 was the number every organization seemed to agree on. In December 1997, Voice of the Martyrs estimated that there were 60,000 Christians in North Korea. In February 1998, they upped their estimate to 60,000 to 100,000.[12] North Korea claims that there are only 12,000 (and 500 house churches). Dr. Moeller told me, "We're always underestimating" the secret believers. "For decades we underestimated China. . . . So I have a feeling in my own gut that we'll be shocked by the number of believers in North Korea."[13]

BIBLES

As I am writing this chapter, there on the far left corner of my desk sits my maroon Bible with its golden-edged pages. It amazes me that this one book could be so simultaneously hated and loved in a country. On the one hand, the regime will ruthlessly torture and kill anyone who possesses a Bible or dares believe in its message. On the other hand,

Christians will risk their lives to own it (or a portion of it). In all of my years attending churches and traveling internationally on mission trips, I personally have never seen a greater devotion to the Bible than I have seen among the North Koreans.

Jung-Hoon, a North Korean man, finished reading the Bible from cover to cover in two weeks. He regularly does this several times a year. Ms. Kim, a refugee who worked for the propaganda news service in North Korea, copied the entire Bible by hand. She started in May 2003 and finished within five months. She wrote for 16 hours a day. When I asked her why, she said, "I thought that filling my mind with Scripture might help me forget about my terrible past." I have seen three hand-written Bibles in my lifetime. Two were written by North Koreans; the other was written by a South Korean.

Very few North Koreans actually own a Bible, but the ones who do are keenly aware that it may one day cost them their lives. When Missionary Yoo smuggles Bibles into North Korea and gives them to Christian families, she tells the families, "Hide them well." Their creativeness in doing so may very well determine whether they live or die. When I asked Mrs. Shin if she had been afraid to own a Bible in North Korea, she said yes and added, "I dug a deep hole and hid it in the ground. If they find out that I have it, my life is over."

In July 2005, when I asked one refugee if he had ever heard about Christianity in North Korea, he responded, "I never heard of Christianity, but I did hear of a Bible. I worked at a cement factory, and one of the workers left a Bible out on a table in his home. Someone saw the Bible and reported it. The man and his whole family, including kids, were sent to a prison camp. That was the first and only time I ever heard of a Bible in North Korea."

Missionary Lee, one of our Korean-Chinese staff members, was imprisoned for five months in North Korea. While he was in prison, authorities searched the homes of 15 families that he had relationships with and found four Bibles. He recounted:

The North Korean guards tried to force it upon the 15 families to sign a report written about me. The paper said something like, "This brother is . . . a spy working under America. He is detrimental to North Korea and ought to be executed." . . . They were all in utter shock. They all stared at him [the guard] with eyes that seemed to say, "Why would you kill a man as good as he?" They started stepping away from him, refusing to sign the paper. He threatened them, saying that if they didn't sign the paper, they would be the ones going to the execution camps. I began urging them to sign the paper. I told them, "It is I who brought the Bibles into your homes. So if anyone is a criminal, it is I." I pleaded with them again and again to sign. Eventually they did. What I'm truly thankful for is that the seeds of the gospel that were sown in their hearts are still growing and that my labor was not in vain.

We were able to get Missionary Lee safely home after we agreed to pay a ransom of $3,600 to the North Korean government for his release.

Bible smugglers use great creativity to get Bibles into the country. Missionary Lee for many years smuggled Bibles into North Korea using *doenjang* jars. He wrapped the Bibles in Saran wrap and placed them at the bottom of these large, ceramic containers filled with soybean paste. He no longer uses this method, however, since customs officials have caught on—they now take a stick and check the bottom of the containers.

Missionary Yoo has smuggled over 100 Bibles into North Korea. She told me of one particular method: "I bought one box of ramen noodles. Then I opened fifteen out of the one hundred packages, cut the ramen in half, cut out a small empty space in the middle, put a small, miniature Bible[14] in the center, then resealed the packages." But customs inspections are now so thorough that this method is no longer used either. "Now, I am too nervous to carry a Bible with me," Missionary Yoo said. Christian workers generally don't attempt to take Bibles into the country through customs anymore, but they instead smuggle them illegally across the river.

PERSECUTION AND MARTYRS

I asked some of the leading organizations serving persecuted Christians in the world today: How would you compare religious persecution in North Korea with persecution in other countries? Tom White, the executive director of Voice of the Martyrs, commented:

> Pyongyang was the most controlled city . . . I've ever been to. I haven't been to Saudi Arabia. The two most controlled countries in the world, in my opinion, having gone to 130 countries, are North Korea and Saudi Arabia . . . North Korea is the most vicious. . . . North Korea is number one on oppression, on attempted extermination of all Christian belief. Saudi Arabia would be a close race, but on murdering believers we don't hear a lot about that in Saudi Arabia. We hear about beatings. North Korea is probably, on brutality, number one.[15]

Ann Buwalda is the executive director of Jubilee Campaign, an international organization that promotes religious liberty and human rights. She puts North Korea

> within the top three. There are a couple of countries that I would rank at least equally as deplorable as North Korea. But certainly it's within the top three in terms of the horrific treatment of anyone discovered to have a faith in God. My understanding from defectors and testimonies from North Koreans is that there really is no ability whatsoever to have any Christian activity other than a very limited government-approved church.[16]

Dr. Moeller commented:

> There's no other country at the levels that North Korea is . . . [in] systematically persecuting Christians. I often say, on our World Watch List of the top 50 countries, there's North Korea and then there's the other 49 countries. Even Saudi Arabia and Iran, with their systematic religious persecution of believers . . . don't have the

dozens of labor camps and work camps that are set up for political and religious dissidents that tens of thousands of Christians are known to be working in—working literally to death. So North Korea stands alone in its repressive, deeply rooted, horrible treatment of Christians.[17]

Michael Cromartie is the chair of the U.S. Commission on International Religious Freedom and vice president of the Ethics and Public Policy Center. He told me:

Religious persecution is bad in many parts of the world, but it is the worst in North Korea. The level of suppression of religious belief is so strong that it is like a sterile country, totally sterilized from any sort of religious symbolism. Everything in North Korea is overwhelmingly totalitarian, and the persecution of religious believers there is appalling and brutal beyond belief.[18]

Mrs. Oh, a Korean-Chinese staffer who recently returned from North Korea, learned that, in some cases, when a Christian is found out, the person's whole family is abducted. "On the way back, I saw three families being dragged away at a train station," she wrote.

I met Mr. Lee, a refugee who defected to China, in January 2004 the night before he was to return to North Korea to be reunited with his family. A small group of us were gathered for a short service and communion. During the service, he stated, "Here in China I've learned about God, Jesus, and the Holy Spirit. I'm thankful that people here have taught me the Bible. . . . When I go back to North Korea, it will be very hard. I will get beaten, and I might even die. I know a grown man isn't supposed to cry, but"—and he broke down crying. As I put my hand on his shoulder, I could feel him trembling. At the conclusion of our time together, Mr. Lee went around and hugged everyone in the room one by one. It's a hug that I'll never forget.

Escaping North Korea

In April 2003, I met Mr. Rhee, a refugee who had found asylum in South Korea. While in North Korea, he had joined a network of 160 Christians. They had one Bible among them and took turns passing it around, copying as much of it as they could by hand. Mr. Kim was eventually imprisoned for his faith and tortured in unbelievable ways. "I had my fingernails and toenails pulled out," he recounted. "I also had nails hammered into my skin." He showed me the scars on his body. When I asked him how he became a Christian, he replied, "There was an 80-year-old pastor among the group of 160. . . . The pastor was caught and publicly executed, with a statement saying, 'This man believed in Jesus. This is what will happen to all those who believe in Jesus.'"

In North Korean prisons, Christians in particular are not allowed to lift their heads to the sky or acknowledge God in any way. The regime attempts to purge hope and faith from them. In stricter locations, Christians are required to always keep their heads down. As a result, they develop severe hunchbacks or "90-degree curvature of the spine."[19] One political prison camp survivor recalled, "It looked like they [Christians] had soccer balls attached to their backs."

Ironically, a Christian in North Korea may have the best chance of meeting another Christian inside a prison cell. North Korean prisons are a common meeting place for Christians. People risk their lives to have conversations like the following one recounted by a North Korean refugee man:

> One day we were talking, and I said, "A person shouldn't waste his life on trying to eat and live well, but he should strive to live a long life making a difference with the life he lives. And even the money that he does have, isn't how he spends it important as well?" As I was saying this, people were shaking their heads and agreeing. . . . Then In-Soo, whom I had gotten close to, looked at me and asked, "So you mean that all the things that are done under the sun, all of them are meaningless?" I immediately replied that I didn't know, even though I knew exactly where that came from [Ecclesiastes 1:14]. We

made eye contact and tried to read each other. The others around us didn't understand, but we clasped each other's hands and, though we couldn't say anything further, we vowed to each other, "We're going to get out of here alive," since that was a common greeting in there. From that day on, I was so encouraged and strengthened.

We regularly receive reports about Christians executed in North Korea. Pastor Kwon wrote after her visit to North Korea in the second half of 2006:

According to what I had heard, in early February several Christians gathered to worship together but were caught by the National Security Police. Three people were executed by firing squad, and the others were sent to a political prison camp. On February 20, another incident had also occurred. Two people were executed by firing squad and the others were sent to a political prison camp.

Pastor Song reported upon his return from the country:

In April 2005, 47 people were taken from Musan and detained in a remote area, with three people executed by firing squad. From what I had heard, it was because people were studying theology through South Korean Christian radio broadcasts. . . . When it is discovered that a North Korean has gone to China and has become Christian, upon their return they are automatically sent to a prison camp. . . . But my relatives tell me that there are still people who quietly go around evangelizing in North Korea.

Missionary Yoo told me about a family she visited in North Korea in November 2004. Mrs. Oh was widowed in 1997 when her husband died from starvation and disease. She lived with her son, daughter, and younger sister. In 1998, Mrs. Oh's son and younger sister defected to China in search of food and money to bring back to North Korea. In China, both converted to Christianity, but in 1999 they were captured by the Chinese police and repatriated to North Korea. The North Korean authorities learned about their newfound faith. "While the family was called in for questioning by the National Security Police, their home was burned to the ground," Missionary Yoo said. "They weren't even able to save a pair of chopsticks." That year, Mrs. Oh's son and younger sister were executed for converting to the Christian faith. Mrs. Oh now lives with her daughter and granddaughter, who are also Christians. The granddaughter says that she secretly hopes to escape to China one day. In partnership with Voice of the Martyrs, we provide regular financial support to Mrs. Oh's family.

There are many other documented cases of torture and executions of Christians in North Korea. The U.S. Commission on International Religious Freedom,[20] in their 2007 Annual Report, stated:

> There continue to be reports of torture and execution of religious believers, including a January 2005 report of the execution of six religious leaders. Additionally, in March 2006, authorities in Pyongyang sentenced Son Jong Nam to death on charges of spying for South Korea. Son's contact with Protestants in China, his religious conversion, and his private criticism of the North Korean regime reportedly served as a basis for the sentence . . . Neither the State Department nor any other official or non-governmental source has been able to document the number of religious detainees or prisoners. According to some reports, an estimated 6,000 Christians are incarcerated in "Prison No. 15" located in the northern part of the country.[21]

The North Korean church has suffered tremendously over the years, but persevered. Believers pray for religious freedom and long for a day when they will be free to worship as they please. Dr. Moeller recalled an interaction he had with a man nicknamed "The Traveler" who he met at the border:

> [The Traveler] talked about the lamentation of the North Korean church. . . . He said one of the prayers he hears [North Korean

Christians] pray, and it breaks his heart, is "Lord, your children and the people of Israel only wandered in the wilderness for 40 years under your wrath. We are wandering almost 60 years under your wrath." There's a deep feeling of contrition on their part. It's something that we in America really don't deal with very much, which is coming to terms with what it feels like to be generation after generation of secret believers, completely oppressed.[22]

CHRISTIANITY AND THE NORTH KOREAN CRISIS

It is worthwhile to consider for a moment the dynamics of the Christian religion in relation to the North Korean crisis. Recently, Open Doors International acquired secret documents that show that the North Korean regime views Christianity as responsible for the fall of communism in Europe.[23] The government is keenly aware of the growing influence of Christianity. But despite the vast resources it has devoted to try to extinguish any trace of Christianity within the country, Christianity continues to play a vital role in opening up the nation. Refugee interaction with house churches in China, an influx of Korean-Chinese Christians into North Korea, and South Korean Christian broadcasts into the country are eroding the regime's control of the North Korean people.

International Crisis Group, in a report titled "Perilous Journeys: The Plight of North Koreans in China and Beyond," stated, "Christian churches in China were particularly active in supporting the early cross-border survival strategy . . . Hundreds of border crossers passed through each of the fifteen to twenty house churches in this one network alone."[24] It is now widely known that it is primarily the massive Korean-Chinese house church networks that provide a safety net for North Koreans who defect to China. In addition, as with the Underground Railroad in the United States in the nineteenth century, the modern-day Asian underground railroad through which North Korean refugees can gain asylum is largely made up of a network of Christians.

The Korean-Chinese, more than any other single group of people, have unparalleled access to North Korea. They are the most frequent travelers to the country, and because of a common language and culture they can communicate most effectively with the people there. Thousands of Korean-Chinese Christians regularly travel to North Korea as missionaries, not only to spread the Christian message but also to dispute the lies of the regime. They have been more effective in their work than any other group of people. Great credit must be given to them for the role they have played in opening up the country.

EIGHT

Freedom on the Fourth

We hold these truths to be self-evident, that all men are created equal, that they are endowed by their Creator with certain unalienable Rights, that among these are Life, Liberty and the pursuit of Happiness.

—Declaration of Independence, July 4, 1776

July 4, 2003, was probably one of the most unusual and memorable days of my life. On that day I attempted to lead four North Korean teenagers into the British consulate in Shanghai to find refugee asylum. Those who have read *The Da Vinci Code* will remember the scene where Robert Langdon and Sophie Neveu were running from French authorities and considered going to the U.S. embassy for protection. "The three-acre compound is considered U.S. soil, meaning all those who stand on it are subject to the same laws and protections as they would encounter standing in the United States," Dan Brown wrote.[1] Similarly, North Korean refugees running from Chinese authorities will attempt to enter a foreign embassy in order to seek the protection of that government. Their ultimate goal is to obtain asylum in South Korea or another country that is willing to receive them.[2]

In May 2002, while I was still training in southern California, I saw for the first time footage of North Koreans forcibly entering an embassy. I was watching CNN one night when they showed Kim Hanmi's family attempting to push their way past Chinese guards in front of the Japanese consulate in Shenyang, China. The attempt was highly publicized because it was captured on video from a nearby building. I still remember the image of Hanmi, who was two years old at the time, standing safely inside the consulate crying, while just a few feet away, outside the gate, two Chinese guards held down her mother (as pictured on the cover of the book). Hanmi's mother was captured by Chinese authorities, but due to pressure from the international community she was released. The family was granted refugee asylum and now resides in South Korea.

As I was watching, little did I know that just over a year later I would be leading the same type of operation—breaking Chinese laws, running from the police and Public Security Bureau (PSB),[3] and risking years of imprisonment—to help refugees find asylum. Just the other day I joked with my former senior pastor in Chicago, Pastor Min, about how ironic it was that I never regularly lied, paid a bribe, or broke laws until I became a missionary in China. Now it seems to be a regular part of my work.

PASTOR CHA AND THE FOUR REFUGEE TEENAGERS

Pastor Cha, a Korean-Chinese pastor in her late sixties, pastored a booming house church in northeast China with over 100 members. The leaders of the church decided to take in four North Korean refugee teenagers and shelter them. One day when I was in town, Pastor Cha called me and said that she needed to meet with me as soon as possible. We met at the church, and to my surprise she brought two of the girls, Yun-Hee and Min-Jung. Pastor Cha pointed to the girls and said, "They are North Korean refugees. It's getting too dangerous for them to stay here. The house church has been raided a number of times by police, and several refugees have already been captured. They need to go to South Korea. Please help them." She said that the two girls had already escaped once by climbing the walls of the church, but that they might not be as fortunate the next time. "The Chinese government is cracking down hard on churches that are helping refugees right now," she added. "These two need to get out of here as soon as possible." There were two boys at a nearby refugee shelter that needed to be evacuated immediately as well, she said. I was moved by the teenagers' plight and told Pastor Cha that I would do some research and get back to her.

I returned home and set up meetings with experts who knew how to get refugees out of China. The first person I met with was Moon Kook-han, the man who masterminded the Kim Hanmi family attempt at the Japanese consulate. We met at a café in Seoul. After I explained the situation of the four North Korean teenagers, Mr. Moon kindly said that he was willing to help. He then methodically explained how he intended to get the teenagers into one of the embassies in Beijing, walking me through the plan step-by-step. He said he had been blacklisted from China and that I would have to lead the operation by myself. The idea of flying solo made me a bit uneasy. I thanked him for his time and said that I would get back in touch with him if I wanted to proceed.

Shortly thereafter, I visited the embassy in Beijing that Mr. Moon had recommended, and I grew increasingly uncomfortable with the plan. If he had agreed to lead the operation, I would have probably gone ahead with it. But knowing that I would be doing this all by myself, I decided to look for another option.

I met with several other contacts, who overwhelmingly advised that it was a dangerous time to attempt such a thing. There had been so many embassy runs that the element of surprise had disappeared. The Chinese government already had increased security at every foreign embassy and consulate in major cities.

Not being one to give up easily, I met with Jim, the underground railroad "conductor" mentioned earlier, and threw out some random ideas: "How about parachuting off of an adjacent building?" "How about making a catapult machine and launching people over the walls?" He laughed and said, "Go check out the U.S. consulate in Shanghai at the Ritz-Carlton. I took a quick look there once and security seemed to be weak." The next day, I was on a plane to Shanghai.

When I arrived at the Ritz-Carlton, I asked employees at the hotel to point me in the direction of the U.S. consulate. But they said that there was no U.S. consulate in the area. I wasn't sure if Jim was mistaken or if it was my poor Mandarin, so I asked several other people where the consulate was. Finally, someone pointed me to the building next door and said, "There isn't a U.S. consulate but there are several other consulates inside."

As I entered the adjacent building, acting as nonchalantly as I could, I noted the locations of all the security cameras. The building was full of foreign consulates, and I stopped casually by several to ask questions and pick up visa forms. As I chatted with the employees, I tried to observe the level of security in general. After visiting several offices, I came across the British consulate, clearly the largest of all of those I had visited so far. There was only one security guard on duty; I took note of the fact that he was overweight and didn't seem very mobile. I had to walk through a metal detector to enter the office. I then proceeded to one of the windows and asked for a visa form. As I pretended to be reading the forms in a chair, I tried to get a bead on my surroundings and a good feel for the place. The security guard seemed to be a bit careless with security and stepped away from the door several times to chat with people. After watching quietly for about 20 minutes, I strolled out—this was the spot.

Tim Peters, director of Helping Hands Korea, and the *Chosun Journal*, a web-based group covering current events related to North Korea, teamed up to fund the project. The whole thing would cost over $5,000. One expense would go for obtaining fake documentation for the refugees. We had two options: We could make low-quality, fake Chinese IDs that would cost about $30 each, or we could have passports made for about $1,000 each. We decided to play it safe and get the fake passports.[4]

I had never done such a thing before, but I had an idea who would know what to do—Jim, of course. Over the years, he had mentored me on the art of operating under the radar and avoiding detection by Chinese police. He had many years of experience doing NGO and humanitarian aid work in hostile environments. Jim sat me down and coached me on what to do if I was captured and tortured by Chinese authorities. "Most likely, the Chinese won't torture you since you are a U.S. citizen," he said. "The worst that you'll probably get is sleep deprivation. Don't get violent or fight back or else it will make it worse. If they do torture you, you just have to dig down deep and make it through it. Dig deep and you'll find something there that will help you get through." Then he went on to tell me about a time when he was imprisoned in Iran and had all of his fingernails and toenails pulled out. Curious, I tried to learn more, but his eyes watered, and he said, "I don't want to talk about it anymore, but it was pretty awful."

As I suspected, Jim knew someone who could help me with the passports. He arranged a meeting with Johnson, a European living in Bangkok, Thailand. I flew to Bangkok to meet Johnson at a crowded bar in the city. I told him ahead of time what I would be wearing so he could find me. I arrived early, sat down, and waited for someone to approach me. About 15 minutes after the agreed time, a man walked up and said, "Do you have something for me?" "What's your name?" I asked him. When he said that he was Johnson, I gave him an envelope with the refugees' information, pictures, and $1,000 for each passport. It was a very unsettling feeling giving that much cash to a stranger. He took the envelope and said, "I'll e-mail you with instructions in a couple of days," then slipped out the door.

A jumpy 48 hours later, I received an e-mail from Johnson. He told me to fly to another city in Southeast Asia, where the passports would be hidden behind a ceiling tile in one of the airport bathrooms. The e-mail included the flight number of the plane that I should take.

I left Thailand the next day and arrived at the specified airport late in the evening. I followed the directions and found the restroom that Johnson was talking about. I quickly entered, locked the door, located the tile, and found something to stand on. My heart was thumping as I reached up and felt behind the tile—no passports. I wondered if I had the wrong restroom, so I went back outside to see if there was another one matching Johnson's description. There were none, so I went back and checked again. Still nothing.

At that point, I began to worry. I walked distractedly around the airport for a half hour trying to figure out what I was going to do. I reread the e-mail several times to see if I had missed something. I checked my in-box to see if Johnson had written with a change in plans. No word.

I then went back to the restroom to check one last time. Reaching up behind the tile again, I felt a small package. I opened it up and, to my immense relief, the passports were there.

DECISIONS, DECISIONS

When I returned to China, I met with Jim and thanked him for all of his help thus far. Jim had one final word of advice for me. "Mike," he said, "make sure you tell the teenagers all of the risks and dangers involved. Tell them that there is a chance that they might be caught. Tell them that if they are caught, they might die. Because if anything happens, you don't want to live with that on your conscience. That has happened to me and let me tell you it's pretty awful . . . I learned the hard way."

I met with Pastor Cha and the four teenagers and gave them an update. I told them that I had visited the British consulate in Shanghai and that it seemed like a good spot. I also told them that I had fake passports made for them. They were ecstatic. Then I took Jim's advice to heart and said, "Everyone listen to me. You have an important decision to make. What we're trying to do here is very dangerous. Many people have made it to South Korea safely, but many have also been caught. I think the plan looks very good, but there is always a chance of capture. And you know what will happen if you are caught. There are never any guarantees with this kind of thing. No one else can make this decision for you. Each one of you has to make it by yourself. Think this through very carefully."

Yun-Hee whispered, "Is it 100 percent safe?" "It's not 100 percent safe—there are no guarantees," I repeated. She kept begging me for a guarantee that everything would be okay, but I told her again that I couldn't give her one. She exclaimed, "But if we get caught, we'll die for sure!"

I sometimes refer to such teenage refugees as "warrior-kids." At their young age, they have already experienced more suffering than most people have in a lifetime. They have endured one of the worst famines in modern history, they have risked their lives to make the perilous journey into China, and some of them were North Korean prison camp survivors. They are, without a doubt, warriors. But at that moment I was seeing the kid in them and the fear in their eyes. They seemed to wish their parents were there to make the decision for them.

But they thought long and hard, and in the end the warrior in them prevailed. All four decided that they would risk their lives to try to force their way into the British consulate in Shanghai. We then made plans to leave the following week.

Mr. Choe, one of the leaders at Pastor Cha's church, traveled with the four teenagers—with their new identification—on an overnight train ride from northeast China to Beijing. I met up with the group in Beijing, and we spent the night at one of the house churches within our network. The next morning, we got up early and I told the teenagers that they had another major decision to make. "Which country do you want to go to? South Korea or the United States?" I asked them. They stared at me with blank looks on their faces. I tried to imagine what it was like for them, at their young ages and with their limited worldviews, to make such a decision. The four shrugged their shoulders and looked around to others in the room for help. I tried to explain the pros and cons of asylum in both countries and said that it was a decision that they would have to make on their own. After a long period of silence, Yun-Hee, the oldest of the group, said, "I want to go to America." The other three followed her lead and said that they did too.

We had them write letters to President George Bush in hopes that it would increase their chances of being granted asylum in the United States. On July 3, 2003, in a small house church in Beijing, the four North Korean teenagers wrote the following letters to the president:

Your Excellency the President,

My name is Du-Ho. I am currently in the British consulate. I dream of my future in America. Please help me.

Sincerely,
Du-Ho (16)

Dear President of America,

I fled to China because my life in North Korea was so difficult. However, China was not safe either. I want to live in a country where I know I am safe even in my dreams. This is why I'm requesting your help.

Sang-Ki (17)

Dear President of America,

Hello. Even though I know that someone like me couldn't mean much to you, I'm hesitantly writing this letter to you because I believe I am also a creation of God. Because I love America, I desperately want to go to America and live out my dreams. I want to watch my dreams blossom like a flower. I believe that you, Mr. President, will give me hope to do so. I am currently in the British consulate. I will be awaiting your reply.

Yours truly,
Min-Jung (17)

Dear Mr. President,

Hello! My name is Yun-Hee. Because it was hard for me to survive in North Korea, I escaped to the land of China. I am so happy and thankful that by the grace of God, I have this privilege to write to the President of America. I came to China because it was difficult for me to live in North Korea. However, I found no freedom in China and I wasn't able to dream, nor hope to achieve my dreams. I want to go to America where I'll be free. By the guidance of my God, I met many great missionaries in China. That is where I received the gospel message and even experienced my living God who has been with me and guiding me all of my life. I am so thankful to God that He may give me the opportunity to go to America where I'll be free. I want to go to America and be free. Please help us.

Sincerely,
Yun Hee (19)

There was one last thing that we had to do while we were in Beijing. I arranged for Benjamin Lim, one of the most respected foreign journalists in China and chief correspondent for Reuters in China, and Paul Mooney, who was stringing for *Newsweek* and other publications, to meet the four refugees at the train station before we left. In my view, the interviews could serve as an "insurance policy" in case something went wrong; articles released by the reporters could possibly create international pressure for the release of the teenagers. The two reporters were both fluent in Mandarin, and the teenagers seemed to have no problems communicating their stories. After the interviews, I shook hands with Ben and Paul and we boarded our train to Shanghai.

MCDONALD'S IN SHANGHAI

We were on an overnight sleeper train to Shanghai and would arrive early the next morning. A few minutes into the train ride, Min-Jung pinched Yun-Hee, and she screamed, "Ouch! What was that for?" Min-Jung grinned and said, "I just wanted to make sure we're not dreaming." Yun-Hee, a bit upset, shouted back, "You're supposed to pinch yourself then!" The two girls had known each other for many years and were childhood friends in North Korea. They were still very much kids.

As the two girls soaked in the moment, the two boys, Sang-Ki and Du-Ho, laid on the upper bunk beds laughing and playing games on my cell phone. The mood was relaxed, and everyone was having a lot of fun. It was kind of surreal given what awaited us. When nighttime came, no one wanted to sleep, so we played some group games and they told me more stories about their lives in North Korea. It felt almost like a junior high slumber party, where you stay up late into the night telling intimate stories and laughing until your sides hurt. After a couple of hours, I made everyone go to sleep. They would need the rest. After all, the next day, they would be risking their very lives.

We arrived in Shanghai at around 7:30 A.M. on July 4, 2003. Since it was going to be their last meal before entering the consulate, I asked the teenagers, "What do you guys want for breakfast? You can have anything you want." "Anything is fine with us," they said. "Have you ever been to McDonald's before?" I asked them. "No, we've only heard about it," one replied.

I decided that they would have to experience McDonald's, so we made our way over to the nearest one we could find. It was already packed, with lines that almost extended to the door. I forgot that

McDonald's doesn't have breakfast menus in China, so we started off the day with Big Macs, fries, Cokes, and ice-cream sundaes.

"How's the food?" I asked as they devoured their sandwiches. Each of the teenagers let me know that they enthusiastically approved. I didn't have much of an appetite myself, so I took a few bites of my Big Mac and reviewed the game plan with them one last time. "Listen up. Which country's consulate are we going to?" "England." "As soon as you get in the front doors, what are you going to do?" "We take our letters to the windows at the front." In addition to their letters to the president, each of them had the following letter:

I am a North Korean refugee and I request asylum in the United States. I fear being deported by the Chinese police back to North Korea. I have converted to Christianity, and I have been fearfully hiding in China with the help of South Korean missionaries. The penalty in North Korea for contact with South Koreans and for becoming a Christian is harsh imprisonment, torture, and even possibly death. I do not want to return to North Korea. Please help me.

I continued drilling them: "If the guard grabs you, what do you do?" I had instructed them to shout in Mandarin, "Let go of me! Reporters are watching!" That would buy them a few seconds of time to run. I elaborated on what to do if there was a physical struggle, and reiterated, "The Chinese guards by international law are not allowed to physically take you outside the consulate. But if there is a struggle, no matter what, you must not let the guards take you outside the consulate. Your life depends on it. Once you are outside those doors you are no longer protected. You can punch, kick, or bite. Do whatever you need to do, but make sure you don't get pulled outside the consulate." They laughed as I demonstrated punches, kicks, and bites, and nodded their heads indicating that they understood.

Du-Ho, the youngest, seemed very distracted by his first Big Mac. I wasn't sure if he was paying attention, so I asked him, "Du-Ho, what did I just say right now?" He knew that he'd been caught and grinned sheepishly. The other three hit him on the head and yelled at him. Yun-Hee, the oldest of the group, shouted, "Du-Ho! This is important. If you don't understand anything, make sure you ask!" I thought it was a telling moment. They were beginning to look like a team.

I noticed that the people at nearby tables were beginning to look over more frequently and I began to feel uneasy, so I instructed the teenagers, "We're leaving in two minutes. Finish up your food." We quickly left and jumped in two taxis; Mr. Choe took the girls and I took the boys. "To the Ritz-Carlton," I told the taxi driver, and we were off.

STARBUCKS AND THE BRITISH CONSULATE

When we arrived at the Ritz-Carlton, I looked around for a spot where the undersized teenagers could blend in. I saw a Starbucks and figured that there would be enough traffic there for them to go unnoticed. I ordered four frappuccinos—another new experience for them—and sat them down at a table. "Wait here while I go and do one final check at the consulate," I told them. "If you need to use the restroom, go use it now."

I donned my Oakley hat and cheap Polaroid sunglasses and entered the adjacent building. It was a weird feeling knowing that the Chinese PSB would be watching this footage of me in a few hours. I entered the consulate and sat down, a visa application form in hand, and observed my surroundings. The same security guard I had noticed earlier was standing next to the metal detector at the door. A few minutes later, he stepped outside to talk to some people, leaving the door unguarded. I took that as my cue and rushed out of the consulate to get the four teenagers.

I found them slouching in their chairs slurping their drinks. "Let's go. *Now*," I directed them, quietly but firmly. Du-Ho protested, "But I have to use the bathroom." "It's too late. I told you to go before. Let's go!"

Min-Jung stood up slowly. Time seemed to stand still for a moment as I watched her close her eyes, put both of her hands on her stomach, and take a deep breath. I looked at the others to see how they were doing. It was crunch time, and they clearly had butterflies. I thought to myself, "They're only kids. No kid should be put in a situation like this."

We threw out the rest of the drinks and headed over to the consulate. I put on my hat and sunglasses again, and the four teenagers giggled. As we rode the elevator up, I pointed at the camera: "See this? This is a video camera. They're going to be watching this footage after this is all over." "Really?" they gasped. "Hi," I said as I waved at the camera; the kids laughed. I was nervous, but was trying to keep things light for them.

When we arrived at our floor, we congregated at the corner about 15 yards from the front door of the consulate. I peeked around the corner and saw the guard back at his post. We had missed a golden opportunity. The teenagers were now clearly panicking, and I had to keep them calm. "Everything is going to be alright," I tried to reassure them. "Take some deep breaths." They were pacing, fidgeting, and breathing heavily, and I began to worry that someone would take notice.

I coached them one last time: "Here's the plan again. I'll walk together with you to the front door. Walk slowly and don't run. Walk right up to the security guard and give him this visa form to distract him. Yun-Hee, you go first since you're the oldest and your Mandarin is the best. After Yun-Hee gives him the form, I want the rest of you to slip past the metal detectors. Du-Ho, since you're the biggest, you go last. Make sure you make it through the metal detectors. Once you pass them, you're inside the consulate. Make sure you make it inside. Min-Jung, while Yun-Hee is talking to the security guard, take your letter to one of the women working at the windows." I gave them one last smile and said, "Let's go."

I then walked with them to the front door and gave each a slight push. The first three walked through as I had instructed, and Du-Ho practically ran through. They were in. I wanted to stay and make sure that everything went okay, but I knew that the place would soon be surrounded by Chinese police, so I quickly made my escape.

STRUGGLE WITH THE CHINESE GUARD

I jumped in a taxi. "Where to?" the driver asked. "That way. I'll tell you as we go," I replied. I changed my clothes in the car, and when we were a good distance away from the consulate, I asked the taxi driver to pull over. I looked for the nearest pay phone and called the teenagers on the cell phone that we had left with them. Yun-Hee answered. She was crying uncontrollably. "Teacher!" she exclaimed when she heard my voice. "I'm so scared." "What happened?" I asked, worried that the plan had failed. "The guard, he grabbed me and tried to drag me out," she cried. "I thought I was dead for sure. I was so scared." "Are you all okay now?" "Yes, we are," she assured me.

I breathed a sigh of relief. "I'm sorry," I said. "I'm so sorry you had to go through all this. It's over now. You're going to be out of China soon." "Teacher?" Yun-Hee said. "Yeah?" "Thank you so much. Thank you." I told her she was welcome and asked to talk to the others.

Min-Jung picked up the phone. She was also crying and clearly shaken by the whole incident, but overall she seemed to be okay. I talked to the boys next. They weren't crying, but spoke very softly, almost in a whisper. After talking to everybody, I said, "It's not safe for me to talk for too long. I have to go, but remember that Jiyon is going to call you." We had arranged for Jiyon Lee, a Crossing Borders U.S. staff member, to call and stay in touch with the teenagers. After I hung up, I called Jiyon in the States to let her know that the kids were safely inside the consulate and that she could contact them.

I later learned the complete story. The Chinese guard had violated international law, as I had suspected he might, and tried to drag the four outside of the consulate. But the teenagers fought for their lives, kicking and screaming, and yelling, "Let me go! Reporters are watching!" That had scared the guard and bought them a few seconds. One of the British consulate employees came out and rescued the four refugees, taking them inside just in time. Within minutes, 30 police officers surrounded the consulate, securing the area and looking for anyone who might have taken video footage of the incident since the teenagers had said that the media was watching.

Later that afternoon, Benjamin Lim wrote a news wire for Reuters stating, "Four North Korean teenagers slipped into the British consulate in Shanghai on Friday and requested political asylum, the latest in a string of such defections in Chinese cities."[5] About a week later, Senator Brownback commented, "'I think it's very important that they [the four teenagers] be allowed to come here as a statement of our support for freedom and liberty, and against the tyranny of Kim Jong Il and his regime."[6]

In the end, the U.S. government did not grant asylum to the refugees, and they were sent to Seoul instead. But we believe that they paved the way for other refugees to reach the United States. About 30 North Korean refugees have since found asylum in the States. About a year later, President Bush signed into law the North Korean Human Rights Act of 2004, which made North Koreans eligible for asylum in the United States.

Usually it takes months for North Koreans seeking asylum to be cleared to leave China, but the four kids made it to South Korea within a matter of days. South Korean President Roh Moo-hyun was scheduled to visit Shanghai later that week to meet with President Hu Jintao, and the Chinese authorities wanted to avoid any unwanted media attention on the teenagers when Roh Moo-hyun arrived.[7]

After the arrival of the teenagers in Seoul, the *Korea Times* reported, "The four, aged between 15 and 18, are believed to be in good health and are undergoing questioning by South Korean intelligence authorities. . . . They initially wanted to go to the United States, but Washington rejected their demand, citing its position that it does not accept North Korean defectors."[8]

A few days later, a contact inside the Chinese government called me and warned, "Mike, I've been hearing some things. Get out of the country as soon as possible and don't come back until I tell you to." I had always wanted to spend some time in Australia, so I called a good friend of mine in Sydney. After I briefly explained my situation, he invited me to stay with him until things settled down in China.

MCDONALD'S ON THE OTHER SIDE

After the teenagers were finished with their required orientation, I flew out to Seoul to meet them. We scheduled a reunion dinner and met at a subway station. When I saw them, I couldn't believe my eyes. They looked completely different in their South Korean clothes; the girls were wearing make-up. I gave them all hugs and asked, "Where should we go for lunch?" "Anywhere is fine with us," they replied. Smiling, I asked, "How about McDonald's?"

We then headed over to the nearest McDonald's and ordered up a cheap feast. I still didn't know a lot of the details of what happened after I had dropped off the teenagers at the consulate, so I barraged them with questions. "What was the third country you went through on your way to Seoul?" I asked, knowing that China's policy is to send refugees to South Korea via a third country. "The Philippines," they answered. "How long did you have to stay at the consulate in Shanghai?" "Four days." "How was your first plane ride?" "Oh, my! It was so amazing,"

Yun-Hee exclaimed. "It was so beautiful. I couldn't stop looking at the clouds!" The other three also said they'd loved their first plane ride.

Du-Ho told me with a big grin, "Teacher, I started boxing lessons." In China, he had said that once he made it out of China he would take lessons. "Oh, yeah?" I responded with a smile and a jab in his shoulder. "Then we'll have to spar sometime."

Then Yun-Hee's expression turned serious and she related, "Teacher, the Chinese authorities had one condition before we went to Seoul. They said that they had to meet with us before we were allowed to leave. It was so scary meeting with them. One of the Chinese policemen had a picture of you with your hat and sunglasses. They asked us who you were." This came as no surprise to me, as I had prepped the kids on how to answer that question. They told me that they had given the Chinese PSB their prepared response: "His name is David. He's a Korean American from the United States. We don't know much else about him other than the fact that he helps refugees."

I leaned back in my chair and enjoyed the moment. I had envisioned it—celebrating with the teenagers on the other side—in China. Everything had worked out perfectly. July 4th, of all days—the four had found their freedom on Independence Day. And it was unheard of for North Korean refugees to be flown out of China so quickly. I wish I could say that I was clever enough to plan out those two details, but I didn't. Things just kind of worked out that way.

NINE

Asian Underground Railroad

The function of freedom is to free someone else.

—Toni Morrison

With my God I can scale any wall.

—Psalm 18:29

With the increased security at embassies and consulates in China, many North Korean refugees are turning to the 6,000-mile underground railroad in Asia to gain asylum. It is a treacherous journey. The underground railroad begins in North Korea and runs through China and several countries in Southeast Asia, mainly Cambodia, Vietnam, Myanmar, Laos, and Thailand. The goal is to make it safely to Bangkok, where the refugees report to the South Korean embassy. After several months of interviews and confirmation that they are not spies, they are allowed passage to Seoul. Had they been allowed to proceed straight from Pyongyang to Seoul, they would have traveled a mere 120 miles.

A NORTH KOREAN WOMAN SICK WITH TB

In October 2003, Pastor Kim, an elderly mentor and director of a U.S.-based mission organization that has operated in China for over 15 years, called me and said, "When you get to the border, meet Mrs. Lee. She's a North Korean refugee and is very sick with TB. She almost died several weeks ago, but we got her some medicine just in time. She needs to get to South Korea soon so that she can get medical treatment. Can you help her get to South Korea?" I told him that I would meet with Mrs. Lee as soon as possible to assess her situation.

When I returned to my home at the border, I visited Mrs. Lee and her Korean-Chinese husband, Missionary Lee, at their home. Her husband helped her as she came out of her room to greet me. She had a bright smile on her face but seemed in a very weak physical state. We exchanged introductions, then talked about her health. "I caught TB in a North Korean prison," she said. "Because I am a refugee, I cannot get medical treatment here in China. If I don't go to South Korea soon, I will probably die."

For the next several days, I couldn't get Mrs. Lee out of my mind. I knew that attempting to forcibly enter another embassy or consulate would be very risky and that there was a high chance of failure. If I wanted to help Mrs. Lee get to South Korea, we would have to utilize the underground railroad. But while I now had some experience working the consulates, I knew next to nothing about the railroad.

After giving the matter a great deal of thought, I decided that I would try to help Mrs. Lee. When I told her the news, she clapped her hands in excitement and squealed like a little child. Then she covered her mouth and cried. After regaining her composure a few minutes later, she whispered, "Thank you. Thank you so much."

"There is going to be a lot of hiking," I advised her. "Do you think you will be able to handle it?" "Teacher, it won't be a problem," she enthusiastically replied. "No matter how hard it is, I'll keep on going." "You should start training now," I said. "Start by taking short walks and then increase the distance over time."

My colleagues and I decided to take two other North Korean refugees on the underground railroad as well: Ms. Kim, the woman who wrote out the Bible by hand, and So-Young, the young girl who, like Ms. Kim, had been a victim of sex trafficking. Both had suffered horribly, and we wanted to help them get to Seoul.

UNDERGROUND RAILROAD 101

I met with some of the leading experts on the underground railroad, including Pastor Chun Ki-won, who is sometimes referred to in the media as the "Asian Schindler." His organization, Durihana, has helped more than 500 refugees escape to South Korea through the railroad. After I told him about the three refugee women, he kindly agreed to help them. He also told me a little about his experiences working in Southeast Asia, and I learned a great deal. When I asked him what his plan was for the three women, he pulled out a map and pointed to a town in southern China. "Get the women here and call me in Seoul when you get there," he said. When I asked for more details, he responded, "That's it. Just get them there and we'll take care of the rest." I then asked him if we should plan some dates. "No," he replied. "Just get the women there and call me." I thanked him for his time and said I would give him a call if I wanted to proceed.

Next, I met with Sang Hun Kim, an amazing South Korean man in his mid-seventies who *Time Asia* included on its prestigious list of "Asian Heroes" along with Asian icons such as Yo-Yo Ma, Yao Ming, and Hideki Matsui. Mr. Kim had been a project manager for the UN's World Food Program for nearly 20 years, helping refugees in places such as Sudan and the Thai-Cambodia border. He had retired in 1994 and dedicated his retirement to bringing about a resolution to the North Korean crisis. He still personally conducts rescues on the underground railroad to this day.

I met with Mr. Kim in Seoul and described the situation of the three North Korean women. "There are two options for you," he responded.

"You can go north to Mongolia or you can go south to Southeast Asia. I think Southeast Asia is a good option right now . . . I would say that there is a 60 to 70 percent success rate using that route." When I asked if he would be willing to help the North Korean women himself, he said that he could not since his resources were reserved for "high value" North Koreans who could provide incriminating evidence against the regime. But he gave me some helpful tips on how to operate on the underground railroad.

Next, I returned to China to meet with my friend Jim, who had years of experience with the railroad. When I asked for his advice, he named a small village in southern China and said, "Go to the China-Laos border and find some farmers in the area. Tell them you're hungry and ask them for a meal. While you're eating, get a feel for them and see if they might be willing to help you. They know how to get across the border. Pay them $12 to $24 for the meal and ask them to get you across the border. Do a test run in and out of the country by yourself."

Three plane rides later, I arrived at the airport nearest to the village Jim had named. From there, I had to take a bus for another 10 hours towards the border. When I got off the bus, I saw a number of motor-bike-taxis waiting for customers. I jumped on one and the driver asked, "Where do you want to go?" "To the border," I replied. A few minutes into the ride, the driver turned around and asked, "Where at the border?" "I don't know. Anywhere near the border," I shouted above the roar of the bike.

It took two and a half hours to get to the border village. As we neared the village, I said, "I want to go to Laos.[1] Can you tell me how to get there?" The taxi driver pointed down the road towards the customs office and said, "It's that way." "No, I don't mean like that," I told him. "I want to go that way," and I pointed to the mountains.

Getting the picture, he nodded and said, "I have some friends who live over there in the mountains. Let me ask them." "How do you know people there?" I asked. "I used to live there," he replied. It was rather amazing. Out of all the motorbikes I could have jumped on, I chose one whose driver grew up in Xai,[2] the border village I was going to.

When we arrived, the driver made a phone call and said, "I think I might be able to help you. We'll go see my friend, Mr. Zhao, in the morning." It was around 9:00 P.M., so he helped me find a place to stay that night.

The nicest accommodation in the village was a dirty, rundown place that cost $1.20 a night. The bed sheets were filthy and sticky. It was so hot that I had to open the windows, which had no screens, and sleep with the bugs and mosquitoes. There was one outhouse for all of the guests in the place's 15 rooms.

The next morning, Mr. Chen, the motorbike-taxi driver, picked me up and took me on a 40-minute ride into the mountains to meet his friend Mr. Zhao. We met in a small schoolyard while the children were on recess running around. I shook hands with Mr. Zhao, and in my limited Mandarin explained that I wanted to get in and out of Laos illegally. Mr. Zhao said, "We can take you into Laos but we can't go any further with you. We must drop you off there." "That's fine," I responded. "But the drop-off point must be past the Lao security checkpoint that is one kilometer in, or else it doesn't help me." (From my research, I had learned that there was an additional military checkpoint one kilometer into the country.) Mr. Zhao squatted down and drew a map in the dirt explaining where, exactly, we would be dropped off. We agreed on a price of $12 for each person who would be illegally crossing the border into Laos.

If Mr. Zhao could keep his end of the deal, I had my route into Laos. I was halfway there. Now, I just had to figure out how I was going to get back into China after the mission was completed. Since I would be leaving China illegally with the refugee women, I would also have to return illegally, as I would not have an exit stamp on my passport. The final piece of the puzzle was finding someone in Laos who could help me re-enter China.

THE DEAD ZONE

In actuality, the distance to Lu Chong,[3] the Laotian village directly across the border where we would be dropped off, was only about four kilometers. However, access to the main road leading into Laos was restricted and reserved for military and commercial trucks. It was a "dead zone." No one was allowed in without a permit. So on my test run I had to take an eight-hour bus ride—circling the mountains—to the official customs office. After passing through customs into Laos, it was another four-hour bus ride to Lu Chong.

Jim said that there was a significant Chinese population in Lu Chong since it was near the Chinese border, so upon arriving I immediately began looking for Chinese with whom I could communicate. I finally found a Chinese man who owned a small Chinese restaurant. I walked in and introduced myself, saying that I had just come from China, and asked, "Do you know how I can get to the Chinese border? I would love to see the border." Pointing towards the mountains, he said, "Take this main road all the way down." "How can I get there?" "You can get there by car or rent a bicycle," he said. "How long does it take by bike?" I asked. "Not long. Around 30 minutes," he replied.

As I had an hour or two of sunlight left, I rented a bike and headed towards the border. It turned out to be a grueling 45-minute uphill ride. As I finally approached the border, I made mental notes of the layout of the government buildings and the guard stations. On the left was a little stream that looked like it led into China, but there were barbed-wired fences blocking access to it. The mountains were to the right of the customs office, but there was no way to proceed in that direction without customs officials noticing.

I stopped at the red-and-white bar that blocked vehicles from entering the dead zone and stared down the road as far as I could see. China was only two kilometers away. I wondered if I could somehow slip in without anyone noticing. I looked around, but there were too many guards. As I was considering my options, a guard approached me and said something to me in Laotian. I pointed towards the dead zone and asked, in English, "Can I go in there to take a quick look?" He shook his head.

The sun was quickly setting, so I had to return to town. I was pretty discouraged and had no idea what my next step was going to be. I decided to get up early in the morning and return to check the place out again.

Forty-five minutes later, I was back in my room soaked in sweat from the bike ride. In the bathroom, there was no showerhead or hot water, only a faucet and a red bucket filled with water bearing a thick layer of bugs on the surface. I cleaned out the bucket, refilled it with water, took a cold shower, and went to bed.

The next morning, I headed to the market and found someone who would drive me to the border. I tried to negotiate a round-trip, but he said that he couldn't wait around and suggested that I try to catch a return ride with someone else. When I arrived at the border, I took another look around to see if I could find any holes in the system, but there were none. There was simply no way I could slip past the customs officials unnoticed. Thirty minutes had passed, and I was starting to get frustrated. The sun was hot, and I was tired. After another 30 minutes, the guards began to get suspicious and came over to ask me some questions. I told them that I was a tourist just taking a look around. I finally admitted defeat to myself and concluded that it couldn't be done—not here, at least.

There were no taxis or cars around, so I started walking back, hoping a car would pass sometime soon. I walked for about 40 minutes in the scorching sun, then stopped to drink some of the bottled water I had packed. I looked to the mountains on the right and estimated that there were about 20 different mountains on the horizon. "One of those mountains has got to lead to China," I thought to myself. I was now feeling optimistic, so I picked one of the mountains and just began hiking, hoping that it would somehow lead me to China. But after several hours of dead ends and failed attempts, I returned to the main road and continued treading towards town.

By that point, I worried that I might be getting dehydrated, so I stopped to take another water break. I stood there on the side of the road, dead tired, looking around for a clue as to what I should do. There wasn't a single soul in sight. The mission was hanging by a thread in my weakened state. I began to seriously contemplate giving up and at that moment asked God for a miracle.

Just a few seconds later, I saw an elderly man walking towards me in the distance. As he got closer, I could tell that he was a tribal person from the mountains. He was a small man and walked with an unusual gait, carrying an axe in one hand. His clothes were torn, and his skin was dark and leathery.

I felt a glimmer of hope as I realized that he was probably familiar with the mountains and might be able to help. I waited until he got closer, then said in English, "Hello. Do you speak English?" He gave me a confused look and didn't answer. I tried again in Mandarin: "Hello. Do you speak Mandarin?" To my surprise, he answered, "Yes, I speak Mandarin." "I want to go to China. Can you help me?" I asked him. He pointed down the road to the customs office where I had just come from. "No, not there," I said. I then pointed to the mountains: "That way. If you can help me, I can pay you some money."

He nodded and said, "Follow me."

YAO AND AKHA TRIBESMEN

His name was Shan. I could tell from his accent and limited vocabulary that he wasn't Chinese. I learned that he was from the Yao tribe that inhabited the mountains of northern Laos. Yao was his first language, and

Akha (the name of another tribe living in the mountains of northern Laos) was his second language. Mandarin was his third. He said that he had picked it up because he lived along the Chinese border. Mandarin was also my third language (after English and Korean), so our language skills were somewhat comparable.

Shan walked fast on the gravel, barefoot, without any hint of pain. We hit a small stream, and he crossed first. He waited patiently as I took off my socks and shoes. I grimaced in pain as I stepped on the sharp rocks at the bottom of the stream. I stopped several times to rest my feet and wondered if I could withstand the pain enough to make it across. As Shan watched with curiosity, I contemplated either turning around or putting my shoes back on and getting them wet. "He must think I'm the biggest sissy right now," I thought to myself. I finally reached the other side without shoes. Shan continued to wait patiently as I sat down to dry off my feet and put on my socks and shoes.

After hiking for nearly an hour, we arrived at an Akha tribal community in the mountains. Shan spoke with an Akha tribesman and explained why I was there. The two men looked very similar. The Akha man was also small, with dark, leathery skin, and carried a machete.

Shan turned to me and said, "He'll show you the way to China. But he doesn't speak Mandarin." I tried to think of any last details that needed to be covered with Shan before leaving. "When I get into China, I need to be past the Chinese border checkpoint," I told him. "Yes. You will not have to worry about the checkpoint," Shan answered. "If you don't take me past the checkpoint, it does me no good," I pointed out. "Yes, yes, I know," Shan replied, slightly annoyed.

Shan then held out his hand, signaling that it was time to pay him. I gave him $6 for the introduction and I was off with the Akha tribesman. I'll call him Ah Soh—I never learned his real name.

He and I began our journey on a trail that ascended into the mountains. The path was simple enough at first, but as we got deeper into the mountains, it grew more complicated. We jumped from path to path and changed directions more frequently. It was like a maze. "There's no way I would have figured this out on my own," I mused.

Ah Soh was clearly a skilled trekker. He walked amazingly fast as he swung his machete nonstop to clear out any branches and make it easier for me to follow. Still, I was having a hard time keeping up with him. After 45 minutes, I signaled that I needed a break and pulled out two water bottles from my bag. I offered him one, but he didn't take it. I chugged half the bottle and tried to regain my breath. Five minutes later, he signaled that it was time to get moving again.

We passed a community of Akha homes made of wood and straw nestled deep in the mountains. Every 10 to 15 minutes, we came across tribesmen who were hard at work cutting wood. Each time we had to stop as they asked my guide questions about me. The thought occurred to me that Ah Soh probably knew that I was traveling with money— more than he might make in a lifetime. The Akha tribesmen could easily mug me and take all of my money; no one would ever know. From then on, I kept a little more distance from Ah Soh and his machete.

After another hour had passed, I motioned that I needed another break. Ah Soh took a bunch of leaves from the nearest tree and made seats for both of us. He then pulled a small plastic bag from his pocket and offered me some of its contents. But I declined, unsure what it was. When he began smoking it, I realized it was opium. I recalled the numerous signs back in town that said, "Don't support the drug trade. Don't buy opium from locals." Then another thought hit me: These were drug-trade routes that we were using. Yao and Akha tribesmen smuggled drugs in and out of China. I was amused by the thought that we were utilizing drug trafficking routes to free human trafficking victims.

After walking a little more, we reached the peak of the mountain and began our descent. I was relieved, as I had finished all of my water and wasn't sure how much more uphill I could handle. We picked up our pace, and about two hours later we arrived at a road at the foot of the mountain. I heard some talking and abruptly stopped. Ah Soh said,

"*Bu pa* (Don't be afraid)," apparently one of the few Mandarin phrases he knew. He motioned for me to follow him, and I proceeded with caution. I then saw Chinese writing on a sign at the side of the road. We were in China! I had never been so happy to see Chinese writing in my life. I could hear construction workers speaking Mandarin.

Ah Soh stuck out his hand and asked for his money, but I wasn't ready to pay him quite yet. Using sign language and drawing on the ground, I asked if we were past the Chinese customs office. He didn't understand. We stood for a few minutes, trying to communicate like a couple of cavemen, grunting and motioning back and forth to each other. He finally understood what I was asking and said, "*Bu pa,*" again. Without a hint of fear, he walked up to the Chinese construction workers and asked if one of them would take me into town when they headed back. One of them nodded. I paid Ah Soh his $6 and hopped into one of the trucks.

As we headed into town, I observed that we were on the same main road as the one on the Laos side of the border. It was a relief to be able to communicate in Mandarin again, and I asked the driver, "How far are we from town?" "About two kilometers," he replied. "There aren't any more border checkpoints on this road, right?" "There is a checkpoint," he responded. "It's about two kilometers out."

Shan and Ah Soh had lied to me. I was livid. I wasn't past the security checkpoint, but in the dead zone. My mind raced as I panicked and tried to figure out what I was going to do. Just then the driver stopped about 200 yards before the Chinese checkpoint and declared, "I can't take you any further. You'll have to get off here."

STUCK IN THE DEAD ZONE

I kept walking along the main road until I was about 50 yards from the checkpoint, then stopped to take a good look around. There were five

Chinese guards on duty, and there was no way I could get past them unnoticed. I looked off to the right and the left to see if there were any alternative routes, but there were none. I would either have to go through the Chinese checkpoint or turn around and head back the way I came. I briefly entertained the thought of hiking back to Laos, but I knew that there was no way I would be able to navigate those mountains on my own.

It was a terrible feeling being stuck in the dead zone, with Chinese border patrol on one side and Lao border patrol on the other. I must have sat there for hours trying to come up with a plan. In my desperation, and for lack of better options, I finally walked towards the five guards while praying that I would pass by unnoticed. The adrenaline was pumping, and my heart thumped louder and louder with each step. As I got closer to the guards, I avoided making eye contact, but I could feel their gaze. I was scared out of my mind, but I kept putting one foot in front of the other while continuing to pray. I actually walked several steps past the guards and thought I was off the hook when one of them shouted, "Hey!" and motioned with his hand for me to come over to him. My heart sank. He asked for identification, and when I gave him my U.S. passport, he sent me inside the customs office.

There, customs officials carefully examined my passport. "This isn't a real U.S. passport. This is a fake," one proclaimed. They didn't think I was really an American but one of the local villagers. Out of all the problems I could have encountered, I definitely wasn't expecting this one. I was slightly insulted that I could pass as one of the villagers and wondered what I looked like at that point. I tried to convince them that I was an American. "Listen to my Mandarin," I said. "Can't you tell that I'm not Chinese? My first language is English." Then I opened my bag and showed them the contents. I was carrying a couple of English books and U.S. currency. The customs officials shouted back and forth to each other trying to arrive at a consensus before deciding to call in an English translator.

The translator arrived an hour later and began the interrogation process. "How did you get in the dead zone?" he grilled me. "I just walked," I replied, trying to be as general as possible. "No one stopped you?" "No. I just walked."

After five hours of interrogation, the guards grew frustrated with my generalities and informed me, "We're going to have to send you back to Laos." I was relieved that they weren't going to arrest me and agreed to return to Laos on the next truck headed down the main road. A few minutes later, I was back in Laos. The driver dropped me off around 50 yards before the Lao checkpoint. I mentally prepared myself to go through the same ordeal with the Lao border patrol. I was exhausted and hungry and really wasn't in the mood for more interrogation. I braced myself and walked towards the gate. I walked through the gate and, to my surprise, none of the guards noticed. They were busy playing foot volleyball and didn't see me walk through. I headed down the road back towards the village without a single person looking over at me. Relieved, I eventually caught a ride back to town. I was back to square one.

I took the eight-hour bus ride back to Xai village in China, thinking that we might have to call off the mission. I tried to figure out how I was going to break the news to the North Korean women. They were going to be devastated. I decided to speak with Mr. Zhao again to see if there were any other options first.

When I returned to Xai village, I met with Mr. Chen, Mr. Zhao, and one of their friends, Mr. Wen. I gave them a full report on my experiences. They laughed, seemingly amused by the hardship I had endured. "I need you to bring me back into China safely after the project is completed," I told them. They talked for several minutes and concluded that they couldn't do it. I added that if they couldn't help me get back into China, there would be no deal and we would be returning to northeast China. I also said that I could pay more money if they could bring me back in.

They talked again, this time arguing amongst themselves. Finally, Mr. Zhao said, "Mr. Wen and I will go with you and wait in Laos with you. Then we will come back together." He grabbed a stick and mapped out a plan in the dirt. "This plan is much more dangerous for us," Mr. Zhao said almost predictably. "We want $100 for each person . . . Also, if you want to walk it will take many hours and it will be a very difficult hike. We can provide a truck for you. It will drop you off near the border. You will still have to hike, but it will be much shorter. Another truck will pick you up on the Laos side. If you want to use the trucks it will cost an extra $250." I thought of Mrs. Lee, who was sick with TB, and said, "Let's use the trucks."

Despite the high cost of the mission, I was happy to see that all of the pieces were finally coming together.

CHINA TO LAOS

When I returned to northeast China, Pastor Cha, So-Young's pastor, called me and said, with deep sadness in her voice, "So-Young has been captured and is being sent back to North Korea." I was devastated by the news, but I continued with the project.

Now we were down to two refugee women. To be on the safe side, we decided to have them travel separately. Missionary Lee would escort Mrs. Lee, while I traveled with Ms. Kim. We took various modes of transportation and reconvened in Beijing.

Upon our arrival, I arranged for Benjamin Lim from Reuters and Paul Mooney, the stringer for *Newsweek* and other publications, to interview the two women. We agreed that their stories would be released after the women's safety was ensured. After completing the interviews, we turned in for the night at a house church in Beijing.

The next day was Sunday, so we attended the house church service. After the service was over, I met privately with Pastor Shin. "The leaders of our church will be praying for you," he assured me. I was reminded that there were friends, pastors, and churches from all over the world praying for the project, and I was deeply encouraged.

After several days of travel, we arrived at a small, remote town in southern China. Mark, a friend and a missionary in the town, set us up with housing for the night. The next morning, I met with Mark for some southern noodle soup and explained what we were doing. He too assured me, "My wife and I will be praying for you." After breakfast, Mark helped us purchase our bus tickets to our next destination.

That afternoon, we took a 10-hour bus ride towards the border. When we arrived at another bus station, I located Mr. Chen, the motorbike-taxi driver, and told him to get a few of his friends to take all of us to the border. Several hours later, we finally arrived at our destination. I got some rooms at the same rundown motel and told everyone that they had one night to rest before we made the big journey the next day.

Early the next morning, we went to the local market to pick up some food and water for the hike. Our transportation then arrived and took us into the mountains to Mr. Zhao's home. When we got there, Mr. Zhao asked for the money. He folded up one of the $100 bills several times and rubbed it against one of the walls in his home to see if the ink left green streaks. He was pleased to see that it did. Apparently, that was his method of testing for counterfeit money.

When a van arrived, the six of us boarded and headed further into the mountains. About 30 minutes later, we arrived at our drop-off point. We then exited the van and began hiking.

Mr. Wen led the way. He was younger than Mr. Zhao and clearly very familiar with the area. He was walking fast, and I had to ask him to slow down for Mrs. Lee several times. No more than 20 minutes into the hike, Mrs. Lee needed a break. Due to her weak lungs she was having a tough time keeping up. We took a five-minute water break and then continued.

After another 30 minutes, we had to take another break for Mrs. Lee. She was beginning to cough, and I was concerned that someone would hear us. As the terrain became more challenging, Mrs. Lee began to cough louder and more frequently. We had only walked for one hour and had three more to go. I was beginning to worry: Would she be able to make it?

I could tell that Mr. Zhao and Mr. Wen were getting irritated, as I hadn't informed them that we would be taking a sick person along. Due to the frequent breaks, we were now running out of water. Mr. Wen picked a large leaf from a tree and used it to scoop up water from the streams. I asked him if the water was okay for me to drink, and he said, "It's okay for me, but I'm not sure if it's okay for you since you are a foreigner." I played it safe and didn't drink any.

We started hiking again when suddenly both of the straps on my $3 imitation JanSport backpack ripped. I was upset, as I had to carry the backpack in my arms the rest of the way; I vowed to never buy fake Chinese items again. At that point, Mrs. Lee collapsed on the ground. She started to cry and moaned that she couldn't hike any more. She was out of breath, coughing hard, and clearly in pain. "I don't have any more strength," she cried. "Just go ahead without me. I'll just stay here and die."

Although I knew that I shouldn't have been, I was irritated with her, since she had told me that she would have no problems with the hike. Mr. Zhao and Mr. Wen came over to me and said, "What are we going to do about her?" I put my hand on Mrs. Lee's shoulder, and with all the intensity I could muster up, I looked her in the eyes and said, "You're not going to die here. You're going to make it. We'll take a little break here and then we're going to finish this hike. We'll carry you if we have to." I said a quiet prayer for her, and a few minutes later we got up and kept on walking.

I still don't know how, but we finished the four-hour hike. As we walked across an unguarded bridge that marked the border of China and Laos, I smiled and told Missionary Lee and the women, "We're in Laos now." After we crossed the bridge, we found a place to hide and ate some of the bread we had packed for lunch. After we finished eating, Mr. Wen checked his watch and signaled that it was time to go. We walked a little bit more, and, sure enough, there was a truck waiting for us. We boarded the truck and made the one-hour drive down the mountain to the closest village. I looked over at Missionary Lee and the women and could tell that they were fascinated with the scenery and the thought of being in another country.

After nearly an hour had passed, I could see Lu Chong and recognized some of its buildings. As I began to celebrate, I noticed a car rapidly approaching us in the distance. As it got closer, I saw that it was a gray van with tinted windows. It abruptly stopped in front of us and blocked the narrow road. Six Lao border patrol soldiers jumped out of the van and approached us with their AK-47s pointed at us.

I stepped forward and slowly pulled my U.S. passport out of my back pocket, careful not to make any sudden movements. They signaled to follow them and took us to the police station. At the station, we were strip-searched, and the captain and an English translator interrogated us for five hours. At first, their attitude towards us was very hostile; they asked questions like, "Where did you come from?" and "Why did you illegally enter our country?" Then they lightened up, and I explained, "These women are North Korean. They are fleeing an oppressive regime. I am trying to help them get to South Korea." The police captain was confused, since he didn't know much about the situation in North Korea. "Why can't they go back to North Korea?" he asked. "What crime have they committed?" I tried to explain that they didn't do anything wrong, but he was having a hard time understanding.

After listening to everything I had to say, the captain stated, "I'm sorry. We must return them to the Chinese authorities." The women, as if on cue, began to cry bitterly, though they didn't understand a word that was being said. I pleaded with the captain, "You can't send them

back to China. China will return them to North Korea and they will
be executed. That's why they are crying." I suggested, "We'll pay a fine,
but please let us pass through your country. I am only trying to help
them get to the South Korean embassy in Bangkok."

The captain had all of our possessions confiscated, including our
identification and money. "You will be under house arrest tonight," he
declared. "We will meet again in the morning and we will give you our
decision then." Mr. Zhao and Mr. Wen were sent to the local prison.

The women's future hung in the balance as we awaited the police
captain's decision. We turned in early that night, but none of us were
able to get much sleep.

In the morning, we reconvened at the police station and the captain
gave us his decision: "We must charge you $1,000 per person . . . After
you pay the fine, we will let you pass through. But if you are captured
later, you must not mention us. We cannot help you." I translated for
the women, and they shouted in joy and then cried again. It took a few
moments for them to regain their composure. They then stood up and
bowed to the police captain and said repeatedly, "Thank you. Thank
you." The captain handed me back my items and I immediately
checked to see if all of the money was there. I was running low on cash
at that point and wasn't sure if I would have enough to complete the
project. I flashed my Visa and jokingly asked the captain if he would accept a credit card. Apparently, he found that amusing and chuckled.

I was happy with the deal and tried to negotiate one more. I said to
the captain, "There are many more women like these in China. If I
bring more people in the future, can we arrange a deal? Maybe I can
pay you $400 for each person and you let us pass through." He liked
the suggestion and said, "Next time, we'll provide an escort for you." I
said, "Maybe I'll come back in the future to discuss the details. Can I
come the same way through the mountains again?" He smiled and said,
"Sure. Come back any time."

It had been my responsibility to get the women safely into Laos. Once we were there, a man I will call Dean, who had worked the underground railroad for many years, would take care of the rest, since his specialty was traveling between Laos and Thailand. Due to our arrest, we were a day late, so I was afraid that he might have already left. We hurried to the rendezvous point, and sure enough Dean was there waiting for us. He was clearly upset. "What took you so long?" he shouted at me. "I was about to leave without you!" I explained that we were under house arrest for two days and were just released. He reacted as if he heard that sort of thing every day and said, "Oh, really? Let's go—we're running late." We decided it would be best if Missionary Lee waited in town to reduce the number of people traveling.

The rest of us jumped into Dean's truck and headed towards the Mekong River. It was a very bumpy ride, and I began to get motion sickness. I stuck my head out the side of the truck to fix my gaze on the mountains to help the motion sickness go away, but Dean pulled me inside and said, "Keep your head down. There are snipers in the mountains."

Several hours later, we arrived at the Mekong River as the sun was setting. During dinner, Dean and I got to know each other; it was the first time we had met. He asked the women many questions and learned about their suffering. Mrs. Lee began to cry and spoke of how much she missed her husband. "I already miss him so much," she said. "Teacher, you have no idea how much he has sacrificed for me. He gave up his own comfort and even his own safety to be with me. I don't know how I can ever repay him for his kindness to me. I really wouldn't be alive today if it weren't for him."

After we finished dinner, all of us were exhausted, so we retired to our separate cabins. After washing up, I said good night to Dean, put down my mosquito net, and turned in for the night.

Early in the morning, we congregated at the river. As Dean made preparations to leave, he said, "I hope we don't run into any problems.

Security has been very tight lately." I shook his hand, wished him luck, and said, "See you in Bangkok." He and the two women boarded the speedboat. It was Mrs. Lee and Ms. Kim's first boat ride, and they looked nervous. Dean warned them, "Get ready. It's going to be a long and bumpy ride." After traveling down the Mekong River for four to five hours, they would arrive at the Golden Triangle, the point where Myanmar, Thailand, and Laos meet.

I returned to town where Missionary Lee was waiting and tried to figure out how we were going to get back into China. We headed to the police station to ask for their help when we ran into Mr. Wen on the street. Happy to see him, I asked, "What happened to you two? Where have you been?" "They sent us to the local prison," he replied. "It was disgusting in there. They kept Mr. Zhao and let me return to China and get some money to pay for our release. They said that they would hand us over to the Chinese authorities unless we paid them." I knew that it was my responsibility to pay for their release, so I paid the money and asked the police to take us back to the same spot where we entered the country.

As the police drove us up the mountain, I rapidly tried to take down directions in case I ever had to do this again on my own. On my notepad, I wrote, "Take big red dirt road north, after 100 yards turn right, five minutes later take small white road east, take the first right, take the third left . . . ." I soon gave up, as there were too many turns and details. A little under an hour later, the truck dropped us off at the same bridge where we had entered the country.

We hiked back to China. After a couple of hours, Mr. Wen abruptly stopped and said that he and Mr. Zhao wanted to be compensated for all of the trouble they had been through. I refused to pay them, and we got into a heated argument. Mr. Wen shouted, "You don't know how disgusting it was in that prison! We were in there because of you!" I argued back in my broken Mandarin, "You guys are the ones that told us we would have no problems. We were caught because of you!"

Mr. Wen then threatened us: "We're going to leave you here in the mountains then. You find your way back on your own." "You guys try and leave on your own," I retorted. "We'll just follow you."

When he realized his threats were not working, Mr. Wen tried a softer approach. "Boss, come on," he said to me. "You have a lot of money. What is a little bit of money to you?"

But I still refused to pay him and we continued hiking, now in a bad mood. Two hours later, we were back in Xai village. Missionary Lee and I took the 10-hour bus ride north to the nearest town with an airport. When we arrived, we said our good-byes, and Lee took a train back to northeast China while I boarded a plane to Bangkok.

CELEBRATION ON KHAOSAN ROAD

After I arrived in Thailand, I checked into my room at a motel on Khaosan Road, a popular spot for backpackers. I made a phone call and was relieved to learn that the women had safely made it to Bangkok. However, I later learned that there had been some close calls along the way. The Mekong River is heavily guarded since it is a border area. It is very difficult to cross illegally from Laos into Thailand, as there are many Lao, Thai, and Burmese police patrolling the area in boats. But Dean was able to successfully navigate the river and get the women into Thailand due to his many contacts and knowledge of the area.

Dean, Mrs. Lee, Ms. Kim, Chung (another person who had helped out with the project), and I gathered later that evening at a local restaurant on Khaosan Road to celebrate. Both Jim and Sang Hun Kim happened to be in town for work, so they joined us for dinner. When I arrived at the restaurant, I saw Mrs. Lee and Ms. Kim smiling like I had never seen them smile before. I hugged both of them; we didn't say much. We just gave each other smiles that seemed to acknowledge all that we had been through together.

I did all of the introductions, then we sat down and ordered up quite a meal. The waitress came over and Jim, Sang Hun Kim, Dean, and I, being well-versed in Thai food, each shouted out three or four of our favorite dishes. In the middle of the meal, I walked over to Dean and said, "Thank you. You did a great job. Thank you for helping these women. We couldn't have done it without you." He replied, "No. You did a great job. You had the more difficult part." I told him I thought his job was harder.

As we feasted, Dean and I recounted the saga for everyone from beginning to end. Hours later, after the final details had been told, Jim turned to me and said, "Mike, you've definitely got some higher power on your side." I had to agree. I said a brief prayer and thanked God for the successful completion of the project.

We had arrived in Thailand on a weekend, so on Monday the women went to the South Korean embassy to request asylum in South Korea. Mrs. Lee was immediately put under hospital care. The doctor told her that she wouldn't have survived another three weeks without medical treatment.[4]

TEN

Heroes

Just before we were shipping out, he asked me, "Why you going to fight somebody else's war? What, do you all think you're heroes?" And I didn't know what to say at the time, but if he asked me again, I'd say, "No, nobody asks to be a hero. It just sometimes turns out that way."

—From the movie *Black Hawk Down*,
at the end as Eversmann (played by Josh Hartnett)
is sitting next to the dead body of a fellow soldier

When I was in North Korea, I bought a book titled *Kim Il Sung Biography,* a Pyongyang-endorsed biography of the former dictator's life. While at the China North Korea border, I tried to read the book, but it was difficult because of the unorthodox use of English. I ended up skimming the book, but I still remember well these two sentences in the final chapter: "The world has seen many renowned heroes. But in no age or in any country has there been found a national *hero* such as General Kim Il Sung."[1] How backwards! I thought to myself. The real heroes in North Korea are the people who have suffered under Kim Il Sung's and Kim Jong Il's tyrannical reigns.

The Merriam-Webster's Online Dictionary defines "hero" as "an illustrious warrior" and "one that shows great courage." As I reflect on the people in my life who have displayed the most courage and the qualities of a warrior, I realize that I met most of those people at the China–North Korea border. During my four years there, I met an amazing group of individuals. The border draws courageous souls. If I were to put together a list of heroes in my life, the people I met in Northeast China would be at the top of it.

My heroes arrived at the border from many different places. I sometimes refer to the border region as the "Korean conjunction." The Korean culture, language, and food there attract Koreans from all over the world. At the border I met and worked with Korean Australians, Korean Kiwis, Korean Uzbeks, Korean Tajiks, Korean Kazakhs, Korean Russians, Korean Japanese, Korean Canadians, Korean British, Korean Americans, Korean Chinese, South Koreans, and North Koreans. In my experience, the border region has the most diverse representation of Koreans anywhere.

In May 2003, I was in my first year of work in China when a South Korean NGO worker asked me to attend an important meeting. We met at a small café tucked away in a corner of a city near the border. Four people attended: a South Korean, a Korean Chinese, a North Korean, and a Korean American. We were all Korean, speaking the same language, yet we were quite different from each other. It would be nearly impossible to get that mix of people in the same room in any other part of the world.

The China–North Korea border also attracts fascinating people from all walks of life: activists, missionaries, reporters, businesspeople, professors, English teachers, and government workers. Because of its proximity to North Korea and the presence of North Korean refugees there, it has become a melting pot for intelligence activity. Government workers, activists, missionaries, and agents flock to the border to get the latest word on North Korea. North Korean agents there try to gather intelligence, infiltrate networks, and sabotage the work of activists and missionaries. These agents will sometimes employ extreme measures, even abduction and murder. Pastor Kim, the elderly pastor with over 15 years of experience operating in China, once visited me there and warned of imminent danger: "You think you're safe here? You feel safe?

Right now, living here and with all the work you're doing, you have about a 50 percent chance of getting caught and kidnapped by North Korean agents." He reminded me that the area was a hotbed for spies and tried to convince me to move further inland.

ACTIVISTS AND MISSIONARIES

When I first arrived at the border, I was the youngest and most inexperienced person there—the rookie. Veterans showed me the ropes and allowed me to observe their operations. They made themselves available and patiently answered my incessant questions. They played a crucial role in my maturation. As I watched them make sacrifices and put themselves in harm's way to help the North Korean refugees, I learned how I should approach my own work.

Others whom I did not know influenced me from a distance. Pastor Chun Ki-won was arrested in December 2001 while helping a group of North Korean defectors reach Mongolia. He spent 220 days in jail. I heard about his arrest while in southern California preparing to leave for the field. I was shocked by the news, and I learned from colleagues that he had suffered a great deal in prison. It was a wake-up call.

Hiroshi Kato, a 62-year-old Japanese humanitarian aid worker and director of Japanese NGO Life Funds for North Korean Refugees, also influenced me from a distance. He frequently traveled to the China–North Korea border to help refugees. His work was so effective that the North Korean government offered $3,600 and a Mercedes-Benz to any North Korean agent in China who abducted him. On November 1, 2002 (just two months before I would move to China), Norbert Vollertsen forwarded me an e-mail from Life Funds for North Korean Refugees saying that Mr. Kato was missing. The e-mail read, "We have done our best to locate Mr. Kato, but we still cannot find him, and none of our friends or contacts in that area has been able to locate him. This is a matter of grave concern." They speculated that either the Chinese authorities had arrested him or that he was abducted by North Korean agents. They later learned that Chinese police had seized Mr. Kato from his hotel room and imprisoned him. After a week of interrogation and sleep deprivation, he was released because of increasing international pressure.

I did not know these two men at the time, but their cases, in particular, set a tremendous precedent for me as I prepared to leave for the China–North Korea border. As I began my journey, these two men were larger-than-life heroes who had risked everything to help the refugees. The sacrifices that they made deeply challenged me; I made it my goal to go to China with the same level of courage.

Pastor Chun and Mr. Kato suffered in prison, but other workers made the ultimate sacrifice of giving up their lives. In January 2000, Reverend Kim Dong-Shik, a South Korean missionary, was abducted in China by North Korean agents because of his work with defectors. South Korean intelligence suspects that up to 10 North Korean agents were involved in the kidnapping.[2]

In 2002, a friend introduced me to a Korean woman at a church in Chicago and said, "This is Mrs. Kim. Her husband was kidnapped by North Korean spies." At that time, I didn't know who Reverend Kim was, so I wasn't sure if I had heard her right. "Excuse me?" I said. "Could you say that again please?" My friend repeated herself. I then bowed and introduced myself to Mrs. Kim, saying that I was sorry about her husband. I later learned that her husband was Reverend Kim Dong-Shik.

In an interview with *The Daily NK* on May 7, 2007, Mrs. Kim said through tears, "I heard stories about my husband's death in 2005 . . . North Korea wanted my husband to convert to the Juche ideology and deprived him [of] his meals. His weight decreased quickly from 190 pounds to nearly 77 pounds on the brink of his death . . . Now, we will begin a campaign for his ashes to be sent home."[3] It is believed that

Reverend Kim died within a year of capture because he refused to deny his Christian faith.

Shortly after arriving in China in 2002, I read about two South Korean missionaries, a married couple, who were found murdered in their home in the border town of Hunchun, China, which I had visited several times. "Dead alongside them were four North Korean refugees they were sheltering," the *South China Morning Post* reported.[4]

In 2004, when Missionary Lee visited North Korea, he met a North Korean man who confessed to killing "two missionaries who were evangelizing North Koreans." When Missionary Lee told me about the man, I immediately wondered if he was the one who had assassinated the missionary couple.

I also had to wonder why I was coming across all of these stories of imprisoned and assassinated missionaries and activists so early in my missionary career. Perhaps it was because I needed their examples to show me the attitude required to approach North Korean refugee work. As the dangerous nature of the work began to sink in, I found the strength to proceed through them.

KOREAN-CHINESE STAFF

The second group of heroes in my life is the Crossing Borders Korean-Chinese staff. In *The Art of War*, Sun-tzu wrote, "Without using local guides, you cannot exploit the lie of the land."[5] During my year of intercultural studies at the Fuller School of World Missions, one of the important lessons I took away was to engage the locals with humility and to empower them. Crossing Borders adopted this philosophy early on; we recognize that the strength of our organization is, in fact, our local staff.

Zhao, a Korean-Chinese friend, had just graduated from college and expressed his interest in helping me with my work. He was young, and

I wasn't sure if he knew what he was getting into. Out of concern, I told him, "I want to make sure you understand what the consequences may be for you if you get caught." He wouldn't let me finish the sentence and interrupted, "Mike, my parents are pastors. Our home is a church. We face these kinds of dangers every day. You don't need to worry about such things."

Persecution is a way of life for Zhao and other members of our local staff. They recognize that it is a price they must pay in order to continue the work. For them, there is no alternative. They cannot grab their passport and leave the country when trouble hits.

Some of my most memorable moments in China were when I studied passages in the Bible on the topic of persecution with our local staff. In our weekly meetings, we studied stories in the Book of Acts and discussed how we could apply their lessons when we met resistance in our work. Every staff member would share a personal persecution experience and make a commitment to be stronger in similar situations in the future. Pages of Scripture that were once foreign to me came alive and began to make sense.

From time to time, I treat our local staff to a nice meal. At one of those dinners, people began to spontaneously tell their persecution stories. Such telling is never done to show off, since everyone has his or her own experiences. As I looked around the room, I realized that every one of the staff members had been imprisoned for North Korean refugee work. Our staff has suffered the whole gamut of costs of persecution—from being on the run to being captured, interrogated, imprisoned, beaten, and tortured.

In June 2003, I interviewed Pastor Choe, who had been housing refugees for many years, and asked him to talk about some of the challenges he faced in doing refugee work. "Of course, it's been hard," he told me. "Chinese people who help refugees get in trouble by the Chinese government. The punishment is going to prison and paying a heavy fine. But we are also a church here, so if we are caught, the punishment will be much heavier . . . If I go to prison, I go . . . I know of some families that have been shot and executed for helping refugees. So if we aren't ready to die, we cannot do this kind of work."

In the summer of 2004, after we sent Missionary Lee to North Korea, North Korean National Security Police captured Missionary Lee and imprisoned him for five months. He was starved, beaten, and tortured, and he suffered unbelievably in prison; he nearly died more than once. Several of the guards were students in tae kwon do and judo and used him as a punching bag to practice whenever they got bored. It was a miracle that he came out alive. Upon his release, he wrote a report on his experiences:

I was interrogated daily. During those 10 days of the interrogation process, my liver pain worsened and I began to feel severe pain in my kidney and heart. My whole body continued to shake uncontrollably and I couldn't make it stop. When I would try standing up, I collapsed on the floor.

I've been absurdly accused [of] partnering with spies from America. They have convicted me of "partaking in the destruction of our Great Leader's regime in North Korea." . . . They've accused me of threatening the political system as well as the power of North Korea. With all the crimes above and more, they've concluded to keep me in the prison camps. After all, to them, I didn't even deserve to live. . . . The prison camps in North Korea are like a living hell.

A Security Department official from Pyongyang kept swearing at me saying, "Our people didn't do anything bad in China during the cultural revolution of China. But you've partnered with America and have done horrible things in my country. China has been imprisoning and even executing my people. So now we have the right to imprison and execute the Chinese as well. I will not forgive you, Lee!" Then he yelled at the official next to him to throw me into the prison. By now, I hope you realize that when they say they are going to kill someone, they will do it. I knew that very well.

Concerning issues of fees, they told me that they would let go of me if I stole two Chinese cars for them. He assured me that there have been people who survived because they agreed to do that. I told them, "Not only do I not know how to drive, but even if I did, I will not steal even if you threaten to kill me. So kill me if you're going to kill me!"

When the security police learned that Missionary Lee could not drive, they gave him a second option. "Why don't you become a drug dealer?" Missionary Lee replied, "Kill me—I can't do anything like that."[6] The police then told him that he could be released after paying $10,000. "For nearly two months, I told them that I had no such money," Missionary Lee recounted. "But my body was deteriorating daily. Because of malnutrition, I began to black out every morning and felt very faint. So after compromising with them, we agreed upon $3,600."

As soon as we received the news about the $3,600 ransom, we gathered the money and paid for Missionary Lee's release. Upon his return to China and partial recovery, we met in a small café. The first thing he did was hand me the report he had written and recount his experiences in prison. He broke down in tears and said, "I really thought I was going to die in there." Then, at the end of the meeting, he stated, "The Chinese police have tight surveillance on me right now. When things die down, I would like to start helping refugees again." He begged, "Please let me continue with the work." I was amazed that this man who had just spent five months in a North Korean prison wanted to begin helping North Koreans again so soon. I suggested that we talk about it later when Chinese surveillance had waned. Later that night, I read his six-page report. At the end of it, he wrote a postscript to me:

Teacher, if I had chosen to give up my life in North Korea, we could have saved that money. I'm sorry for spending that money and coming back alive. It cost $3,600. I know it's not a small sum of money and I can't help but to feel like I've wasted a lot of money. Please forgive me. I know you are very understanding. It really isn't that I was afraid of dying. Even now, every morning when I wake up, I am amazed that I'm alive, living in my very own house.

Many of our other local staff members have sacrificed greatly for our work. But we all get discouraged at times. I've had several moments with some of our key staff members when, over a cup of tea, they've acknowledged that they want to quit sometimes. I've told them that I sometimes feel the same way. Then we'll encourage each other and re-mind ourselves of the importance of our work and make a renewed commitment to press on. We all have a burning desire to help the suf-fering people of North Korea.

We hold quarterly local staff retreats where we gather to study the Bible, pray, discuss strategy, and recalibrate our mission and vision. After every retreat, without fail, a staff member or two will come up to me and say, "Teacher, I really needed this retreat. These days I have been contemplating giving up the work because it's so difficult. But after this retreat, I feel strengthened and will continue on."

Security issues and the constant threat of imprisonment, abduction, torture, and assassination will wear down the most committed and faithful of workers. On July 12, 2003, after only seven months in the field, I wrote in my journal, "It has been an unbelievably heavy burden dealing with things such as prison, torture, and death for the staff and for the North Koreans. Lately I've had to deal with a type of stress I have never experienced before. . . . I am completely drained mentally, physically, and emotionally." I only devoted four years of my life to live in China, but many of our local staff have committed the rest of their lives to the difficult work of helping North Koreans.

I have had to learn stress management in a new way. I carefully sched-ule leisure activities and breaks from the field in order to keep my sanity. But the local staff do not have the option to just pick up and leave. Nor do they have U.S. passports that might serve as get-out-of-jail cards (or negotiating tools at the very least). Day in and day out, they engage in some of the most difficult humanitarian aid and mission work in the world today.

NORTH KOREAN REFUGEES

At the top of my list of heroes are the North Korean refugees. I know of no modern-day group of people that has displayed greater courage. The refugees have taught and inspired me with their lives. They have battled and survived oppression, persecution, famine, sex trafficking, and gulags. They are among the unsung heroes in the world today.

On April 23, 2004, a teenager who described himself as a Caucasian American studying tae kwon do contacted our organization and asked us to forward the following e-mail to our refugees:

> You are the greatest heroes to the world because you have shown that no country or leader, no matter how cruel and despotic, can ever crush the spirit of freedom . . . You have shown me that freedom is something that we must all fight for. You are heroes to me because of the incredible courage you have shown, and the resolve, and I admire you so much for that.

Recently I visited my friend Ed Sul, who works for the U.S. Peace Corps in Fiji, for a few days of scuba diving. While we were diving, he updated me on his work and shared a quote by Lila Watson, an Australian Aboriginal woman. Apparently, it is a quote that every Peace Corps worker is exposed to early on in his or her two-year service. It reads, "If you have come to help me, you are wasting your time. But if you have come *because your liberation is bound up with mine*, then let us work together" (emphasis added).

There's a lot of truth in that short statement. When I first set out for China, I was not only following a calling but also doing something that

I had to do because I knew it would change me forever. Even before I jumped on that plane to China, I knew that I would be deeply impacted by the people I met there, more than they would be by my work. In moving to the China–North Korea border to help some of the most destitute people in the world today, I feel that I have been liberated. As much as I have taught them, they have taught me more. In helping them, I have gained a greater sense of purpose and fulfillment; they have forever changed my life.

ELEVEN

Restoring Lives

He who saves one life saves the world entire.

—Babylonian Talmud, Sanhedrin, 37a

At the end of 2004, Crossing Borders made a strategic shift from helping refugees find asylum in South Korea to setting up long-term shelters in China. We believe that this has prolonged our work and allowed us to operate somewhat unhindered in China for many years. Our mission is now "to restore the indigent." Restoration has become a catchword in our organization; we focus all of our resources on helping the individual find complete restoration—physically, emotionally, socially, and spiritually.

When refugees enter our Crossing Borders shelters, they can choose from two paths: Stay in China or return to North Korea. We provide the tools, resources, and the support necessary for them to either begin a new life in China or return to North Korea to help their families there. To those who stay in China, our commitment is to do whatever is in our power to help them live safe and happy lives. The vast majority, if they are cautious and listen to our instructions, will not be captured in China. It is usually the ones who take risks or are careless with security who are apprehended.

After a while, a surprising number of refugees do decide that they want to return to their families in North Korea. We provide them with the needed financial resources, perhaps enough to start a small business, and pay their way out of prison, if possible. We teach and encourage them to help other North Koreans in need upon their return, and many of them do. Those who return to North Korea will often come to China several times a year to meet with our staff to report on the situation inside North Korea and receive additional support.

RESTORE LIFE SHELTERS

Refugees are in survival mode when they first enter our Restore Life shelters.[1] It's difficult for us to have any kind of intelligent conversation or do any long-term planning with them when they arrive in this state. They are mainly concerned with food, medicine, shelter, and safety. After their treacherous journey, our first obligation is to feed them, since they are usually extremely weak, thin, and malnourished. A recent North Korean defector typically appears lifeless and rarely smiles. The Chinese police in northeast China are trained to identify North Koreans who have recently defected by their yellowish skin tone. For this reason, those who have just arrived are at the greatest risk and must hide indoors until their physical condition normalizes.

When a refugee enters our shelter, it takes awhile for their stomach to adjust to eating solid food. I once bought dinner for a refugee family that had been in China for only three days. As we ate at the shelter, I noticed that the grandmother wasn't eating much and said, "Grandmother, you're not eating too much. Does the food taste okay?" She smiled and said, "The food is so good. I'm just not used to digesting this kind of food."

The first few weeks with refugees are usually a bit awkward. On top of being somber, they are hostile at times. When I meet someone who has just defected, it's always the same: They sit as far away from me as possible in the other corner of the room and do not make eye contact.

Even though we are feeding and sheltering them, they don't trust us and wonder what it is that we might want from them. The North Korean regime has taught them to distrust all foreigners.

When our U.S. director of operations and his wife visited the border, we went to a shelter to see a refugee family that had just arrived in China. The family of five and four Crossing Borders staff crammed into a small room. One of the sons stood up to close the curtains before we began talking. The family members wouldn't make eye contact with us and looked down at the ground as we spoke. They barely talked and were clearly scared. I commented to my teammates in English, "I'm glad you get to see how refugees are at this stage. This is how they are when they first come to China. . . . After a few months, you'll see that they change radically. They'll begin to smile and laugh."

The concept of receiving help is foreign to them. Having lived in a society where it is the survival of the fittest, they are not used to this sort of kindness and generosity. Sometimes they will ask us flat out, "Why are you helping me? What is it that you want from me?" One commented, "I have never received such a deep love from anyone in North Korea. [There] it's rare to find support between family members. How can I not be overwhelmed when a complete stranger, and a foreigner at that, lends a helping hand like this?"

When I first signed up for refugee work, I had no idea that providing medical help would be a regular part of my job. But some North Koreans cross the river with serious illnesses for which they need immediate medical attention. If a hospital visit is possible or there is a doctor willing to take the risk of examining the refugee, we set that up immediately. We once took a medical survey of 200 refugees within our network. We found that almost every single one of them had a sickness or disease of some sort, and about half of them had major illnesses.

After their immediate physical needs are taken care of, we usually begin teaching them Mandarin. We either pay a trusted university student or find volunteers at the local house churches to tutor them. Language skills are very important if they want to successfully assimilate into Chinese culture. And their ability to speak Mandarin might one day save their lives. A couple of our refugees were questioned by police on the streets and spoke the language well enough to get off the hook. Because of the various minorities in China, there are many people there who are not fluent in Mandarin. While in the United States you would be hard-pressed to find a second-generation minority who isn't fluent in English, in China there are many people who were born and raised in China who are not completely fluent in Mandarin. With a minimal level of Mandarin, a North Korean refugee could potentially pass as Korean-Chinese.

Perhaps one of the most rewarding parts of my work is witnessing the transformation that takes place in the lives of the refugees. With the passing of time, they carry themselves with a level of confidence that wasn't there before. There is newfound dignity and self-respect. They smile, laugh, and joke. In essence, they are restored and transformed. One refugee woman, who stayed in one of our shelters for a year, said, "We've lived like animals all of our lives. I never knew what it's like to feel like a human being until now."

We sometimes have the refugees write thank-you letters to donors. Those letters often show their transformation. Mi-Sook, a young refugee woman, wrote, "I have been living in despair and in tears without any hope to live. I have left my family and cried very often because it was so hard to live in this foreign country at a young age. Under oppression and discrimination, I lived asking why I have to live like this. . . . Then some people provided shelter, clothes, and much food to eat. I am so happy. Even though I haven't met you, I thank you for reaching out to me. I have a new dream now. I now dream about reaching out to other poor people who are without hope."

When we spend time with the refugees, we consider it a high priority to make them laugh. I have referred to this as our "Ministry of Fun and Laughter." One of the benefits of a young organization full of people in our twenties and thirties is that we can be silly. One of my good friends, Brian, who is an accountant for a large corporation and works part-time as the finance director for Crossing Borders, once visited the China–North Korea border. We took an overnight train to visit one of our women's shelters in an adjacent province. In the shelter, there were two women (one aged 30, the other 20) who were both victims of sex-trafficking, and a 13-year-old orphan girl.

Brian has always been the type that could easily make people laugh (when he was younger, he aspired to be a stand-up comedian and even performed once), so immediately upon arriving he suggested, "Mike, let's play some games." He introduced us to a game called "*jae-meet-tah*," which means "this is fun" in Korean. The game starts off with a beat that you make by slapping your hands on your thighs and then clapping while chanting *jae-meet-tah* over and over again. The objective of the game is to keep from smiling or laughing while chanting "this is fun"— if you do either, you lose. You can make faces and do things to try to make others in the group laugh, but you are not allowed to break a smile. The last one to keep from laughing wins.

It's a ridiculous game, which perhaps is the reason why people laugh so hard while playing it. Knowing the background of the women and how much they suffered made the experience special. It was truly precious to see them smile, laugh, and roll on the ground as if they didn't have a care in the world. Around 8:00 P.M., the electricity went out, but we lit some candles and kept on playing. Their usual bedtime was 9:00, but we kept on playing until 11:00, when their overseeing pastor, an elderly woman in her sixties, woke up to all the noise and came into the room. She was concerned about the safety of the refugees and said, "Be careful. Make sure you don't attract any attention from the neighbors." We were in a bit of dilemma. The environment was a somewhat dangerous one, but we were having so much fun that nobody wanted to stop. We looked at each other for a brief moment and decided to keep on playing into the night. It's been almost a year since I've left the field, and these are the kinds of moments I cherish.

THE WORKING HANDS PROJECT

After making sure their basic needs are met, the next step is to find employment for the refugees. However, their illegal refugee status and inability to speak Mandarin make this difficult. For example, Jae-Hoon, an 18-year-old refugee, said he wanted to learn graphic design, so we enrolled him in a class since he was one of the better Mandarin speakers among the refugees. But within a few weeks he dropped out because he wasn't able to keep up with the language. Ji-Hae, a refugee in her early twenties, said that she had always wanted to be a hairstylist. We spent several hundred dollars and bought her all of the supplies she needed to begin beauty school. Shortly after she began training at a local beauty shop, however, the owners learned that Ji-Hae was a refugee, and she had to flee the scene.

Many times, an employer will learn that a worker is a refugee and continue to employ them. But after the refugee has worked for one or two months, the employer will refuse to pay them, knowing that they can't do anything about it. Mrs. Huh, a refugee in her forties, came crying to one of our staff, "I worked day and night at a restaurant for two months and now the owner won't pay me because he knows I'm a refugee."

In 2005, we launched the "Working Hands Project," a small, nonprofit business in China employing North Korean refugees. The refugees work full-time embroidering items within the safety of their own homes. We then sell these items in various countries throughout the world. We pay the refugees very well (around four times what they would normally make doing similar work) and all of the proceeds go directly towards helping other refugees in the shelters. Many Working Hands employees are sending money back to their families in North Korea or saving up so that they can one day return to North Korea and start a business.

Restoring Lives

Benjamin Lim from Reuters visited a Crossing Borders shelter and interviewed one of the women in the Working Hands Project. In an article titled "Women the Most Vulnerable of North Korean Refugees," he wrote:

Rhee—not her real name—had been dying from abdominal inflammation last year and fled to China with her mother to seek treatment. Because her belly was so distended, she began to float as she waded across the Tumen river which marks the border and was almost washed away. . . . She recovered after treatment by a South Korean doctor in China and is now able to work. No Chinese hospital would have admitted her and anyway she could not have afforded the bill.

"North Korea was too oppressive. We were constantly harassed," she said in an interview. "I want to spend the rest of my life in China," said Rhee, who makes twice as much as an average urban Chinese worker and is now learning Chinese.

Crossing Borders, an Illinois-based non-profit Christian organization, employs Rhee and several dozen other Korean refugees to stitch the mini-crosses which it then ships and sells to Christian donors in South Korea, the United States and Europe.[2]

When I first began refugee work back in 2003, one local staff member expressed frustration that our humanitarian aid sometimes seemed to go into a black hole: "Teacher, you give me $50 and then tell me to give it to the poorest people. I give it to them, and it's only enough to buy food. They can't buy anything else. And then I come back, and you give me $50 again and the cycle just continues." Another local staff member recently argued, "They [the refugees] need us to provide something for them, such as a greater sum of money to start a business to do on their own, instead of giving them free handouts all the time. Then, they will feel a sense of ownership and accomplishment. They will also learn how to provide for themselves."

Through the Working Hands Project, the refugees have attained a certain level of independence and self-sufficiency. There is a Chinese proverb, "Give a man a fish and you feed him for a day. Teach a man to fish and you feed him for a lifetime." That's what we have been trying to do through this project. By teaching the refugees skills and employing them, we're trying to make them self-sufficient and restore their dignity and self-esteem. As the months go by, the refugees in the Working Hands Project begin to carry themselves differently. They wear nicer clothes, and the women put on make-up for the first time. They have an air of confidence and self-worth that was not present before. With a newfound sense of pride, they say things to me like, "Teacher, I want to take you out for lunch sometime." Soon after we began the Working Hands Project, one of the refugee mothers made dinner for me. She used the shelter's funds to prepare an elaborate meal, and afterwards I pulled her aside and offered to pay for the meal as I was accustomed to doing. Proudly, she said, "Don't worry. This one's on me."

SECOND WAVE SHELTERS

In 2004, we started underground orphanages for children of North Korean descent who were abandoned, neglected, or underprivileged. When the children first come into these Second Wave shelters, they too look malnourished, like homeless children off the streets. Oftentimes, they walk in with ragged clothes, dirty and smelly. Most come from dysfunctional homes; many have been abandoned. Once one of our Korean American staff, Hannah, interviewed several of these children (which was quite a task) and asked them about their family backgrounds. Kyoung-Mi, an eight-year-old girl, said, "My parents cannot take care of me because they are too poor, and there is no school for me to go to where I live." Eun-Joo, a nine-year-old girl, told us, "My dad died in January 2006. I do not know where my mother is." When we asked one girl about her family, she replied that she didn't know anything about them. When we asked her how old she was, she said, "I don't know my birthday."

Although the children don't generally smile when they first arrive at our shelters, it doesn't take long before they do. Soon they are playing with everyone, running around, screaming at the top of their lungs. We consider it a high calling to make sure that these children who have already suffered enough for an entire lifetime are now taken care of. Perhaps one of the greatest responsibilities our organization has is making sure that they have hope and a future.

We currently have four Second Wave shelters. Each is overseen by what we call a "caretaker" and at least one assistant caretaker. The children are enrolled in the local schools and are provided with food, clothing, medicine, and other miscellaneous items. The caretakers are some of the most impressive people I have met. Not only do they live with the children while also caring for their own, they subject themselves to great risk. One of them recently confessed to me, "I was so afraid and couldn't get a good night's sleep until we received all of the necessary [fake] identification for the North Korean children."

When I visit the Second Wave shelters, I see them full of kids running around, playing and screaming loudly. I will often shake my head and say to the caretakers, "I don't know how you do it." The energy of the caretakers is incredible, as is their profound love for the children. During a July 2008 visit, Mrs. Choe, one of the caretakers, told me about one child they took in:

> He is nine years old and doesn't sleep very well at night. His schoolteacher knows he is a North Korean orphan and told us not to keep him. She says that he's been hurt too much and that he's a bad kid. In my eyes it doesn't seem that way, but that's what the teacher keeps on saying. [My husband] Mr. Choe holds him for awhile every morning, and he seems to be getting better. We pray for him, and we care for him. Every morning, he'll come into our

room and sleep under our blanket for awhile. . . . His mom is a
North Korean refugee and was caught. His dad is Chinese and is a
gangster. . . . He's been hurt so much.

The caretakers have made a commitment to consider these children
their family. When we ask them how long they plan on caring for the
children, they say that they will raise them as their own until the children
become young men and women.

People who visit our Second Wave shelters often comment on how
happy the kids seem. A Crossing Borders director wrote about his visit
to a Second Wave shelter in an article for our newsletter titled "Mina's
Story":

> Outside their window is a neighborhood like any other apartment
> in the area. It has an open space for them to play soccer and bad-
> minton. I could hear their laughter from a block away, it rises above
> the constant honking and changing of lanes, the airplanes that
> screech overhead.
>
> When I approached them they ran to me with open arms. They
> wanted to be held and played with. I swung them around by their
> arms until I became dizzy, after a while I had to turn them away. I
> shared food and candy with them. I could barely communicate
> with them but they seemed similar to the children I encounter
> back in the States.
>
> Throughout my stay with them, I had to remind myself that
> they are orphans, that if they didn't have Crossing Borders, they
> wouldn't have a home, they wouldn't have a surrogate mother to
> tend to their wounds and hold them when they were scared.
>
> But there is one that sticks out with me. I had heard her story
> before I met her but seeing her in all her scruffy glory made the
> story real. It's one thing hearing her tale and another to play with
> her. Her story crossed from intellect and became huggable, lovable
> flesh and bone. Her name is Mina and she is an orphan. Her father
> is dying and her mother has abandoned her. Somehow she made it
> to us. . . . She is oblivious to her sordid past. Rather, she carries on

with the carelessness of a child with all the riches in the world. She begs to be twirled like any other child would. . . .

There is a saying that it takes a village to raise a child. Mina will never get to meet the village that raised her. She will never get a chance to thank all the faithful people giving and praying for her needs. It is a very unique village we have created. She will grow up in a family like none other, but it is a family nonetheless and we are committed to raising this child.[3]

Through our shelters, children who might have ended up in gangs or brothels now have a chance at life. We stress education and encourage them to dream. When we ask the children what they want to be when they grow up, they now reply like any other kid would—nurse, firefighter, teacher, and police officer are some of the occupations they mention. Hyun-Jung, a seven-year-old girl, said, "My future dream is to become a doctor so I can cure 'mother' [the caretaker] when she gets sick." Kwang-Ho, a nine-year-old orphan boy, stated, "I want to be the president [of China] when I grow up." If a boy like Kwang-Ho, who was once abandoned, is now dreaming of becoming the president of China, we must be doing something right.

Through Restore Life, Working Hands, and Second Wave, we regularly witness tremendous transformations in the lives of refugees and children at the China–North Korea border. By applying both humanitarian aid and faith effectively, Crossing Borders is, I believe, a model for the future.

TWELVE

The Future of North Korea

Do not withhold good from those who deserve it, when it is in your power to act.

—Proverbs 3:27

Speak up for those who cannot speak for themselves, for the rights of all who are destitute.

—Proverbs 31:8

We continue to receive encouraging reports about positive changes inside North Korea. Political and cultural shifts are occurring largely because of the flow of refugees back and forth from China. As they cross the border, the refugees carry information from the outside world that they inevitably share with their neighbors and other villagers. "Mass defections from North Korea strike at the heart of the Kim regime, giving the lie to the myths upon which North Korean rule is based," as Nicholas Eberstadt and Christopher Griffin wrote in *The New York Times*.[1]

Our staff members who travel in and out of North Korea have observed the changes in the political climate there. "The government's policies have loosened quite a bit," Mrs. Soh, who visited in early 2006, noticed. "North Koreans are openly criticizing the government these days." The next month, Pastor Yoo wrote, "Even when a few of the people gather and talk, there is a lot of discontent towards the government.

It has become part of everyday speech to say that the government under Kim Il Sung was much better than the current regime under Kim Jong Il."

When I asked Mrs. Park, a North Korean who lived in a village bordering China, how many people in North Korea knew that Kim Il Sung and Kim Jong Il were not really gods, she replied, "Everyone in my village knew. They just couldn't say anything about it because they would be punished." When did people begin figuring this out? "Ever since the famine," she said. "When there was no food and the famine got really bad . . . people were asking, 'If Kim Jong Il and Kim Il Sung are gods, why can't they feed us?'"

As we've seen, a surprisingly large number of refugees in China desire to return to North Korea. Jong-Cheol, a young man, said, "There's so much need, and I want to help . . . I plan on settling down over there, and if it gets too hard, then I can come back." Hye-Su, a teenaged girl, reflected, "I thought I'd be happy with a lot of food. In North Korea, I dreamed of eating pork for dinner. But now that I'm here, I want to go back to North Korea. Now, I realize there's nothing that can truly satisfy human beings. . . . I think it's best to live with my parents in North Korea." When I asked Jang-Ho why he wanted to return home, he replied, "My family is there. My friends are there. But most of all I want to help my country become a better one."

Tens of thousands of refugees return to North Korea every year. According to Michel Gabaudan of the UN High Commission for Refugees, about 50 percent of North Koreans in northeast China end up returning to North Korea.[2]

Yet refugees in China often comment on the deep sense of betrayal they feel when they learn that they have been deceived by the North Korean regime all of their lives. Kim Hyun Hee, the North Korean spy who smuggled a bomb onto the Korean Air flight, killing 115 passengers, described how she felt after arriving in Seoul: "I couldn't shake the feeling that the first twenty-six years of my life had been something of a sham. I felt a surge of hatred for Kim Il Sung as I realized in one brief moment that all my work and plans and training, indeed my entire life, had been founded upon lies."[3] Ms. Ryu, another refugee, recalled, "In North Korea, we were taught that the eyes of the whole world were on Kim Il Sung and Kim Jong Il, and that every other country was poorer than North Korea. I was so shocked when I came to China and found that this wasn't true."

North Koreans are learning the truth about the world: North Korea is not a "paradise on earth," as the regime teaches. And the level of fear there has been steadily decreasing over the years. That is tremendously important. With fear declining, there is great potential for change. And as North Koreans discover the truth, the regime's grip loosens further. Tom White, the executive director of Voice of the Martyrs, commented, "Our friends who work there say that much of [the regime's] control is deteriorating. Pyongyang is now the last bastion of super-control, being the capital city. The rural area is becoming like the 'Wild West.'"[4]

INFORMATION AGE

The information age is coming to North Korea. People are hungry for information from the outside world, and the most daring ones risk their lives to obtain it. Some illegally own short-wave radios and listen to foreign broadcasts. Wealthier families obtain South Korean dramas on DVDs and other items on the black market. Barbara Demick reported in the *Los Angeles Times*, "Smugglers carry chests that can hold up to 1,000 pirated DVDs. South Korean soap operas, movies about the Korean War and Hollywood action films are among the most popular. Even pornography is making its way in."[5]

After refugees arrive in our shelters and get settled in, they devour any available information. We make sure that there are television sets in the shelters for them to watch the Chinese news and South Korean cable television. As they watch, they learn more about the world. For many, reading becomes one of their favorite hobbies in China, because for the first time, they have access to real information. "In North Korea, we can't read anything besides what the government gives us," one woman said. "Now that I've escaped, I love to read books and learn from the outside world." Ambassador Mark Palmer, in his book *Breaking the Real Axis of Evil*, stated, "In closed societies, the written word acquires special, almost magical, power. There is a huge thirst not only for books from abroad on almost every subject but also for materials from within."[6]

Young Howard, the executive director of Open Radio for North Korea, reported in the *International Herald Tribune*:

> The iron curtain on North Korea has been lifted little by little in recent years by hundreds of thousands of refugees who have fled across the border to China. With their increasing use of Chinese cell phones, they are providing near-instantaneous news to the outside. . . . These developments have created a new flow of information. According to defectors, people in North Korea now believe that in China even dogs eat better than they do. They also know that the Chinese can criticize the top leaders of their government, at least in private (the penalty for such dissent in North Korea is death). Of late, South Korean pop songs, soap operas and movies have become quite popular via Chinese cassette players and VCRs smuggled across the border. . . . People now realize that Kim is neither their god nor their helper. Some feel he is an obstacle.[7]

The North Korean authorities are taking desperate measures to curb the flow of information: tightening security at the border, punishing border patrol soldiers who take bribes and allow refugees to cross, giving harsher punishments to repatriated refugees, and executing border-crossers in some cases. The regime has also outlawed cell phones. North Korea introduced mobile phones in 2003, but then in May 2004 quickly banned cell phone usage in an effort to block information.[8] Despite the ban, however, about 20,000 North Koreans had access to cell phones as of early 2005.[9] Several North Koreans reported that the National Security Police now have machines that detect cell phone activity. One local staff member who visited the country in mid-2006 heard that "North Korea has obtained wiretapping equipment from Shanghai so they can tap and source the location of all telephone calls." In June 2007, South Korea's government-affiliated think tank, the Korea Institute for National Unification, reported that public executions of those who "circulate South Korean leaflets and sell videos and use cell phones are on the rise."[10]

There have also been shifts in North Korean culture, as South Korean culture is taking root in cities like Pyongyang. One Pyongyang elite complained to me, "These days, North Korean teenagers are imitating South Korean teenagers by dying their hair. Young people in Pyongyang are also trying to speak with a Seoul accent." When I asked him why the government would allow this, he answered, "The government can't control it."

SOUTH KOREA

Some look to South Korea as a model for North Korea and reason for hope. "One of the most positive models for a liberated North Korea is the example of South Korea," Mark Palmer wrote. "In a single lifetime, South Korea has risen from being considered a hopeless backwater under dictators to joining the Organization for Economic Cooperation and Development—the club of the world's richest democracies."[11] Michael Breen remarked, "[South Korea] moved out of the paddy fields and into Silicon Valley in one generation. . . . These are a people who are making miracles." But "there is another miracle to come," Breen says. The "final part of the Korean healing will be the reunification of its bitterly divided halves."[12]

The more I get in touch with my roots and learn about the history of South Korea, the more impressed I am by the achievements and resolve of the South Korean people. South Korea continues to enjoy economic success; it currently boasts the eleventh-largest economy in the world. The country's increasing prominence in the world is reflected in the appointment of South Korean Ban Ki-moon as the UN secretary general.

In 1998, South Korea adopted the "Sunshine Policy" (a term that the international community still uses but that South Korea has not used for many years) as its foreign policy toward North Korea. This highly controversial policy attempts to engage North Korea while avoiding topics or actions that might provoke or anger the country. With the policy, South Korea took the topic of human rights off the negotiating table; the government actively discourages and in some cases prevents North Korean refugees in Seoul from testifying about the human rights violations they experienced.

South Korea's silence on human rights has puzzled many in the international community for years. While the United States, Japan, and some European countries have called North Korea to account for its human rights violations, South Korea has remained mute. The UN General Assembly has met every year since 2003 to vote on resolutions urging North Korea to fully respect human rights, and the resolutions have always passed. In 2003, South Korea did not show up for the vote, and in 2004 and 2005—when 84 countries voted in favor of condemning human rights violations in North Korea—it abstained. In 2006, however, in response to North Korea's nuclear test, South Korea for the first time voted in favor of the resolution. Many in the international community lauded South Korea's vote. However, in 2007, South Korea once again abstained from a vote condemning North Korea for its human rights abuses. Park Sang-hak, a former North Korean refugee now based in Seoul, commented, "How can South Korea claim to play a role in the international community when it turns its back on a universal value of mankind?"[13] The good news is that we can hope to see some positive changes with the new administration. The newly elected South Korean president, Lee Myung-bak, has already been taking a tougher stance on North Korea regarding its nuclear ambitions and human rights record.

I asked Tim Peters, the director of Helping Hands Korea who is based in Seoul, about South Korea's policy towards North Korea and its silence on human rights violations. He commented:

> I think that a large share of the ambivalence that South Koreans show toward North Korea has to do with the fact that many in the South have, in the past few decades, become rather nouveau riche. Remember, South Korea is now an OECD[14] member country. They're quickly approaching this $20,000 per capita income mark, which seems to be the golden target at which their economic leaders are aiming. But by the same token, many middle- and upper-class South Koreans are thinking, "We have to protect this status. Anything that would disrupt our upward trajectory to greater economic success and personal wealth needs to be avoided at all costs." So, it's not hard to understand that the specter of having distant North Korean relatives "camped out" on their doorstep after a sudden North-South reunification is hardly an attractive thought for most South Koreans, even if few would admit it publicly. . . . The leadership of North Korea understands that supremely well, and they can manipulate South Korea by rattling their sword or doing a nuclear test.[15]

Michael Horowitz, a senior fellow at the Hudson Institute, offered a different theory on South Korea's silence:

> When East Germany collapsed and they opened up the Stasi files in East Germany, they found as many as 30,000 West Germans who were implicated; they were receiving payments. [In] some cases [they] were spies. They were in journalism, they were in the churches, they were in the business community, they were in the universities, they were in the political community. And I believe in South Korea today, large numbers of people wake up every morning and they may talk about Sunshine Policy, but the first thing in

their mind is, "Whatever happens, keep those files in North Korea locked. Because if Kim Jong Il loses power, I will go to jail or I will be disgraced." And I think Kim Jong Il has got many influential South Koreans—and we will know the truth of this before long—subject to blackmail.[16]

Critics of the Sunshine Policy argue that it has ignored North Korean human rights violations for far too long and allowed North Korea to act without accountability. Chuck Downs, a former senior Pentagon official and author of *Over the Line: North Korea's Negotiating Strategy*, commented:

> It's a policy driven by hope but not experience. The experience with North Korea is that they never respond positively to favorable treatment. They abuse people who give them favorable opportunities. Unfortunately, the only way you can get them to do what you want them to do is by pressure and force. That's the way they treat their people and that's the only way they understand foreign policy. . . . The North Korean government will abuse any opportunity you give them. They'll take it and run.[17]

On the other hand, those who support the Sunshine Policy argue that it has prevented hostilities from getting out of hand. To bring up the topic of human rights would be a nonstarter in negotiations, they say, and therefore unproductive. Professor Armstrong, director of the Center for Korean Research at Columbia University, says:

> This sort of policy may not be a great option, but the alternatives don't seem to be any better. At the moment, addressing the human rights violations in North Korea directly doesn't get anybody anywhere. Until North Korea becomes involved with the outside world enough that it actually does have a stake in international opinion, I don't think there's much we can do. So on the whole, I think a cautious and realistic policy of engagement is the least bad option of how to deal with North Korea.[18]

I also asked the Honorable Song Young-Sun, a member of the South Korean National Assembly, for her thoughts on the Sunshine Policy. She told me:

> The Sunshine Policy operates under the assumption that if we give, they will change. If we give them unconditionally, they will change unconditionally. But it does not work that way. The more we give [Kim Jong Il] unconditionally, the more he becomes vicious. We have to change our approach. How? Action to action. Behavior to behavior. West Germany did it perfectly. Every single assistance, they calculated in terms of price and they traded for the equivalent. Give us 10 people, we will give you 10 packs of rice.[19]

Song added that South Korea now refers to its foreign policy towards North Korea as the "Engagement Policy." But "in terms of what we have done in the last ten years, Sunshine Policy is a more accurate description," she said. "We didn't engage North Korea; we have never engaged them. We have only been a donor. We have only been giving things away. Engagement means that there is a mutual obligation and duty. There is commitment."[20]

FROM THE EXPERTS

I interviewed 15 leading figures involved with the North Korean crisis and asked them what steps they would suggest to resolve it. Here are their answers.

Ambassador Mark Palmer served in policy positions in the State Department in the Nixon, Ford, Carter, Reagan, and first Bush administrations. He was U.S. Ambassador to Hungary from 1986 to 1990 and witnessed firsthand the impact that refugees can have in a struggle for justice as thousands of East Germans fled through Hungary in 1989. He argued:

> We need a comprehensive approach to resolve the problems with North Korea . . . The problem is the dictatorial nature of the

regime, which represents a threat to its people first and foremost but also to its neighbors. So the goal has to be to help North Koreans achieve democracy, and that requires a number of things. One, it seems to me that we need to be present in Pyongyang; that is, we should have an embassy and a very, very active outreach program to the North Korean people, including cultural, sports, and other exchanges. Two, we need a much fuller program of communicating with the North Korean people through radio and eventually television, VCRs, and all other means of communicating with them directly as well. And three, I strongly favor a really active program of supporting the North Korean people in their effort to organize themselves and to bring democracy through the kind of color revolutions that we have seen in Ukraine . . . and other countries over the last 40 years—without a shot being fired, peaceful revolutions in over 60 countries.[21]

Willy Fautré is the director of Human Rights Without Frontiers International, an organization whose main goal is to influence Belgium and European Union institutions on human rights issues. He told me:

A German foundation . . . organized an exchange of German and North Korean journalists. I couldn't believe it, but, really, four North Korean journalists visited their colleagues in Germany. Of course, they were monitored by their embassy, but at least they could see how people are living in Germany or in Europe in general. And they talked with other journalists in Germany. Afterwards, German journalists went to North Korea.

North Korea needs a civil society, and for the moment it is nonexistent. So, why not try to promote such exchanges? Why not try to have language teachers from North Korea meeting Belgium language teachers? They would just talk about methodology, about their students, about their job, and not at all about politics. . . . Through such contact, they would cease to demonize "Westerners," they would compare their ways of living and would want to reach the same standards. The same could be done with physicians, nurses, and so on from other European countries. The more people will think differently from the official discourse from Pyongyang, then the bigger the rift will be between the regime and the population. . . . Basically, I am in favor of all sorts of exchanges between North Koreans from various backgrounds and "colleagues" from developed and democratic countries. I think that Europe could play a major role in the building of a North Korean civil society of free-thinking minds, which is necessary to start a promising Asian Helsinki process.[22]

Sang-Hun Kim is a 75-year-old South Korean activist who focuses on obtaining incriminating evidence against the North Korean regime. He was included on *Time Asia*'s list of "Asian Heroes." He argues:

We need to get as much information and evidence as possible on crimes against humanity perpetuated by the North Korean regime. . . . It is an unforgivable crime that they are committing and have been committing for decades. Why do we remain silent on it and only talk about their nuclear program, which is not a crime?[23]

Ambassador John Miller is the former director of the State Department Office to Monitor and Combat Trafficking in Persons and a former congressional representative from the state of Washington. He told me:

I believe we should take a page out of the Reagan administration book in negotiating with the Soviet Union. I was in Congress then. Secretary of State Shultz and Ambassador Max Kampelman negotiated all sorts of security, nuclear, and armament issues with the Soviet Union, but at the same time they kept raising the issue of human rights. It was always part of a package. And I am very concerned that we apparently are ignoring this lesson of successful negotiation with a totalitarian government. With regards to North Korea we are allowing ourselves to negotiate separately—for example, on the nuclear issue—while ignoring the pathetic, brutal conditions of those in North Korea. When you look back at what President Reagan, Secretary of State Shultz, and Ambassador Kampelman did, they got progress on a whole basketfull of issues. They made progress on disarmament and nuclear issues, but they also got progress on human rights. They got progress, and they started in those negotiations the process of *perestroika*.[24] We should be doing the same in our negotiations with North Korea.[25]

Lord David Alton is chair of the British–North Korean Parliamentary Committee and has served in the British parliament for the past 28 years. He says:

As we grapple with the security issues posed by North Korea, we must hold in equal tension these human rights issues. What, then, might be a thoughtful and intelligent response to North Korea? One thing is clear: Fifty years of isolation have not worked, and attempting to starve a patriotic and proud people into submission will not work either.

In addition to the six-nation talks, the U.S. has had welcome bilateral discussions with Pyongyang. Like the United Kingdom, it should establish an embassy and diplomatic relations. "Helsinki with an Asian Face" would be a positive and constructive move and could hardly be portrayed as rewarding the regime. For Pyongyang, it is the United States that matters. It is the major player involved, and it alone can guarantee the security that North Korea craves. That is precisely the successful approach used by Ronald Reagan and Margaret Thatcher during the worst years of the Cold War. As a precedent we might also keep in mind the normalization of U.S.-Libyan relations in 2004.

In many respects, North Korea's mad dash to develop a nuclear weapon is a sign of weakness and desperation, and we should see it thus. When I stood at Panmunjom[26] on the North Korean side of the border, where the 1953 cease-fire was signed, it was hard not to think of Berlin and the Cold War that divided and devastated large swaths of Europe. Is it so unrealistic to demolish this wall too, and to actively seek the reunification of the two Koreas? North Korea is often called "the hermit kingdom" and "the land that never changes," but for the sake of its people and its neighbors we should devote our energies to disproving that proposition.[27]

The Future of North Korea

The Honorable Hwang Woo-Yea is a member of the South Korean National Assembly and the secretary general of the Grand National Party (GNP). He is also the standing co-chair of the International Parliamentarians' Coalition for North Korean Refugees' Human Rights (IPCNKR).[28] He asserts:

> There are various problems related to the North Korean crisis. Of those problems, however, I think that the issue of North Korean defectors and refugees is the most urgent. Therefore, efforts to resolve the problem can result in positive consequences. North Korea is not an open society. Consequently, young North Korean citizens are severely restricted from traveling abroad to acquire new knowledge, skill, and the experience of a free society. Fortunately, there are 100,000 to 400,000 North Korean defectors living in China and Northeast Asia. If we could bring them to South Korea and teach them about the system of a free and open society, and introduce them to a new worldview, they will serve as valuable leaders when North Korea becomes a reformed country.
>
> Therefore, I think that cultivating human resources is the most effective way to help North Korea in its path to becoming a developed country. The international community's help is crucial in achieving this goal. We must not merely ensure the North Koreans' survival and protect their basic human rights, but we must foster them as leaders who can contribute to the development of North Korea. In this regard, we should respect them and provide them with opportunities and support. I think that this is the most important step to be taken in resolving the North Korean crisis.

Representative Ed Royce (R-CA) is a member of the U.S. House of Representatives and IPCNKR. He observes:

> To ensure his survival, Kim Jong Il controls the dissemination of all information, which is crucial to maintaining a system based on lies. The propaganda is so great, malnourished defectors report that they believed their country was more prosperous than South Korea. Many

believed that they lived in a socialist paradise. Broadcasts on Radio Free Asia, a surrogate broadcast agency, help combat this propaganda, offering a truthful alternative to the falsehoods fed to North Koreans by the Kim Jong Il regime. Some ex-party officials have said that they now know that it's the government of Kim Jong Il that is responsible for the woes of their country. There are cracks in the armor of the Hermit Kingdom; it is time to intensify our broadcasting efforts. Radio could help to fundamentally change the political system and end the refugee crisis.[29]

Suzanne Scholte is president of the Defense Forum Foundation and a leading North Korean human rights activist. She advises:

We have to engage and reach out to the people of North Korea, and we have to do that by getting more information into that country about our concern and care for them. We have already seen the success of what Free North Korea Radio [a defector-based radio station that broadcasts into North Korea] has been able to do, which to me is very key, because there is nothing more powerful than North Koreans living in freedom talking to North Koreans living in enslavement.

In addition, there are quite a few NGOs that have projects sending in by balloon pamphlets and information. Some of these are Christian organizations sending in Christian messages along with radios and food. Others are sending in political messages and true history about North Korea . . . For example, one South Korean NGO is sending in a single sheet of information of true history and true facts about the death and destruction the regime has caused. The information is written across a photo of Kim Jong Il, which means no one from North Korea can destroy the pamphlet because it is a crime against the regime to deface a photo of Kim Jong Il.

We know that these pamphlets are having a tremendous impact because in meetings between North and South Korea, the North Koreans have complained bitterly to the South Korean government about these balloon projects and the information that is being sent into North Korea. North Korean delegations have actually brought to talks with the South these orange pamphlets and demanded that this propaganda be stopped. So we know the regime is feeling the impact of it.[30]

Hiroshi Kato, the director of the Japanese NGO Life Funds for North Korean Refugees, commented:

In recent days, four North Korean defectors in a small boat with a motorcycle engine crossed the Sea of Japan and reached the Japanese shore. It is a very rare case. But another 20 to 30 vacant boats also reached the Japanese shore. This means that there are many people trying to cross the Sea of Japan by boat, but these people in the vacant boats were unfortunately unsuccessful . . . They were struck down by rough waves and storms . . . I think we will see more North Koreans defecting by the sea route in the future. We must try to help them to also use this method.[31]

Chuck Downs, the former senior Pentagon official and foreign policy advisor to the U.S. House of Representatives Policy Committee, told me:

The cause of the crisis on the Korean peninsula is the refusal of the corrupt and self-serving Kim regime to permit its people to govern themselves. Kim Jong Il understands better than anyone else that to let his people participate fully in the political process would mean the end of his regime and, more than likely, a threat to his personal security. Even food itself serves him as a mechanism to oppress the people of North Korea, so the politically disenfranchised become refugees merely to sustain their survival. The rest of the world should acknowledge that starving North Koreans are in fact political refugees. Political change is clearly required to address the fundamental crisis, and the actions of Kim Jong Il will determine whether that change will come about through his removal by war, revolution, assassination, flight, or natural causes. The rest of the world must attend to these developments more carefully and creatively than we have in the past. In spite of our avowal of human rights and democracy, the U.S. and its allies have a peculiar tendency to assist failing regimes in the pursuit of stability instead.[32]

Istvan Szent-Ivanyi is a Hungarian politician, an elected member of the European Parliament, and the vice-chair of the parliament's Delegation for Relations with the Korean Peninsula. He argues:

We need an overall consensus among the major players. Not only between the U.S. and the European Union, but it should also involve China, Russia, South Korea, and Japan, who are major players in the whole issue. If we can agree on a strategy towards North Korea, we can be successful. Otherwise, unfortunately, we may fail because the North Korean leadership can see an escape route and find a way out. . . . The second point, and absolutely the key in my mind, is the refugees. I remember . . . when East Germany collapsed and Hungary accepted the refugees and allowed them to leave the country . . . That was the final blow to the East German Communist regime. Definitely, it's very important to persuade the Chinese leadership to accept the refugees. . . . And the third point, which is important, is that humanitarian aid that we provide . . . should reach the targeted people . . . not the party leadership and the party elite, but the people. . . . That means that we need to have some monitoring mechanics for that.[33]

Representative Masaharu Nakagawa is a member of the Japanese House of Representatives and a co-chair of the IPCNKR. Here's his view:

I appreciate the effort of the six-party talks. The present effort should be continued. I think it is highly important for the related countries to take united action based upon collaborative policies toward the North Korean government. The human rights agenda for the refugees, abductions, and harsh conditions for the nationals of North Korea such as gulags should be implemented on the multinational negotiating table in the framework of the six-party talks. Humanitarian aid programs should be resumed on the condition that foods and medicines are distributed directly to the people by UN staff. The process should be monitored by third countries so that immediate information on the social conditions of North Korea can be obtained. . . . We should be prepared for a sudden change of the Kim Jong Il regime.[34]

Tim Peters, the director of Helping Hands Korea and a leading North Korean human rights activist who was featured on the cover of *TIME Asia*, asserted:

The more we can energize anyone who has a heart for the suffering, including Christians particularly because they seem to be in the majority of those who are already helping actively in China, the better. . . . I believe that we need to continue to educate, challenge, recruit, and equip a larger number of individuals to meet the needs of North Koreans in crisis. As a Christian, I would go to my own community of fellow Christians first, and educate them as to what the opportunities and challenges are to help persecuted brothers and sisters in China—in this context, referring to North Korean refugees.

Of course, that's what our Catacombs movement is all about. In a sense, it's looking past the more traditional, structured, above ground Christian community that is operating in countries that have freedom of religion. The Catacombs is a way of explaining to Christians that we're moving into an era in which an ever-growing proportion of Christians will need to learn how to operate in an underground fashion . . . I'm encouraged that more and more volunteers are stepping forward as their eyes are opened to this fundamental fact. I really think that's the future in China, North Korea, and globally.[35]

Michael Horowitz, another leading North Korean human rights activist, told me:

A handful of Korean American leaders are more powerful than George Bush, are more powerful than Hu Jintao, are more powerful than Ban Ki-moon, are more powerful than anybody you could name in bringing down the regime in North Korea. If the Korean American community went to Congress . . . if every Korean American church had a sign that said "Let my people go. Freedom for the North Korean people," Kim Jong Il would not survive. . . . It is the leadership of the Korean American community, their gaining a sense, which they do not have, of the power they have to shape events. A major American political figure told me just the other day, "If you could get the fifty leading Korean businessmen to spend three days in Washington talking to everybody, saying 'sanctions against China for helping North Korea or we will oppose the party that opposes the sanctions the most,' the president would pass a Jackson-Vanik[36]-type law that would force China to have to choose between Kim Jong Il and their own economy."

America's political parties know—and know much better than Korean Americans do—how important the Korean American community will be in our country's twenty-first-century life . . . But Koreans are defensive, and I understand that. As a Jew I understand that. When Hitler was rising to power and Franklin Roosevelt at one point wanted to appoint a Jew to the U.S. Supreme Court . . . Roosevelt was visited by a delegation of leading Jews who begged him not to do it because they thought that it would make Hitler too angry and would make Jews in America too visible and too subject to discrimination. I see the same defensiveness on the part of the Korean American community. The power is in the hands of the Korean American community . . . To me it is a very simple thing: Energize the Korean American community and it will happen.[37]

Michael Green served as the special assistant to the president for National Security Affairs and senior director for Asian Affairs at the National Security Council. He advises:

The debate about North Korea policy frequently drives people into two opposing camps. Either we engage them or we contain them and wait for their regime to collapse. It's a very artificial debate. It's a debate that's perpetuated by election politics in the U.S.

and by the media. And it's a damaging debate because the reality is to deal with North Korea you need a full toolkit. You need to engage them both bilaterally and multilaterally. You need to work with your allies. You need to deter them. You need to constrain their ability to obtain dangerous materials or export them. You need to press on human rights. You need to find ways to expand aid in a transparent way to help the North Korean people but also to be ready for the day when there's reunification. You need to do all these things at once. Politically it's not a very catchy slogan to say that North Korean policy is complex, so we need to work on multiple fronts. But that's the reality. This is not a policy problem that lends itself to a very simple answer such as bilateral engagement versus containment. We need to be prepared to use pressure, to use inducements, to use our allies, to work with China, and to address human rights at the same time we deal with the nuclear issue. That requres a full toolkit, not a simple binary choice.

MULTIPLE EFFORTS AND A FREE NORTH KOREA

You have heard a wide variety of opinions, strategies, and policies on the North Korean crisis. Clearly, there is no one correct answer to the question of how to resolve it, no single strategy or policy. The magnitude of the task will require efforts at multiple levels. A mixture of strategies must be applied to bring about change in North Korea.

Throughout my four years in China, I had the unique opportunity to build relationships with many North Koreans. I befriended not only refugees but also government officials and tae kwon do athletes. I cherished those friendships and enjoyed the time I spent with my North Korean friends. But at the same time, there was always something of a barrier between us. I could never fully be honest with them, and they could never fully be honest with me. They had their secrets, and I had mine. There were some things that we couldn't talk about.

The North Korean national tae kwon do team during an exhibition in Yanji, China (July 2004, author photo)

Many times, my North Korean friends asked me, a bit suspiciously, what I was doing in China. I recall a time when my two tae kwon do masters, Master Chung and Master Park (a 33-year-old, 6' 4" sparring champion), confronted me and said, "Mike, tell us what you're really doing here in China." I managed to dodge the question, but I imagine that they will feel betrayed when they learn about this book and the true nature of my work at the China–North Korea border. It pained me to build those friendships under a facade, but that was the way it had to be. If they ever come across this book, I hope that they will know that while I could not be completely transparent with them, I genuinely cherished their friendship. Some of my greatest memories in China are with North Korean friends such as Master Chung and Master Park.

I've often thought that in another world Master Park and I, being similar in age, might have been the best of friends. We both loved sports and we got along extremely well. I spent a great deal of time with him and his family. His wife was also a sparring champion in North Korea and spent some time training me as well. Master Park and I worked out hard together, and he trained me for my first full-contact tae kwon do tournament. Our friendship grew, but there was always that artificial wall between us erected by the North Korean regime. He was a Kim Jong Il loyalist and a full believer in North Korean ideology. I, a Christian Korean American, adamantly opposed everything he believed in.

I look forward to the day when there will no longer be a wall between North Korea and the rest of the world. It is becoming increasingly clear that there are cracks in the current North Korean system and that it is only a matter of time before that wall will come tumbling down.

But the international community must continue to move forward on all fronts. I have always been a proponent of multiple efforts at multiple levels to resolve the North Korean crisis. We need an abundance of advocates for North Korean human rights in various governments, NGOs, and churches around the world. Effective government policies in Washington and other places must be supplemented by work on the ground with the refugees at the Tumen River in China. We also need to get mass media into North Korea and work with the 10,000-plus refugees in Seoul. And it is crucial that people attempt to implement change inside North Korea through official channels. Resolving the North Korean crisis will require joint efforts of the international community. As each person plays their part, change is inevitable. We will one day soon see a free North Korea.

EPILOGUE

There and Back Again

Since I've returned to the States, I've spent much time reflecting on my four years at the border. I often tell people that it was the most amazing ride of my life, and that I wouldn't trade those years for anything. That much is probably clear from what I have written so far. But there's more that I don't often talk about.

During my four years at the border, I experienced some of the greatest victories of my life but also some of the most crushing defeats. I had both mountain-top highs and valley lows. I experienced God in the most profound ways, but at times found myself asking, "God, where are you?" There were occasions when I enjoyed a type of camaraderie that I never knew existed, and then there were other times when I felt extreme loneliness. I called some of my closest friends in the United States at all hours and confided, "I just need to talk to someone right now," and then they would stay on the phone and talk with me for hours. Sometimes I wanted nothing else than to do this work for the rest of my life. Other times, in my final year, I lacked the motivation to continue.

In March 2007, I visited my good friend D. C. and his wife, Amy, in New York. Amy was a Peace Corp worker in Mali, West Africa, for two years, so we had several conversations about our overseas experiences. One night, I was describing how I felt about my time in China, and she pulled a book off the shelf called *A Walk in the Woods* by Bill Bryson and read a passage to me. Bryson had hiked the Appalachian Trail from

Georgia to Maine with an old high school buddy and documented the experience. The two of them had made it all the way to Maine, but in the end had decided not to complete the journey and quit early. One day afterward, Bryson's high school friend asked him, "So do you feel bad about leaving the trail?" Bryson wrote:

> I thought for a moment, unsure. I had come to realize that I didn't have any feelings towards the AT [Appalachian Trail] that weren't confused and contradictory. I was weary of the trail, but still strangely in its thrall; found the endless slog tedious but irresistible; grew tired of the boundless woods but admired their boundlessness; enjoyed the escape from civilization and ached for its comforts. I wanted to quit and to do this forever, sleep in a bed and in a tent, see what was over the next hill and never see a hill again. All of this all at once, every moment, on the trail or off. "I don't know," I said. "Yes and no, I guess."[1]

After Amy finished reading, D. C. asked me, "So, is that how you feel?" It definitely was. Bryson, in that short paragraph, had captured my sentiments perfectly. Up until that moment, I was having a difficult time articulating or understanding my mixed feelings about my time in China. It was then that I realized that anyone who has undertaken an extremely daunting task, or been in environments of intense danger or extreme suffering for an extended period, probably experienced such feelings.

Those closest to me, in my inner circle, saw the work increasingly take its toll on me over the years. They could tell that I was delighted and absolutely loved what I was doing, but that at the same time I was exhausted. I felt an internal peace, but there was no denying the fact that I was tired and burdened with stress. Every year when I returned to the United States for the holidays, my friends commented on how quickly I seemed to be aging.

In my final year at the border, I read Billy Graham's autobiography, *Just As I Am*, in an attempt to find some encouragement and strength to finish my work. He said something about his 1957 crusade in New York (one of his most successful ones) that just gripped me. "But New York also took a toll on me physically," he wrote. "I left drained; I had lost twenty or more pounds. I have said in later years that *something went out of me physically in the New York Crusade that I never fully recovered* [emphasis added]."[2]

Billy Graham's words stopped me dead in my tracks. As I packed all of my belongings to go home for good, I wondered if I would ever fully recover.

Towards the end of my service in China, D. C. said to me, "You remind me of Frodo." I braced myself for one of the many jokes I get from friends who refer to me as a hobbit because of my hairy feet. But instead he made a somewhat insightful comparison of me and Frodo that, unfortunately, neither of us can now recall. Since D. C. made that comment, I have watched *The Lord of the Rings* movie trilogy several times and found myself identifying with the main character. In one of the final scenes of *The Lord of the Rings: The Return of the King,* Frodo Baggins writes the final paragraph to a book by his uncle Bilbo Baggins titled *There and Back Again.* He concludes his journey: "How do you pick up the threads of an old life? How do you go on when in your heart, you begin to understand there is no going back? There are some things that time cannot mend. Some hurts that go too deep . . . that have taken hold."

I suppose a lot of times I feel like Frodo coming back after a long and arduous journey, having enjoyed the most amazing experiences but also feeling a bit beaten up. I have come to grips with the fact that there are some things that time cannot mend and some hurts that go too deep.

Sometimes, those in my inner circle will ask me, "If you could go back in time, would you do it again?" That question is a no-brainer for me. Without hesitation, I always say that I would. Despite all of the hardships I've endured, it's difficult to imagine my life without these last four years in China. They have become such an important part of who I am. Through my time in China, I discovered a part of myself and was "liberated." While that self-discovery did cost me something, it is priceless to me nonetheless, and I would not trade it for anything in the world.

Our organization, Crossing Borders, is my pride and joy. It gives me great satisfaction to know that I am a part of something bigger than myself. I have the deepest admiration for each and every member of the U.S. and Chinese staff who make such tremendous sacrifices for our work. During my time in China, they were my closest companions. Together we experienced the astounding things that happen when you combine faith and humanitarian aid.

When I take a step back and look at the lives of all of the people we have touched in China and North Korea, it becomes clear that, without the slightest doubt, it was all worth it. One of the things I have learned is that helping the oppressed, the persecuted, the abused, and the abandoned yields great rewards and an enormous sense of fulfillment. I cannot recall a time when I have felt more alive or fulfilled. It has been my greatest joy and privilege to witness the transformations in the lives of the North Koreans we have served. Their stories have also taught me something about how to live my own life. They have inspired me to live it to the fullest. The North Koreans, the refugees, and the children will always be in my prayers and a significant part of who I am.

Notes

INTRODUCTION

1. Ken Gire, *Windows of the Soul: Experiencing God in New Ways* (Grand Rapids, MI: Zondervan Publishing House, 1996), 76, 82.

2. An honorific way of addressing someone in the Korean culture.

CHAPTER 1: THE NORTH KOREAN MIND

Chapter opening quote: Thomas J. Belke, *Juche: A Christian Study of North Korea's State Religion* (Bartlesville, OK: Living Sacrifice Book Co., 1999), 1.

1. Michael Breen, *Kim Jong-Il: North Korea's Dear Leader* (Asia: John Wiley & Sons, 2004), 114.

2. In Su Choe, *Kim Jong Il: The People's Leader* (Pyongyang: Foreign Languages Publishing House, 1983), 65.

3. Author interview, 30 May 2007.

4. Kim Il Sung is Kim Jong Il's father and was the first Communist dictator of North Korea, from 1948–1994.

5. Belke, *Juche*, 5.

6. Breen, *Kim Jong-Il*, 3.

7. James Brooke, "Where Is North Korea's Leader? Train Blast Raises Questions Unanswered by Propaganda," *International Herald Tribune*, 30 April 2004.

8. Michael Breen, *The Koreans: Who They Are, What They Want, Where Their Future Lies* (New York: Thomas Dunne Books, 2004), 137.

9. Belke, *Juche*, 9.

10. From an unpublished interview with The Voice of the Martyrs on 25 October 2005. Used by permission. www.persecution.com.

CHAPTER 2: INSIDE THE HERMIT KINGDOM

Chapter opening quote: Jasper Becker, *Rogue Regime: Kim Jong Il and the Looming Threat of North Korea* (Oxford: Oxford University Press, 2005), 218.

1. Michael Breen, *The Koreans: Who They Are, What They Want, Where Their Future Lies* (New York: Thomas Dunne Books, 2004), 124.

2. North Korea is often referred to as the "hermit kingdom" because of the extent to which it is isolated from the rest of the world.

3. Becker, *Rogue Regime*, 131.

4. Becker, *Rogue Regime*, 43.

5. Michael Breen, *Kim Jong-Il: North Korea's Dear Leader* (Hoboken, NJ: John Wiley & Sons, 2004), 144.

6. Becker, *Rogue Regime*, 137.

7. Becker, *Rogue Regime*, 271.

8. Becker, *Rogue Regime*, 196.

9. Edward Kim, "Putting Kim Jong Il on a Diet," *Chosun Journal*, www.chosunjournal.com/2006/11/29/putting-kim-jong-il-on-a-diet (29 November 2006).

10. fermented and seasoned vegetables (usually cabbage) that is a popular Korean dish

11. Barbara Demick, "Glimpses of a Hermit Nation," *Los Angeles Times*, 3 July 2005.

12. Bill Bryson, *A Walk in the Woods: Rediscovering America on the Appalachian Trail* (New York: Anchor Books, 1998), 183.

13. Becker, *Rogue Regime*, 132.

14. Kang Chol-Hwan, *Aquariums of Pyongyang: Ten Years in the North Korean Gulag* (New York: Basic Books, 2001), 77.

15. Because the value of the North Korean Won (KPW) fluctuates to such a great degree, it is difficult to pin an exact USD equivalent. Conversions were calculated at the time of writing.

16. "Korea, North," *CIA World Factbook*, www.cia.gov/library/publications/the-world-factbook/geos/kn.html (13 December 2007).

17. Author interview, 24 May 2007.

18. a low-cost Korean alcoholic beverage

19. Author interview, 10 July 2007.

20. James Dao, "Aftereffects: Asian Arena; North Korea Is Said to Export Drugs to Get Foreign Currency," *New York Times*, 21 May 2003.

21. George Orwell, *1984* (New York: Signet Classics, 1949), 6.

CHAPTER 3: FAMINE

1. Jasper Becker, *Rogue Regime: Kim Jong Il and the Looming Threat of North Korea* (Oxford: Oxford University Press, 2005), 20.

2. Becker, *Rogue Regime*, 33.

3. Becker, *Rogue Regime*, 205.

4. Becker, *Rogue Regime*, 34.

5. Becker, *Rogue Regime*, caption in photo spread.

6. Kang Chol-Hwan, *The Aquariums of Pyongyang: Ten Years in a North Korean Gulag* (New York: Basic Books, 2001), 141.

7. Michael Breen, *Kim Jong-Il: North Korea's Dear Leader* (Asia: John Wiley & Sons, 2004), 151.

8. Bjorn Lomborg, "Take Your Vitamins," *Foreign Policy*, May/June 2007.

9. Choi Sung Chul, ed., *Human Rights in North Korea* (Seoul: Center for the Advancement of North Korean Human Rights, 1995), 233.

10. Lindsay Beck, "North Korea facing 1 mln tonne food shortage— WFP," *Relief Web*, www.reliefweb.int/rw/RWB.NSF/db900SID/JBRN-6ZNG3N?OpenDocument (26 March 2007).

11. Audra Ang, "Millions may starve in North Korea: UN," *Brisbane Times*, www.brisbanetimes.com.au/news/world/millions-may-starve-in-north-korea-un/2007/03/28/1174761555038.html (28 March 2007).

12. Author interview, 10 July 2007.

13. Breen, *Kim Jong-Il*, 122.

CHAPTER 4: ROAD TO REFUGE

1. Helie Lee, *In the Absence of Sun: A Korean American Woman's Promise to Reunite Three Lost Generations of Her Family* (New York: Harmony Books, 2002), 1.

2. "Perilous Journeys: The Plight of North Koreans in China and Beyond," *International Crisis Group*, www.crisisgroup.org/home/index.cfm?id= 4469 (26 October 2006).

3. The amount of money a North Korean must pay a border guard to cross the river has consistently increased over the years. As of July 2007, North Korean border guards were charging $260 to cross the river. In some cases, guards would not even accept that amount for fear of being punished by authorities.

4. "North Korea: Border-Crossers Harshly Punished on Return," Reuters, www.alertnet.org/thenews/newsdesk/HRW/a157192a346177742fe9f20 5535894ef.htm (6 March 2007).

5. "Perilous Journeys."

6. From an unpublished interview with The Voice of the Martyrs on 25 October 2005. Used by permission. www.persecution.com

7. "Perilous Journeys."

8. "Perilous Journeys."

9. The United Nations High Commissioner for Refugees was established "to protect refugees and resolve refugee problems worldwide." www .unhcr.org

10. "Perilous Journeys."

11. Kurt Achin, "N. Korean Defectors Testify About Human Rights Abuses Back Home and in China," VOA News, www.voanews.com/english/2005-03-16-voa27.cfm (16 March 2005).

12. "The Status of North Korean Asylum Seekers and the U.S. Government Policy Towards Them," Department of State Report, Washington, D.C., www.state.gov/g/prm/rls/rpt/43275.htm (11 March 2005).

13. "Perilous Journeys."

14. Melanie Kirkpatrick, "Let Them Go," *Wall Street Journal* (15 October 2006).

15. Kirkpatrick, "Let Them Go." Yanbian Prefecture is an ethnic Korean autonomous prefecture in Jilin Province.

16. Carter J. Eckert, Ki-baik Lee, Young Ick Lew, Michael Robinson, Edward W. Wagner, *Korea Old and New: A History* (Cambridge: Harvard University Press, 1990), 273.

17. Carter J. Eckert et al., *Korea Old and New*, 273.

18. Author interview, 1 June 2007.

19. James Brooke, "A Human Face on North Koreans' Plight," *New York Times* (21 August 2002).

20. "The requirement that a person must be outside his country to be a refugee does not mean that he must necessarily have left that country illegally, or even that he must have left it on account of well-founded fear. He may have decided to ask for recognition of his refugee status after having already been abroad for some time. A person who was not a refugee when he left his country, but who becomes a refugee at a later date, is called a refugee "*sur place*." (Definition taken from the UN-HCR "Handbook on Procedures and Criteria for Determining Refugee Status.")

21. Author interview, 15 May 2007.

22. Author interview, 8 May 2007.

23. Author interview, 19 July 2007.

24. Author interview, 9 May 2007.

25. The International Parliamentarians' Coalition for North Korean Refugees' Human Rights (IPCNKR) is a coalition of parliamentarians from 19 countries (including South Korea, the United States, the United Kingdom, Japan, and Mongolia) "demanding that North Korean refugees be given official UN refugee status and calling for the end of North Korean human rights abuses" (quote from IPCNKR website, www.ipcnkr.org). The stated goals of the IPCNKR are to avoid further defection, get recognition of refugee status of the Free North Korean Immigrants, build refugee camps, and strengthen international cooperation to improve human rights of the Free North Korean Immigrants.

CHAPTER 5: SEX TRAFFICKING

1. Author interview, 21 June 2007.

2. "Trafficking in Persons Report," U.S. Department of State (June 2007).

3. According to the U.S. Department of State 2007 "Trafficking in Persons Report," North Korea is known to export labor to other countries such as "Russia, the Czech Republic, Poland, Romania, Libya, Bulgaria, Saudi Arabia, Angola, Mongolia, Kuwait, Yemen, Iraq, and China."

4. Donna M. Hughes, "How Can I Be Sold Like This?" *National Review Online* (19 July 2005), 3.

5. Hughes, "How Can I Be Sold Like This?"

6. "Perilous Journeys: The Plight of North Koreans in China and Beyond," *International Crisis Group*, www.crisisgroup.org/home/index.cfm?id= 4469 (26 October 2006).

7. "A Girl's Right to Live," report published for the United Nations Commission on the Status of Women on behalf of The Working Group on the Girl Child, Geneva, 2007.

8. Valerie M. Hudson and Andrea M. Den Boer, "'Bare Branches' and Danger in Asia," *Washington Post*, www.washingtonpost.com/wp-dyn/articles/ A24761-2004Jul2.html (4 July 2004).

9. Author interview, 21 June 2007.

10. "North Korea: Imminent Execution," *Amnesty International*, web .amnesty.org/library/Index/ENGASA240012007?open&of=ENG-PRK (15 February 2007).

11. Abraham Lee, "Combating Human Trafficking in China: Domestic and International Efforts" (congressional testimony on behalf of Crossing Borders before the Congressional-Executive Commission on China, Washington, D.C., 6 March 2006), cecc.gov/pages/hearings/2006/20060306/ index.php

12. There is no word for God in the North Korean vocabulary. The literal translation of the word So-Young used would be "god of heaven" or "god in the sky."

13. Judith Herman, *Trauma and Recovery: The Aftermath of Violence—from Domestic Abuse to Political Terror* (New York: Basic Books, 1997), 1.

14. Herman, *Trauma and Recovery*, 2.

15. Lee, "Combating Human Trafficking in China."

16. Lee, "Combating Human Trafficking in China."

17. Herman, *Trauma and Recovery*, 74–75.

18. "Trafficking of North Korean Women in China," *Refugees International*, www.refugeesinternational.org/content/article/detail/890 (28 July 2003).

CHAPTER 6: GULAGS

1. David Hawk, "The Hidden Gulag: Exposing North Korean's Prison Camps," report for the U.S. Committee for Human Rights in North Korea, Washington, D.C., 2003.

2. Robert Windrem, "Death, terror in N. Korea gulag," MSNBC, msnbc.msn.com/id/3071466 (15 January 2003).

3. Michael Breen, *Kim Jong-Il: North Korea's Dear Leader* (Asia: John Wiley & Sons, 2004), 132.

4. Suh Sung, *Unbroken Spirits: Nineteen Years in South Korea's Gulag* (Lanham, MD: Rowman & Littlefield, 2001), 17.

5. Windrem, "Death, terror in N. Korea gulag."

6. Windrem, "Death, terror in N. Korea gulag."

7. Windrem, "Death, terror in N. Korea gulag."

8. Jasper Becker, *Rogue Regime: Kim Jong Il and the Looming Threat of North Korea* (Oxford: Oxford University Press, 2005), 87.

9. Hawk, "The Hidden Gulag."

10. Hawk, "The Hidden Gulag."

11. Choe Sang-Hun, "Born and raised in a North Korean gulag," *International Herald Tribune*, www.iht.com/articles/2007/07/09/news/korea.php?page=1 (29 November 1996).

12. Jung A Yang, "Escape From 'Total Control Zone', North Korea's Papillon," *The Daily NK*, www.dailynk.com/english/read.php?catId=nk00100&num=2051 (11 May 2007).

13. Choe, "Born and raised in a North Korean gulag."

14. Becker, *Rogue Regime*, 90.

15. Becker, *Rogue Regime*, 90.

16. Kim Hyun Hee, *The Tears of My Soul* (New York: William Morrow and Company, 1993), 8.

17. Barbara Demick, "Glimpses of a Hermit Nation,"

CHAPTER 7: CHRISTIANITY AND NORTH KOREA

Chapter opening quote: "Quotations of Leader Kim Jong Il," *The People's Korea* (Tokyo: DPRK web magazine), 13 May 1998.

1. Yoido Full Gospel Church, "History: The Church at Yoido," english .fgtv.com/yoido/history2.asp (11 June 2007).

2. Tom White, *North Korea: The Battle Continues* (Bartlesville, OK: The Voice of the Martyrs, Inc., 1996), 1.

3. Thomas J. Belke, *Juche: A Christian Study of North Korea's State Religion* (Bartlesville, OK: Living Sacrifice Book Co., 1999), 142.

4. Belke, *Juche*, 52.

5. Belke, *Juche*, 60.

6. "Annual Report of the United States Commission on International Religious Freedom," U.S. Commission on International Religious Freedom (May 2007), 154.

7. Author interview, 6 June 2007.

8. "USS *General Sherman* Incident," GlobalSecurity.org, www.globalsecurity.org/military/ops/sherman.htm (21 May 2007).

9. Jasper Becker, *Rogue Regime: Kim Jong Il and the Looming Threat of North Korea* (New York: Oxford University Press, 2005), 68.

10. Belke, *Juche*, 134.

11. Billy Graham, *Just As I Am: The Autobiography of Billy Graham* (San Francisco: Harper San Francisco and Zondervan, 1997), 631.

12. Belke, *Juche*, 148.

13. Author interview, 6 June 2007.

14. Some organizations have produced small, pocket-sized Bibles for the purpose of distribution in North Korea.

15. Author interview, 30 May 2007.

16. Author interview, 29 May 2007.

17. Author interview, 6 June 2007.

18. Author interview, 31 July 2007.

19. Becker, *Rogue Regime*, 85.

20. "The United States Commission on International Religious Freedom was created by the International Religious Freedom Act of 1998 (IRFA) to monitor violations of the right to freedom of thought, conscience, and religion or belief abroad, as defined in IRFA and set forth in the Universal Declaration of Human Rights and related international instruments, and to give independent policy recommendations to the President, Secretary of State, and Congress." U.S. Commission on International Religious Freedom 2007 Annual Report.

21. "Annual Report of the United States Commission on International Religious Freedom," U.S. Commission on International Religious Freedom (May 2007).

22. Author interview, 6 June 2007.

23. Eric Leijenaar, "North Korea Christians on Edge as Nation 'Celebrates' 65th Birthday of Leader Kim Jong-Il," *BosNewsLife* (16 February 2007).

24. "Perilous Journeys: The Plight of North Koreans in China and Beyond," *International Crisis Group*, www.crisisgroup.org/home/index.cfm?id=4469 (26 October 2006).

CHAPTER 8: FREEDOM ON THE FOURTH

1. Dan Brown, *The Da Vinci Code* (New York: Doubleday, 2003), 117.

2. According to an International Crisis Group report titled "Perilous Journeys: The Plight of North Koreans in China and Beyond," 95 percent of North Korean defectors resettle in South Korea. As of July 2006, about 8,741 North Koreans have been granted asylum in South Korea. In addition, hundreds have resettled in Europe, roughly 100 in Japan, and about 30 in the U.S. On February 17, 2007 (Kim Jong Il's birthday), the 10,000th defector arrived in Seoul.

3. The Chinese equivalent of the Federal Bureau of Investigation (FBI)

4. For security reasons, the country where the passports were made will remain nameless.

5. "Four N. Koreans Defect in Shanghai, Two in Korea," Reuters (4 July 2003).

6. "US eases entry for refugees from N. Korea," *The Strait Times* (11 July 2003).

7. "Four Teenage North Korean Defectors Arrive in Seoul," *The Korea Times* (9 July 2003).

8. "Four Teenage North Korean Defectors Arrive in Seoul."

CHAPTER 9: ASIAN UNDERGROUND RAILROAD

1. I have spoken with several activists operating on the underground railroad, and we have concluded that because the routes have already become

so widely publicized, it would not be a problem to specifically mention Laos in this chapter.

2. not the real name of the village

3. not the real name of the village

4. In November 2004, Crossing Borders undertook its final rescue project. We no longer help refugees go to South Korea. To ensure a longer presence in China—underground railroad workers are usually captured by authorities within a year—we decided to focus on helping refugees either live safely in China or return to North Korea.

CHAPTER 10: HEROES

1. Bong Baik, *Kim Il Sung Biography* (I) (Beirut: Dar Al-Talia, 1973), 558.

2. Andrew Salmon, "Seoul charges suspect in North Korea kidnapping case," *International Herald Tribune* (15 December 2004).

3. Yong Hun Kim, "Pastor Kim Dong Shik Abducted, Now Dead for Refusing to Deny Jesus," *The Daily NK*, www.dailynk.com/english/read.php?cataId=nk00100&num=2033 (7 May 2007).

4. Jasper Becker, "Persecuted Church Fights Secret War," *South China Morning Post* (17 June 2001).

5. Sun-tzu, *The Art of War* (New York: Penguin Group, 2002), 42. [Translated by John Minford].

6. From an unpublished interview with The Voice of the Martyrs on 25 October 2005. Used by permission. www.persecution.com

CHAPTER 11: RESTORING LIVES

1. "The purpose of the Restore Life program is to bring complete restoration to the refugee—physically, emotionally, socially and spiritually—through providing basic needs such as food, clothing, shelter, medicine and schooling or job training." Excerpt from Crossing Borders Portfolio.

2. Benjamin Kang Lim, "Women the most vulnerable of North Korean refugees," Reuters (27 July 2005).

3. Crossing Borders newsletter, First Quarter 2006.

CHAPTER 12: THE FUTURE OF NORTH KOREA

1. Nicholas Eberstadt and Christopher Griffin, "Saving North Korea's Refugees," *The New York Times* (19 February 2007).

2. Author interview, 19 July 2007.

3. Hyun Hee Kim, *The Tears of My Soul* (New York: William Morrow and Company, 1993), 150.

4. Author interview, 30 May 2007.

5. Barbara Demick, "Glimpses of a Hermit Nation," *Los Angeles Times* (4 July 2005).

6. Mark Palmer, *Breaking the Real Axis of Evil: How to Oust the World's Last Dictators by 2025* (Lanham, MD: Rowman & Littlefield, 2003), 73.

7. Young Howard, "The real threat to Kim," *International Herald Tribune* (25 February 2005).

8. Sang-min Joo, "N.K. preoccupied with controlling regime: experts," *The Korea Herald* (18 November 2004).

9. "Perilous Journeys: The Plight of North Koreans in China and Beyond," *International Crisis Group*, www.crisisgroup.org/home/index.cfm?id= 4469 (26 October 2006).

10. "N. Korea ups executions of cellphone users," *The China Post*, www.chinapost.com.tw/international/112428.htm (15 June 2007).

11. Palmer, *Breaking the Real Axis of Evil*, 262.

12. Michael Breen, *The Koreans: Who They Are, What They Want, Where Their Future Lies* (New York: Thomas Dunne Books, 2004), xi, 11–12.

13. Jack Kim, "South Korea puts ties with North ahead of UN vote," Reuters, www.reuters.com/article/latestCrisis/idUSSEO238753 (21 November 2007).

14. The Organisation for Economic Co-operation and Development (OECD) "brings together the governments of countries committed to democracy and the market economy from around the world to: support sustainable economic growth, boost employment, raise living standards, maintain financial stability, assist other countries' economic development, contribute to growth in world trade." From the OECD website.

15. Author interview, 14 May 2007

16. Author interview, 8 May 2007.

17. Author interview, 31 May 2007.

18. Author interview, 1 June 2007.

19. Author interview, 10 July 2007.

20. Author interview, 10 July 2007.

21. Author interview, 30 May 2007.

22. Author interview, 17 May 2007. The Helsinki Accord is the agreement signed in 1975 by 35 countries (including the United States and the Soviet Union) in Helsinki, Finland. The document reduced tension between the East and the West during the Cold War. In addition to addressing security issues, the Helsinki Accord addressed human rights, making it one of the most important human rights documents of all time.

23. Author interview, 17 May 2007.

24. Literally means "restructuring." The Merriam-Webster Online Dictionary defines the word as "the policy of economic and governmental reform instituted by Mikhail Gorbachev in the Soviet Union during the mid-1980s."

25. Author interview, 21 June 2007.

26. A village in the Demilitarized Zone (DMZ) that straddles the border of North and South Korea. It is the place where the 1953 cease-fire agreement was signed at the end of the Korean War.

27. Author interview, 14 July 2007.

28. The International Parliamentarians' Coalition for North Korean Refugees' Human Rights (IPCNKR) is a coalition of parliamentarians from 19 countries (including South Korea, the United States, the United Kingdom, Japan, and Mongolia) "demanding that North Korean refugees be given official UN refugee status and calling for the end of North Korean human rights abuses" (quote from IPCNKR website; www.ipcnkr.org). The stated goals of the IPCNKR are to avoid further defection, get recognition of refugee status of the Free North Korean Immigrants, build refugee camps, and strengthen international cooperation to improve human rights of the Free North Korean Immigrants.

29. Author interview, 20 July 2007.

30. Author interview, 15 May 2007.

31. Author interview, 14 June 2007.

32. Author interview, 7 June 2007.

33. Author interview, 11 June 2007.

34. Author interview, 14 June 2007.

35. Author interview, 14 May 2007. For more information on the Catacombs meetings in Seoul, visit www.helpinghandskorea.org or email Tim Peters at tapkorea@gmail.com.

36. The Jackson-Vanik amendment, named for its major co-sponsors Senator Henry "Scoop" Jackson (D-WA) and Representative Charles Vanik (D-OH), denied normal trade relations to countries that had nonmarket economies and that restricted emigration rights. President Gerald Ford signed the amendment into law in 1975. In 2006, the "Scoop Jackson Let My People Go Act of 2006" Bill was introduced to Congress. The purpose of the bill is "to limit the total annual value of primary imports from the People's Republic of China into the United States if China continues to take certain actions with respect to North Korean refugees in violation of its obligations under international law."

37. Author interview, 8 June 2007.

EPILOGUE: THERE AND BACK AGAIN

1. Bill Bryson, *A Walk in the Woods: Rediscovering America on the Appalachian Trail* (New York: Anchor Books, 1998), 389.

2. Billy Graham, *Just As I Am: The Autobiography of Billy Graham* (San Francisco: Harper Collins, 1997), 323.

About the Author

Mike Kim was born and raised in Chicago and graduated from the University of Illinois at Urbana-Champaign in 1999. In 2001, he left his financial planning business in Chicago and moved to California to prepare for humanitarian aid work in China. On New Year's Day 2003, he fulfilled his dream, carrying little more than two duffel bags and a one-way ticket to China. Soon thereafter, Mike founded Crossing Borders Ministries, an NGO providing food, clothes, shelter, and medicine to North Korean refugees in China. His organization has aided hundreds of refugees and has established 25 refugee shelters and five orphanages near the border. Mike eventually was granted entry to North Korea in 2004, a time when most American citizens were strictly banned.

Mike travels and speaks widely on the North Korean crisis. He has prepared congressional testimony on the topic of combating human trafficking in China and regularly meets with high-ranking government officials from various countries. He lectures to audiences worldwide about the plight of North Koreans and his experiences in China.

Currently residing in Washington, D.C., Mike is a full-time MBA student at Georgetown University's McDonough School of Business and plans on returning to nonprofit work in the future. In his spare time, he enjoys reading, travel, golf, volleyball, and martial arts. While in China, he received a second-degree black belt in tae kwon do from a North Korean master.